RECORDS MANAGEMENT AND THE LIBRARY

Issues and Practices

INFORMATION MANAGEMENT, POLICY, AND SERVICES
Charles R. McClure and Peter Hernon, Editors

Library Performance Accountability and Responsiveness: Essays in Honor of Ernest R. DeProspo
 Charles C. Curran and F. William Summers
Curriculum Initiative: An Agenda and Strategy for Library Media Programs
 Michael B. Eisenberg and Robert E. Berkowitz
Resource Companion to Curriculum Initiative: An Agenda and Strategy for Library Media Programs
 Michael B. Eisenberg and Robert E. Berkowitz
Information Problem-Solving: The Big Six Skills Approach to Library & Information Skills Instruction
 Michael B. Eisenberg and Robert E. Berkowitz
The Role and Importance of Managing Information for Competitive Positions in Economic Development
 Keith Harman
A Practical Guide to Managing Information for Competitive Positioning in Economic Development
 Keith Harman
Librarianship: The Erosion of a Woman's Profession
 Roma Harris
Microcomputer Software for Performing Statistical Analysis: A Handbook for Supporting Library Decision Making
 Peter Hernon and John V. Richardson (Editors)
Public Access to Government Information, Second Edition
 Peter Hernon and Charles R. McClure
Statistics for Library Decision Making: A Handbook
 Peter Hernon et al.
Libraries: Partners in Adult Literacy
 Deborah Johnson, Jane Robbins, and Douglas L. Zweizig
Library and Information Science Research: Perspectives and Strategies for Improvement
 Charles R. McClure and Peter Hernon (Editors)
U.S. Government Information Policies: Views and Perspectives
 Charles R. McClure, Peter Hernon, and Harold C. Relyea
U.S. Scientific and Technical Information Policies: Views and Perspectives
 Charles R. McClure and Peter Hernon
For Information Specialists
 Howard White, Marcia Bates, and Patrick Wilson

In preparation
Organizational Decision Making and Information Use
 Mairead Browne
Technology and Library Information Services
 Carol Anderson and Robert Hauptman
Microcomputer Local Area Networks and Communications
 Thomas R. Kochtanek
Investigations of Human Responses to Knowledge Representations
 Mark E. Rorvig
Information Seeking as a Process of Construction
 Carol Kulthau
Assessing the Public Library Planning Process
 Annabel Stephens

RECORDS MANAGEMENT AND THE LIBRARY

Issues and Practices

Candy Schwartz
Simmons College

Peter Hernon
Simmons College

ABLEX PUBLISHING CORPORATION
NORWOOD, NEW JERSEY

Second Printing 1995

Copyright © 1993 by Ablex Corporation.

All rights reserved. No part of this publication may be reproduced, stored in a retrieval system, or transmitted, in any form or by any means, electronic, mechanical, photocopying, microfilming, recording, or otherwise, without permission of the publisher.

Printed in the United States of America

Library of Congress Cataloging-in-Publication Data

```
Schwartz, Candy.
    Records management and the library : issues and practices / Candy
  Schwartz, Peter Hernon.
       p.   cm. -- (Information management, policy, and services)
    Includes bibliographical references and indexes.
    ISBN 0-89391-964-0. -- ISBN 0-89391-998-5 (pbk.)
    1. Library science--United States.  2. Records--United States-
  -Management.  3. Business records--United States--Management.
  4. Archives--United States--Administration.   I. Hernon, Peter.
  II. Title.  III. Series.
  Z665.2.U6S38  1992
  020'.973--dc20                                              92-41735
                                                                  CIP
```

Ablex Publishing Corporation
355 Chestnut St.
Norwood, NJ 07648

P

> In order to keep this title in print and available to the academic community, this edition was produced using digital reprint technology in a relatively short print run. This would not have been attainable using traditional methods. Although the cover has been changed from its original appearance, the text remains the same and all materials and methods used still conform to the highest book-making standards.

Contents

List of Figures	x
List of Tables	xii
Preface	xiii

1 Records Management: An Overview — 1
- Records Management, Librarianship, and Archives Management — 2
- Professional Associations, Journals, and Information Services — 5
- What Do Records Managers Do? — 13
- References — 16
- Readings — 16
- Discussion Points — 18

2 Historical Background — 19
- Early History — 20
- Developments in the Modern Age — 23
- Records Management and the U.S. Government — 25
- Conclusion — 33
- References — 35
- Readings — 36
- Discussion Points — 37

3 Systems Analysis — 38
- Problem Solving — 42
- Phases in Conducting a Systems Analysis Study — 45
- Conclusion — 53
- References — 53
- Readings — 54
- Discussion Points — 55

4 Records Inventory — 56
- Making the Case for Records Management — 56
- Preparing for Records Inventory — 60
- Physical Records Inventory — 66
- What Next? — 70
- References — 71

vi Records Management and the Library

Readings	72
Discussion Points	72

5 Records Appraisal and Retention — 74
- Classification — 74
- Appraisal/Analysis — 75
- Retention Scheduling — 80
- Disposal — 87
- Results — 89
- References — 90
- Readings — 90
- Discussion Points — 91

6 Database Management for Records Management — 93
- Commercially Available Records Management Software — 93
- Using a Database Management Package — 95
- Implementation and Costs — 110
- Conclusion — 110
- References — 111
- Readings — 112
- Discussion Points — 112

7 Filing and Storage — 113
- Formats and Materials — 113
- Filing Equipment — 116
- Filing Methods — 118
- Records Centers — 128
- Conclusion — 129
- References — 129
- Readings — 131
- Discussion Points — 132

8 Vital Records and Disaster Management — 133
- Vital Records — 133
- Disaster Management — 135
- Conclusion — 139
- References — 140
- Readings — 141
- Discussion Points — 141

9 Expanding the Role of Records Control — 142
- Reports, Directives, and Correspondence — 142
- Forms Management — 144

Reprographics	146
Micrographics	147
New Information Technologies	152
Conclusion	154
References	154
Readings	155
Discussion Points	156

10 Administrative Considerations — 157

The Administrative Environment	158
Decision Making	160
Working with Upper Management	161
Organizational Charts	161
Staffing	163
Records Management Manual	166
Budgeting and Resource Allocation	168
Space Management	171
Career Choice	172
Establishing a Research Basis for Records Management	174
References	175
Discussion Points	177

11 Evaluation and Planning — 178

Use of Evaluation	179
Basic Evaluation Approaches	180
Planning	181
Action Research	183
Performance Measures	184
Doing a Records Management Study	187
Decision Support Systems	188
Obstacles to Evaluation	191
Accountability	192
The Challenge for the Present and Future	193
References	193
Readings	195
Discussion Points	196

12 Information Resources Management — 197

Information Life Cycle	197
Information Resources Management	200
An Inventory/Locator System	208
Records Management: A Part of IRM	213
Barriers to Overcome	215

Doing IRM as a Records Manager		216
Information Policy		217
References		219
Discussion Points		220

13 Information Policy — 222
- Information Policy at the Corporate/Institutional Level — 223
- The Literature — 223
- Policy Issues — 224
- Policy Framework — 227
- Role of Selected Agencies — 229
- Government Information *Safety Nets* — 233
- Toward National Information Policy — 234
- References — 235
- Readings — 236
- Discussion Points — 238

14 An Overview of the Weston Records Management Project (by Kate Jones-Randall) — 239
- Background — 239
- Library Records Operations — 240
- The Records Management Project, 1988-1989 — 241
- Project Progress — 244
- Results and Outlook — 252

15 MARC AMC and the Government Records Project at the Massachusetts Archives (by Nancy Richard and Kathryn Hammond Baker) — 255
- Development of MARC AMC — 255
- Testing the Format — 256
- Implementation — 261
- Benefits and Obstacles in Using MARC AMC for Records Management — 272
- Conclusion — 277
- References — 278

16 Records Management at the Massachusetts Bay Transportation Authority: Creating an Integrated Information Management System (by Toby Pearlstein) — 280
- The General Context — 280
- The Information Trails — 281
- An Integrated Information Management System — 282

Can the Integrated Information Management System Become a Reality?	287
Progress in Spite of Ourselves	288
Conclusion	290

17 Records Management, Librarians, and the Future   292
    Education for Records Management   292
    Image and "Turf"   293
    Looking Toward the Future   295
    References   296

Contributors   298

Author Index   300

Subject Index   303

List of Figures

1-1.	Library Science, Archives Management, and Records Management	3
1-2.	Coverage of Records Management by Secondary Services	14
2-1.	Organization Chart, General Services Administration	30
2-2.	Organization Chart, National Archives and Records Administration	31
2-3.	Holdings of Federal Records Centers	34
3-1.	Model for Records Management System	39
3-2.	Overview of the Systems Development Life Cycle	43
3-3.	Systems Concepts and Related Activities	46
3-4.	Planning Chart	49
3-5.	A Gantt Chart	51
4-1.	Typical Equipment Codes	63
4-2.	Cubic Foot Equivalent Chart	64
4-3.	Sample Preliminary Survey Coding	65
4-4.	Records Inventory Form	68
4-5.	Files Survey Record	69
5-1.	Guide to Records Retention Requirements	78
5-2.	Retention Guidelines for Library System Records	79
5-3.	Records Appraisal (Attachment to a Records Inventory Form)	82
5-4.	Retention Schedule	83
5-5.	Records Transfer Form Used by the Massachusetts State Archives	85
5-6.	Reference Request Form	86
5-7.	Charge-Out Form	88
6-1.	Data Dictionary Entry	98
6-2.	Database Management Software Evaluation Criteria	99
6-3.	Database Management -- Flat File Approach	102
6-4.	Database Management -- Relational Database Approach	103
6-5.	PFS PROFESIONAL FILE Data Structure	105
6-6.	Columnar Report	108
6-7.	Label or "Bibliographic" Report	109
7-1.	Alphabetical Filing Rules	120
7-2.	Terminal Digit Filing	123
7-3.	Subject Classification Scheme	124
7-4.	Index to Subject Classification	125
7-5.	Subject Arrangement	126
8-1.	The Disaster Kit	138

List of Figures

10-1.	Organizational Chart	162
10-2.	Sample Playscript	167
10-3.	Combination Program-Line Item Budget	169
11-1.	Hierarchy of Planning Components	182
12-1.	Selected Readings on Information Resources Management	198
12-2.	Information Life Cycle	199
12-3.	Records Management as Part of IRM	214
12-4.	Use of Information Facilities in a Public Library	218
13-1.	Selected Source Material on Information Policy	224
14-1.	Records Inventory Form	247
14-2.	Records Inventory Database Sample Record	250
14-3.	Records Control System Sample Record	251
14-4.	EquipInv Sample Record	252
14-5.	Timeline for Weston Records Management Project, September 1988-March 1989	253
15-1.	Government Records in the RLIN Database	259
15-2.	Definitions of Record Types	262
15-3.	Guidelines for Records Schedules and Scheduled Records	264
15-4.	Guidelines for LDA/LDB	267
15-5.	Appraisal Worksheet	269
16-1.	MBTA -- Records Inventory Worksheet	285

List of Tables

1-1.	Associations and Organizations in the United States	6
1-2.	Journals and Newsletters	11
4-1.	Audiovisual Presentations on Records Management	57
4-2.	Elements of the Inventory Form	67
6-1.	Software Directories for Records Management	94
9-1.	Factors Affecting a Microfilming Project	115
14-1.	Records Questionnaire	243

Preface

Librarians and archivists share professional knowledge areas and literatures enough so that each group pretty well knows what the other one does, although they may not be acquainted with all the details. Librarians or archivists who are asked, or who feel it necessary, to take on records management duties, often have no understanding of what constitutes records management, and how it differs from their own practices. Records management as a field is younger than either librarianship or archives, is not as well defined, and lacks a clear educational path. Nevertheless, it shares with the other two professions sufficiently similar goals and procedures that a deeper understanding of records management on the part of library and archives professionals is warranted. More pragmatically, information professionals in corporate, academic, and public libraries are beginning to be looked to as the logical inheritors of records management responsibilities (many of which do not become "responsibilities" until after they have become problems).

Records managers are confronted by a shifting technological landscape, shaped by largely unpredictable developments in information and image handling. This situation is normal for the the practicing librarian. Records managers often have to tread delicately with information users, and this too is true of librarians. Records managers design systems for information acquisition, storage, access, and delivery. None of this is new to the library science community. In fact, for librarians to learn about records management mainly requires adjustments in perspective and vocabulary, and an introduction to standard practices.

Most records management texts assume either no subject background or educational level at all, or are written for students in schools of business administration or computer science. This text is written with the librarian and the library educator in mind. It assumes that the reader is familiar with the basic concepts of library and information science, through on the job experience or professional education, or a combination of the two. It follows closely the course in Records Management taught at the Graduate School of Library and Information Science at Simmons College, Boston, Massachusetts.

The first half of the book reviews standard records management practice. This is followed by a series of issues-based chapters which take up such topics as information policy, evaluation, and information resources management. The last three chapters are case studies of records management in library settings -- one in a special library, one in a public library, and one in a state archives. Each chapter is accompanied by a list of references and suggested readings, and a group of discussion points which could be used in a classroom or study group context.

Candy Schwartz and Peter Hernon
February, 1992

Chapter One

Records Management: An Overview

Records management is concerned with gaining control over the recorded information which an institution (or, for that matter, an individual) needs to do business. For an institution, this would include personnel files, inventory records, constitutions and by-laws, minutes of meetings, policies and directives, financial records of all kinds, contracts, and so on. As individuals in society, our own records include tax returns, wills, birth certificates, and all those other pieces of paper which record our lives and livelihoods. Records management involves exercising control over all phases of the life of an information resource, from creation and organization through dissemination, use, and either permanent retention or destruction.

Records management activities are carried out in academic settings (under the direction of registrars and business managers), in governments at the national, state, regional, and local levels, and in public and private corporations and institutions of all types and sizes. Sometimes records operations are distributed among different branches of an organization, such as data processing, personnel, purchasing and supplies, and archives. Diffusion of responsibility, however, does not lend itself to effective and efficient service, and organizations which recognize this usually concentrate responsibility in a records management department (or in a records manager).

Definitions of records management usually emphasize a systematic approach to planning, and focus on the functioning of business operations. For instance, the following appear in some of the standard records management texts and sources:

o   The systematic control of all records from their creation or receipt, through their processing, distribution, organization, storage and retrieval to their ultimate disposition. (Association of Records Managers and Administrators, 1989, p. 17)

o   Records management is the application of systematic and scientific control to all of the recorded information that an organization needs to do business. (Robek, Brown, and Maedke, 1987, p. 5)

o   Records management is an administrative system by which an organisation seeks to control the creation, distribution, filing, retrieval, storage and disposal of those records which are created or received by that organisation in the course of its business. In this "information age," it is also the means by which the valuable information which is contained in those records is released in support of that business. (Emmerson, 1989, p. 5)

In the same way that librarianship has moved from being reactive (the library as storehouse) to proactive (the library as information service provider and advocate), the focus of records management has shifted. Activities such as records filing, storage, and destruction are still central to the practice of records management, but the current thrust of the profession is also to gain control over the creation and dissemination of internally generated information. This is apparent in the definitions above, and in the content of records management texts and handbooks. It is interesting to note that this shift in emphasis has been accompanied by the creation of titles such as "information resources manager" or "information and records manager," much in the same way that terms such as "information scientist" or "information specialist" have evolved to reflect new outlooks on librarianship. Information resources management implies both a way of looking at information and a set of skills and tools to bring to bear on information control, and is discussed in more detail in Chapter 12.

RECORDS MANAGEMENT, LIBRARIANSHIP, AND ARCHIVES MANAGEMENT

The difference between records management and librarianship or archives management is sometimes a difficult one to grasp, as libraries and archives are largely concerned with records (in that catalog cards or online catalog entries are records of items on shelves or in storage facilities). Certain aspects of library management, such as circulation control and serials control, are examples of records management. However, there are some fundamental differences. Figure 1-1 illustrates some of these differences, and they are discussed more fully in this section.

Records management focuses almost entirely on *internal* records, that is, information which is generated during the course of business, for instance, invoices, personnel files, order forms, contracts, and policy documents, such as directives. Libraries are much more concerned with acquiring, controlling, and disseminating sources which are created by external agencies (authors, publishers, corporate institutions, governments, etc.).

Figure 1-1. Library Science, Archives Management, and Records Management.

LIBRARIES	ARCHIVES	RECORDS CENTERS
	Sources of Materials	
external	*external and internal*	*internal*
	Nature of Information	
recorded knowledge	*institutional history*	*business operations*
	Media	
print/microform	*print/microform*	*print/microform*
audiovisual	*audiovisual*	*audiovisual*
electronic/optical	*electronic/optical*	*electronic/optical*
realia	*realia*	*realia*
	Principal Activities	
collection development	*collection development*	*forms design/ records appraisal*
acquisitions	*acquisitions*	*records transfer*
cataloging/indexing	*description*	*inventory*
filing/shelving	*filing/shelving*	*filing/records storage*
reference/circulation	*reference*	*retention/retrieval*
interlibrary loan		
orientation		
preservation	*preservation*	*protection*
	microreproduction	*microreproduction*
	reprography	*reprography*
	Professional Education	
master's degree	*master's degree*	*degree varies*
accredited programs	*optional certification*	*optional certification*
	Professional Associations	
well identified	*well identified*	*well identified*
	Journals/Indexing Sources	
many journals	*few journals*	*few journals*
small core of sources	*small core of sources*	*scattered sources*

Another difference is that records management is concerned with the *function* of records rather than their intellectual content, whereas libraries emphasize the *content* of items, inasmuch as they represent recorded knowledge. Like records managers, archivists deal with internally created materials, but with an emphasis on their *historical* value. These differences in approach lead to differences in the organization of and access to materials. Library access to collections (through shelf arrangement, catalogs, bibliographies, and indexes) is largely based on subject content. Finding aids for archival collections generally emphasize provenance, thereby serving historical research purposes. In records management, collections are accessed by filing systems and listings which focus on institutional function.

As might be expected, all three groups deal with the same diversity of formats, and use the same tools for information handling. Information may be recorded in print, in graphic form, in microform, electronically, optically, orally, or may be conveyed by a physical artifact (for instance, a collection of shoe samples). The companies which supply libraries and archives with shelving and cabinetry provide the same services for records centers. The catalog cards, databases, and vertical file folders used in libraries and archives for organizing information and making it accessible are also used by records managers. Filing, indexing, and classification are activities common to all three groups, as are management tasks, such as staffing, training, budgeting, planning, and policy setting.

One of the most substantial differences between records management and either library science or archival studies is the absence of a standard educational path to and through the profession. The master's degree in library science (under a variety of different names) is typically recognized as the entree to professional work in libraries, and in archival studies, a master's degree in either library science or history (or both) is expected. In both these fields, doctoral degrees lead to higher levels of management or to research and teaching. By contrast, there is no widely accepted degree for records management, although the Institute of Certified Records Managers administers a certification program, and a number of undergraduate and graduate programs offer courses or specializations (Association of Records Managers and Administrators, 1991). Records managers tend to have risen through the ranks within a corporation, and those who have graduate degrees may have studied business administration, computer science, history, or library science (Williams, 1987). Records managers in the public sector may be political appointees with little in the way of academic preparation for records administration.

The case can be made for library and information science as a natural home for records managers. Apart from common tools, activities, and resources, both share a strong user services orientation, and both are coming to grips with the impact of new technologies for information storage, retrieval, and dissemination. Furthermore, as cost centers both have to deal with the problems of demonstrating their worth as proactive information providers, whether in profit or nonprofit settings. Relatively new phrases, such as "information resources management" or "information and records management," have found their way into course titles or degree titles in library and information science departments. These phrases reflect an approach which argues that information services are most effectively provided by persons who understand the impact of information in an organization, who can analyze user needs at many levels, and who can coordinate the contributions of all information centers, including libraries, records centers, archives, and data processing facilities.

Librarians should find an introduction to records management useful for a variety of reasons. In a large institution, with an existing records management department, it is important that all parties concerned with information handling understand each others' roles. In small organizations, or in organizations which do not have a formal records management program, librarians or archivists may be able to make a substantial contribution by establishing a program. In fact, small businesses are frequently unaware of their legal obligations with respect to records keeping, and an informed librarian cum records manager can be an invaluable asset.

Library offices contain records which are subject to the same control considerations as the records of any working business. Correspondence and personnel files, worksheets, order forms and invoices, policy statements, systems documentation, statistics on library activities, and maintenance and service contracts are all examples of records which might be found in library offices. A systematic approach to managing records of these kinds would result in benefits with respect to efficient use of space, reduction in duplication of effort, and ease of retrieval and analysis for decision making.

PROFESSIONAL ASSOCIATIONS, JOURNALS, AND INFORMATION SERVICES

Like librarians and archivists, records managers enjoy affiliation with many different professional organizations, and their information needs are addressed by an array of trade literature, scholarly journals, newsletters, and monographic publications. Tables 1-1 and 1-2 provide address and bibliographic information for the associations and journals discussed in the following sections.

Table 1-1. Associations and Organizations in the United States.

Association for Federal Information Resources Management (AFFIRM)
P.O. Box 11967, Alexandria, Virginia 22312
202-453-4126

Association for Information and Image Management (AIIM)
1100 Wayne Avenue, Suite 1100, Silver Spring, Maryland 20910
301-587-8202; FAX 301-587-2711

Association for Information Management (AIM)
6348 Munhall Court, PO Box 374, McLean, Virginia 22101
703-790-0403

Association of Commercial Records Centers (ACRC)
P.O. Box 20518, Raleigh, North Carolina 27619
800-336-9793; FAX 919-546-0545

Association of Records Managers and Administrators
(ARMA International)
4200 Somerset Drive, Suite 215, Prairie Village, Kansas 66208
800-422-2762; 913-341-3808; FAX 913-341-3742

Information Industry Association (IIA)
555 New Jersey Avenue, Suite 800, Washington, D.C. 20001
202-639-8262; FAX 202-638-4403

Institute of Certified Records Managers (ICRM)
P.O. Box 8188, Prairie Village, Kansas 66028
800-825-4276

International Information Management Congress (IMC)
345 Woodcliff Drive, Fairport, New York 14450-4201
716-383-8330; FAX 716-383-8442

National Association of Government Archives and Records
Administrators (NAGARA)
c/o Executive Secretariat, New York State Archives
Room 10A46, Cultural Education Center, Albany, New York 12230
518-473-8037

Table 1-1. (Continued)

National Records Management Council (NAREMCO)
60 East 42nd Street, New York, New York 10165
212-697-0290

Society for Information Management (SIM)
401 North Michigan Avenue, Chicago, Illinois 60611-4267
312-644-6610; FAX 312-321-6869

Associations

The Association of Records Managers and Administrators (ARMA International) is the premiere professional organization for records managers, with well over 10,000 members. The Association was formed in 1975 from the merger of the Association of Records Executives and Administrators (founded in 1955) and the American Records Management Association (founded in 1956). ARMA has 135 local chapters which are organized into 12 regional groups. The chapters and the groups hold regular meetings, and the Association holds one annual conference. ARMA also has about 40 Industry Action Committees which focus on special interests, for example, Advertising, Legal Services, Mineral Mining, Health Care Services, and Police/Law Enforcement. ARMA is active in creating and promoting industry standards and guidelines, presents several annual awards and scholarships, and operates a speaker's bureau. The Association is affiliated with the Institute of Certified Records Managers. ARMA publishes *ARMA News, Notes and Quotes* (a bimonthly newsletter), *Records Management Quarterly* (the principal journal in the field), *Directory of Collegiate Schools Offering Courses and Majors in Records and Information Management* (annual), and various monographs, guidelines, and audiovisual aids.

In the absence of a professional degree track, the Institute of Certified Records Managers (ICRM) administers a series of examinations which lead to certification. To become a Certified Records Manager (CRM), the candidate must pass all the examinations and show evidence of a number of years of experience in records management. The importance of the CRM to employers varies from region to region. The Institute was founded in 1975 and currently numbers some 550 members. ICRM is affiliated with ARMA, and meets at ARMA's annual conference. Publications include *ICRM Newsletter* (three times a year), *Membership Directory* (annual), and *Preparing for the CRM Examination: A Handbook*. This last title is particularly helpful for the extensive lists of readings provided as an aid to those studying for certification. In 1991, ARMA surveyed records managers about their attitudes towards the CRM certificate, and the results might help shape the Association's educational platform.

The Association for Information and Image Management (AIIM) (formerly the National Microfilm Association and the National Micrographics Association) was founded in 1943. Among its 8,500 members are manufacturers, distributors, and users of information and image handling equipment. AIIM has 51 local groups, and sponsors one annual conference with a large trade show. Other activities include several annual awards and scholarships. AIIM maintains a library and resource center, and publishes *Inform* (a journal issued 10 times a year), *fyi/im* (a newsletter), *Information and Image Management* (an annual profile of the information industry), *Information Management Sourcebook* (an annual buying guide), *Resource Center Index* (semiannual), *AIIM Monthly Monitor* (an index to current professional literature), and a number of pamphlets, standards, and reports.

The Information Industry Association (IIA) was founded in 1968 as a trade association serving the interests of the information industries, including publishers, telecommunications companies, database services, hardware and software manufacturers, and so on. IIA represents its 800 (institutional) member constituency to the federal and state/local governments, and works to keep its members well informed on new technologies, regulatory issues, public policy, and marketing. The Association also attempts to facilitate new business ventures among its membership. IIA has an annual conference with exhibits, and it also sponsors various symposia and seminars. IIA publishes *Information Times* (a bimonthly tabloid style journal), *Friday Memo* (a biweekly newsletter), and *Information Sources: The Companies, Products, and People of the Information Industry* (annual).

Founded in 1978 (and known as Associated Information Managers until 1990), the Association for Information Management (AIM) has 1000 members, including information managers and chief information officers in all types of settings. AIM runs a career service, holds one annual conference and a number of regional meetings, compiles bibliographies and statistics, has a speaker's bureau, and presents several annual awards. Its publications include *Conference Proceedings* (annual), *AIM Network* (a monthly newsletter), and *Who's Who in Information Management* (annual).

The Society for Information Management (SIM), founded in 1968, is a professional society for information system executives with almost 2,000 members and 25 local groups. The Society has a strong interest in management information systems, and in the application of new technologies. SIM offers various educational and research programs and awards, and some of the local chapters are very active in developing recruitment and training programs for new professionals. SIM publishes *MIS Quarterly* (a research journal), *Network* (a bimonthly newsletter), *Proceedings* (of the annual conference), and various research reports.

Formerly the International Micrographic Congress, the International Information Management Congress (IMC) was founded in 1962 to serve as an international federation of information management societies. Its membership now numbers over 800 such societies with 30 regional groups. IMC sponsors seminars and exhibitions (including an annual convention) in various parts of the globe, and bestows several annual awards. IMC's main publications are *IMC Journal* (bimonthly) and *IMC Newsletter* (monthly).

Two associations focus on records management in government. The National Association of Government Archives and Records Administrators (NAGARA), founded in 1974, currently has some 345 institutional and individual members. NAGARA focuses on government records and archives at the federal, state, county and local level. The Association provides a forum for information exchange, and promotes research and educational activities. NAGARA represents its community to the government in issues affecting records management, promotes and distributes various guidelines and other materials, and holds an annual conference. NAGARA publications include a *Directory of State Archives and Records Management Programs* (annual), *NAGARA Clearinghouse* (a quarterly newsletter), and *Government Records Issues*, a series of short papers on timely topics. The Association for Federal Information Resources Management (AFFIRM), founded in 1979, has upwards of 275 members. AFFIRM promotes information resources management in the federal government through participation in meetings and symposia on federal information management, and is particularly concerned with issues such as privacy, paperwork reduction, and the impact of new information handling technologies. AFFIRM holds one annual conference and publishes *The Affirmation* (a monthly newsletter) and a *Membership Directory* (annual).

Several smaller organizations are also of interest to records managers. The Association of Commercial Records Centers (ACRC) was founded in 1980, and serves the interests of the commercial records center business, with over 370 members. ACRC holds one annual conference and publishes *For the Record* (a quarterly newsletter). The National Records Management Council (NAREMCO) is not a membership organization, but is instead an independent bureau acting in support of business and government organizations seeking to apply advanced records management systems. NAREMCO, founded in 1948, maintains a speakers' list, in addition to providing research and consulting services.

There are similar societies in most industrialized nations. In the United Kingdom, for instance, records managers turn to the Association for Information Management (Aslib) and the Association of Commonwealth

Archivists and Records Managers (ACARM), as well as the European Information Industry Association (EURIPA). Aslib is particularly worth noting on either side of the Atlantic for its serial publications, *International Journal of Information Management*, *Records Management Journal*, and *Aslib Information* (all discussed in more detail below). Canadian professional associations include the Canadian Information and Image Management Society (CIIMS), the Canadian Information Industry Association (CIIA), and the Canadian Information Processing Society (CIPS).

Records managers in specific industries or professions can often find specialized associations which serve their interests, or might form special interest groups within larger associations. The American Medical Records Association (AMRA), the American Association of Collegiate Registrars and Admissions Officers (AACRAO), and the Nuclear Information and Records Management Association (NIRMA) are examples of the former, and special interest groups can be seen in the Records Management committee of the International Institute of Municipal Clerks and the committee on Charts and Records of the American Association of Hospital Podiatrists. A number of professional groups, such as the Office Automation Society International (OASI), the Business Forms Management Association (BFMA), and the Data Processing Management Association (DPMA), focus on activities closely allied to records management.

Journals and Newsletters

ARMA's *Records Management Quarterly* is the foremost professional journal for records managers. It usually carries four to six feature articles in each issue (including some case studies), as well as book and audiovisual reviews, industry and association news, columns, and letters to the editor. Since ARMA is the largest professional organization in the field, this is probably the most widely read records management serial.

The *IMC Journal*, published bimonthly by the International Information Management Congress, typically contains six or seven special reports and application studies. Other features include a "yellow pages" section with news about the association, new products (including a reader service card for requesting product literature), and international events of interest to records managers, and a "World Bookstore" section with publication announcements.

Inform, the magazine of the Association for Information and Image Management, is a glossy publication with four or five articles each month on optical disk and computer technology and micrographics. Regular columns include "Capitol Comment," "Technology," "Trends," and "Management," and *Inform* also carries book and media reviews, a calendar of events, and many advertisements.

Table 1-2. Journals and Newsletters.

IMC Journal, 1967-
International Information Management Congress
Bimonthly ISSN: 0019-0012 CODEN: IMGCB7

Inform: The Magazine of Information and Image Management, 1967-
Association for Information and Image Management
Monthly ISSN: 0892-3876 CODEN: INFREN

International Journal of Information Management, 1980-
Butterworth-Heinemann Publishers
Quarterly ISSN: 0268-4012

Recordfacts Update, 1987-
Records Administration Information Center
Office of Records Administration
National Archives and Records Administration
3 issues a year

Records & Retrieval Report, 1985-
Greenwood Publishing Group, Inc.
10 issues a year ISSN: 8756-0089

Records Management Journal, 1989-
Aslib, The Association for Information Management
Quarterly ISSN: 0956-5690

Records Management Quarterly, 1967-
Association of Records Managers and Administrators
ISSN: 1050-2343 CODEN: RMGQAB

The *International Journal of Information Management* is published quarterly by Butterworth's in association with Aslib. It is a scholarly journal aimed at professional information managers. Each issue holds six or seven refereed articles, along with a few shorter reports, several book reviews, conference reports, and a calendar of events.

Records Management Journal, another quarterly publication of Aslib, is a relatively new entrant into the list of records management serials (the first issue was published in Spring 1989). The emphasis here is on managerial aspects, practical information, and new ideas. The first few issues carried four or five long articles and several columns, letters, and book reviews.

12   Records Management and the Library

Records Management Journal is scholarly in appearance, with only one or two advertisements in the back cover pages. Aslib also publishes *Aslib Information* 10 times a year, with short articles, news, reviews, and advertisements targeted to a wide audience, including records managers.

Two newsletters targeted specifically to records managers are *Records & Retrieval Report* (10 times a year) and *Recordfacts Update* (three times a year). The former, published by the Greenwood Publishing Group, is intended to provide practical guidelines for cost-efficient records management. Each issue runs to about 15 pages, focuses on one or two specific topics, and carries an index to the previous issues for the year. Issues in 1990 included anti-virus protection products, forms management, labor costs, local area networks, and sabotage. *Recordfacts Update* is available at no cost from the Records Administration Information Center at the National Archives and Records Administration in Washington, D.C. It carries information and news on federal records activities.

Journals in related fields, such as archives management, computer science, library and information science, office management, information resources management, management information systems, and information technology, frequently carry material of interest to records managers. Titles which are most likely to yield useful citations include:

o   *American Archivist*;
o   *Archives*;
o   *Archives & Museum Informatics*;
o   *Bulletin of the American Society for Information Science*;
o   *Datamation*;
o   *Docment Image Automation* (formerly *Optical Information Systems*);
o   *Government Computer News*;
o   *Information Processing & Management*;
o   *Information Systems*;
o   *Information Systems Management*;
o   *Information Week*;
o   *International Journal of Micrographics & Optical Technology*;
o   *Journal of Management Information Systems*;
o   *Journal of Systems Management*;
o   *Microcomputers for Information Management*;
o   *MIS Quarterly*;
o   *MIS Week*; and
o   *The Office*.

Secondary Services

Secondary services are not as fully developed for records management; there is no one indexing service or online database directed specifically to the needs of records managers. Instead, the professional literature is indexed by a wide scatter of print and online secondary services (including *Library Literature*, *Library and Information Science Abstracts*, and *Information Science Abstracts*). Figure 1-2 shows the principal indexing services and online databases in the field of records management, and the degree to which they cover the journals mentioned above.

WHAT DO RECORDS MANAGERS DO?

Separate chapters discuss the activities of records management, as well as broader or overarching issues and activities, such as systems analysis, information policy, and information resources management. For now, a brief outline of activities can provide an overview and set the stage:

o   *Records selection and inventory.* Existing records in an organization must be identified, and their role or value must be assessed.

o   *Records retention and disposition.* A variety of factors dictate the length of time for which a record must be kept and the appropriate methods of destruction or disposal for nonpermanent records.

o   *File organization and handling.* Certain records are needed on a regular basis, and must be organized for effective access. Records which are no longer needed in active storage may still need to be stored for legal, historical, or other reasons.

o   *Reprographics and micrographics management.* Records largely are generated by duplication technologies, and may be stored permanently or temporarily using reprographic and micrographic technologies.

o   *Database and information technologies.* Database management software can be an effective tool for records control, and new technologies present attractive options for records storage and dissemination.

o   *Vital records management.* Vital records are those which are absolutely necessary for the survival of an organization; they must be identified and protected.

o   *Disaster preparedness.* A disaster recovery program for records is essential to the survival of an organization.

Figure 1-2. Coverage of Records Management by Secondary Services.

Journals

Records Management Quarterly (RMQ)
IMC Journal (IMCJ)
Inform (INF)
International Journal of Information Management (IJIM)
Records Management Journal (RMJ)
Records & Retrieval Report (R&RR)
Recordfacts Update (RU)

American Archivist (AA)
Archives & Museum Informatics (A&MI)
Archives (ARC)
Bulletin of the American Society for Information Science (BASIS)
Datamation (DATA)
Document Image Automation (DIA)
Government Computer News (GCN)
Information Processing & Management (IP&M)
Information Systems (IS)
Information Systems Management (ISM)
Information Week (IW)
International Journal of Micrographics & Optical Technology (IJM)
Journal of Management Information Systems (JMIS)
Journal of Systems Management (JSM)
Microcomputers for Information Management (MIM)
MIS Quarterly (MISQ)
MIS Week (MISW)
The Office (OFF)

Indexing Services

AB *ABI/Inform* (online, CD-ROM)
AD *Accounting & Data Processing Abstracts* (print)
AC *Accountants Index* (print, online)
BI *Business Index* (CD-ROM)
BP *Business Periodicals Index* (print, online, CD-ROM)
CD *Computer Database* (online, CD-ROM)
CL *Computer Literature Index* (print)
ER *ERIC* (print, online, CD-ROM)
IS *Information Science Abstracts* (print, online)
IN *Inspec* (print, online)

Records Management: An Overview   15

Figure 1-2. *(Continued)*

LI *Library & Information Science Abstracts* (print, online, CD-ROM)
LL *Library Literature* (print, online, CD-ROM)
MC *Management Contents* (online)
PT *Predicasts F&S Indexes* (print, online)
TI *Trade & Industry Index* (online)

Coverage of Journals by Indexing Services

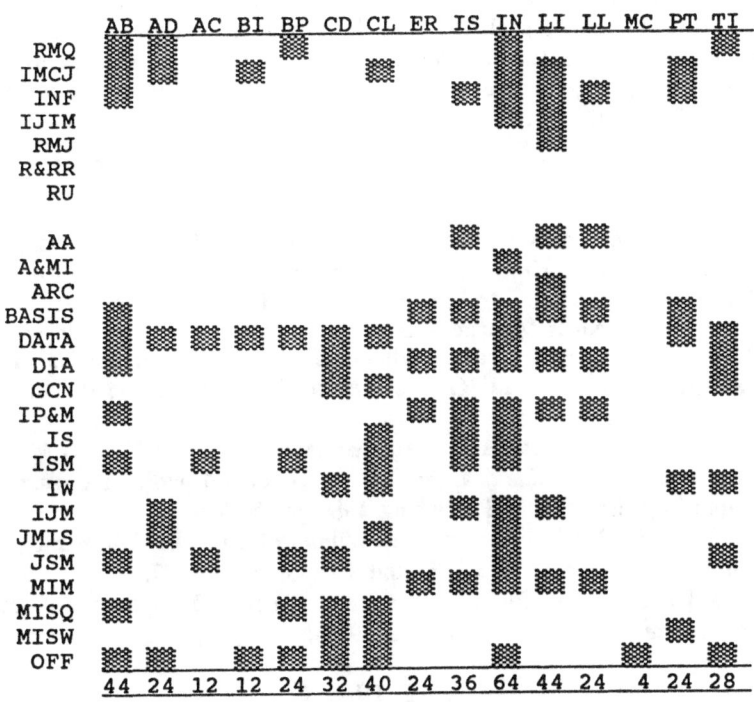

In some cases, coverage is selective rather than comprehensive.

o   *Forms management.* Information is collected, reported, and stored on forms; effective forms design and inventory control contributes to effective records management.

o   *Correspondence, reports, and directives management.* All information carrying resources generated by an organization can be subject to records management control.

o   *Records center management.* As with any department in an organization, managing a records center involves planning, staffing, policy setting, promotion, and similar managerial activities.

These tasks will each be explored in further depth throughout the book. First, however, it is important to understand the historical background of records management, especially as the development of records management in many ways parallels the development of libraries. Chapter 2 explores this history and highlights some of the historical events which have been significant for both fields.

REFERENCES

Association of Records Managers and Administrators. *Directory of Collegiate Schools Offering Courses and Majors in Records and Information Management.* 1991 ed. Prairie Village, KS: ARMA International, 1991.

Association of Records Managers and Administrators. *Glossary of Records Management Terms.* Prairie Village, KS: ARMA International, 1989. (ARMA International Guideline for Records and Information Management)

Emmerson, Peter. "What is Records Management?" In *How to Manage Your Records: A Guide to Effective Practice*, edited by Peter Emmerson. Cambridge, Eng.: ICSA Publishing, 1989, pp. 5-10.

Robek, Mary F., Gerald F. Brown, and Wilmer O. Maedke. *Information and Records Management.* 3d ed. Encino, CA: Glencoe, 1987.

Williams, Robert V. "Records Management: An IRM Perspective," *Records Management Quarterly* 21 (October 1987): 36-40, 54, 71.

READINGS

1. On Librarianship and Records Management

Evans, Frank B. "Archivists and Records Managers: Variations on a Theme." In *A Modern Archives Reader*, edited by Maygene F. Daniels and Timothy Walch. Washington, DC: National Archives and Records

Service, U.S. General Services Administration, 1984, pp.25-45. (Reprinted from *The American Archivist* 30 (January 1967): 45-58.)

Horton, Forest Woody, Jr. "Librarianship and Information Management," *Information Management Review* 4 (Summer 1988): 59-64.

Hubbard, Abigail and Barbara Wilson. "An Integrated Information Management Education Program . . . Defining a New Role for Librarians in Helping End-Users," *Online* 10 (March 1986): 15-23.

Lee, Frank. "Expanding Your Base: The Law Librarian as Records Manager," *Law Library Journal* 80 (Winter 1988): 123-129.

Pemberton, J. Michael. "Library and Information Science: The Educational Base for Professional Records Management," *Records Management Quarterly* 15 (April 1981): 48-53.

Pemberton, J. Michael. "Education for Records Managers: Rigor Mortis or New Directions?," *Records Management Quarterly* 25 (July 1991): 50-54.

Schwartz, Diane G. "New Roles for the Medical Librarian in an Information Management Environment," *Medical Reference Services Quarterly* 6 (Winter 1987): 27-33.

2. Basic Texts

These are some of the best known textbooks in the field of records management. Individual chapters will be listed in the readings throughout this book. New editions of Aschner, Diamond, and Johnson and Kallaus were expected in late 1991, but were not available for review at the time of preparing this text.

Aschner, Katherine, ed. *Taking Control of Your Office Records: A Manager's Guide.* White Plains, NY: Knowledge Industry Publications, 1983.

Diamond, Susan Z. *Records Management: A Practical Guide.* New York: AMACOM, 1983.

Emmerson, Peter, ed. *How to Manage Your Records: A Guide to Effective Practice.* Cambridge, Eng.: ICSA Publishing, 1989.

Johnson, Mina M. and Norman F. Kallaus. *Records Management.* 4th ed. Cincinnati, OH: South-Western Publishing, 1987.

Lundgren, Carol A. and Terry D. Lundgren. *Records Management in the Computer Age.* Boston, MA: PWS Kent, 1989.

Penn, Ira A., Anne Morddel, Gail Pennix, and Kelvin Smith. *Records Management Handbook.* Brookfield, VT: Gower, 1989.

Place, Irene and David J. Hyslop. *Records Management: Controlling Business Information.* 2d ed. Reston, VA: Reston Publishing, 1987.

Ricks, Betty R. and Kay F. Gow. *Information Resource Management: A Records Systems Approach.* 2d ed. Cincinnati, OH: South-Western Publishing, 1988.

Robek, Mary E., Gerald F. Brown, and Wilmer O. Maedke. *Information and Records Management*. 3d ed. Encino, CA: Glencoe, 1987.
Smith, Milburn D. *Information and Records Management: A Decision-Maker's Guide to Systems Planning and Documentation*. New York: Quorum Books, 1986.
Wallace, Patricia E., Jo Ann Lee, and Dexter R. Schubert. *Records Management: Integrated Information Systems*. 3d ed. Englewood Cliffs, NJ: Prentice-Hall, 1992.

DISCUSSION POINTS

1. What files can you identify in your library which might be brought under better control? Are there records which you think are being saved to no purpose? Can the staff find what they need when they want it?

2. What kinds of correspondence files are kept in your library? How much time is spent managing correspondence files? Who makes the decisions as to whether a letter will be saved or discarded?

3. Does your institution have an archives? If so, is it part of the library, or separate? If there is no formal archives, who keeps the items relating to the history of your institution? Is it important to retain institutional memory? If you had to put together a centennial exhibit, where would you look for materials?

4. Does your institution have a records management program? If so, what is the title of the person who is in charge, and what is the relationship of the records management program to the library (and the archives, if there is one)? Do you think the current arrangement is effective?

Chapter Two

Historical Background

Records have been with us from the moment when the first cave dwellers decided that it might be wise to record the results of a hunt, whether for propitiation, or for their own glory, or as a suggestion for techniques, locations of game, and so on. Granted that these records were neither sophisticated nor portable, they were nonetheless records. In fact, what we know about the development of writing systems is largely based on sources which represent business records kept by early societies. The more agrarian, centralized, and wealthy societies became, the more it was necessary to commit to some permanent form vital facts which could not be retained in human memory. Furthermore, that permanent form had to be based on mutually understandable conventions (an "alphabet" or other common symbol system), and it had to be learned by those who would control the "business", i.e., wealth.

Over time, business records have been recorded on stone, pebbles, bone, wood, sticks, string, wax, clay, metal, animal hides (and later parchment), bark, papyrus, textiles, paper, and eventually plastic and other synthetic products (film, magnetic media, and optical media). The implements used to mark these materials with information have included charred wood, sharpened sticks or stones, styli, reeds, beads, brushes, knots (in strings), feathers, quills and pens in various forms, and the whole panoply of printing and duplication technology available for the past 500 years, up to and including laser beams.

Whatever the format, the intention (at least as far as business records are concerned) has always remained the same: to record ownership, accounts, debts, and other information vital to the control of property and people and the flourishing of the state, religious institution, enterprise, or individual. The purpose-based distinctions which we now make among *library*, *archive*, and *records collection* developed very gradually, as social institutions became more complex, and as reading and writing skills were spread among the population at large.

It is the nature of a state (or rather those who manage it and who have an interest in the continuation of the *status quo*) to require certain activities and behaviors of its citizens. Monarchs, emperors, pharaohs, heads of churches, presidents, and other governing bodies usually collect taxes, tithes, or tributes; enact and enforce laws; regulate migration and perhaps employment; and attempt to encourage commerce as long as it is in the best interests of the state. In more enlightened ages, states also provide services to citizens (for instance, public utilities, transportation systems, and medical and other social services). All of these efforts generate records. Furthermore, political units engage with other political units in boundary disputes, wars, and treaties, and they develop contractual arrangements with public and private institutions. These are also record-creating behaviors.

Twentieth-century developments in printing, copying, and computing technologies made for dramatic and somewhat sudden growth in the volume of records documenting interactions between a government and its constituents or other governments. In many nations the response to this growth has been to establish (or strengthen) government agencies and regulations concerned with exerting a more systematic control over records creation, arrangement, retention, and disposition. The same growth was experienced, of course, by private enterprise, and has contributed to the development of records management as a recognized profession (and to subsequent extension in the direction of information resources management).

EARLY HISTORY

Types of Writing Systems

Avrin (1991) provides an excellent characterization of the different systems and stages in the development of writing. *Embryo writing* (really prewriting or protowriting) uses signs which cannot be readily interpreted outside of the immediate frame of reference of the writer or audience. The meanings of cave drawings, by and large, remain obscure even to specialists because they are examples of embryo writing.

Logographic writing is picture-based, although the resemblance to the objects represented by logograms may diminish over time. Logographic writing can be further subdivided into two types: *pictographic writing* and *ideographic writing*. In the case of the former, the image stands for the object, so, for instance, a pictogram of a cow represents just that. Ideograms, on the other hand, may represent concepts related to the object portrayed by the symbol. An ideogram of a cow might represent cattle farming, or prosperity, or milk. Ideograms can play different grammatical roles in the construction of a text passage (they may act as verbs, adjectives, nouns, etc.).

In *phonographic writing*, as opposed to logographic writing, the symbols (phonograms) stand for the sound associated with the object represented by the sign. For instance, a picture of a fish would represent the sound "fish" (if we were looking at English as an example), and could be used in combination with other signs to form words (for instance, "official" or "efficient"). Most of us have played rebus or charades games along these lines.

Most of the systems with which we are familiar today fall into the final category, *phonetic writing*, although the symbols used may be historically derived from phonographic and logographic systems. The symbols used in phonetic writing represent speech elements, either vowels and consonants in alphabetic systems, or vowel and consonant combinations in syllabic systems. This obviously greatly reduces the number of symbols needed for written communication. English, and most western writing systems, are alphabetic. Japanese writing systems (katakana and hiragana) are generally syllabic, and Chinese is one of the few principally logographic writing systems still in wide use (it is also the oldest system in continuous use since the invention of writing).

Early Writing

Although the Sumerians are the first people whose business records have been recognized as such, there is no doubt that earlier societies kept track of property and commerce. Interpretations of early cave wall drawings and marked pebbles found in Southern France have suggested that they might represent records of herd ownership, property demarcation, and the like (Johnson, 1973, p. 13). The use of tally sticks and knotted cords as memory aids can still be found in some present-day societies, and are probably remnants of traditions passed down over the ages (Rider, 1976, p. 3).

By the end of the fourth millennium B.C. the Sumerians were using a mixed logographic and phonographic script to record business information on clay tablets. This writing in its later stages is called "cuneiform" after the Latin for "wedge", since the tool used to make an impression on soft clay resulted in wedge-shaped symbols. Over the next several millennia the various cultures which flourished in the Middle East adopted cuneiform writing, and it appears to have remained widely in use until the sixth or seventh century B.C.

Hieroglyphic writing in Egypt seems to have started in the third millennium B.C. Hieroglyphs may represent pictographs, ideographs, and phonographs, and are found on Egyptian monumental and memorial artifacts as well as in two cursive scripts for religious (hieratic script) and secular (demotic script) purposes. By the third century A.D. the use of hieroglyphics had largely ended, and even their existence remained obscure for many centuries to come (the Chinese, by way of contrast, had an officially standardized system of writing by the third century B.C., and its use continues to this day, albeit modified over time).

As these great nations fell out of power, others rose to greater influence through the first millennium B.C., and these newly powerful societies brought with them the development of alphabetic writing systems. In particular, the spread of alphabetic systems was assisted by a growth in trading and commerce. Among the most influential of these was the Phoenician alphabet, which was eventually adopted by the Greeks, and is the progenitor of Western alphabets.

Early Business Records

It is fortunate that clay was a widely available and inexpensive medium, as it has been well preserved over the centuries. Among the records deciphered from the clay tablets of the Sumerians and other civilizations we find tax memoranda, payrolls, loans, inventories, ledgers, records of money lenders and rates, military inventories of rations and equipment, contracts, trade and agricultural reports, cargo manifests, shipping schedules, commodity prices, and business correspondence. There are even examples of daily records kept on clay tablets, then discarded as the information was transcribed and cumulated into weekly accounts, which were then themselves cumulated over longer periods (Dunlap, 1972, p. 5). One of the other advantages of clay was that it could be imprinted with a permanent seal, which meant that contracts and other official agreements could be "signed" without the requirement of writing ability.

In some cases collections of records were indexed, abstracted, and cataloged. Clay tablets stored on racks or in jars, for instance, were often affixed with tags which noted contents (no doubt for convenience's sake) and/or shelf location. Papyrus rolls might be stored in roll containers made from animal hide or other materials, and also might have tags indicative of content. Catalogs, that is, lists of library holdings or guides to arrangement, have been found on the walls of archives and as separate records inventories.

Johnson and Harris (1976) point to the differentiation of library types as a logical consequence of economic advancement, political complexification, and the passage of reading and writing skills from the ruling elite to the middle/business classes. Early records are mainly found in temple libraries and government archives, as these bodies had property and wealth, and engaged in hiring, financing, borrowing, and exacting monies through taxes and tributes. Religious and ruling bodies kept records of laws, deeds, decrees, proclamations, populations, treaties, diplomatic correspondence, and religious rites and observances. Keeping records occupied a significant portion of time in the business of running an empire, and schools were established to maintain a supply of skilled scribes.

Private commercial agencies and local governments also needed to keep permanent records of their activities. Business archives held by private firms might include tax records (paid rather than collected), inventories, partnership treaties, accounts of agents and expeditions, and other similar kinds of records we would expect any modern commercial enterprise to maintain. Family libraries, in addition to those records representative of a family business, might contain genealogies, family letters, wills, and the like.

DEVELOPMENTS IN THE MODERN AGE

Printing and Reproduction

The significant changes in business records over the ensuing centuries have more to do with the medium on which they were recorded than with their content or organization. Unfortunately, record keeping for business migrated to less durable media, and so the written records of emerging modern society tend to be representative of intellectual life rather than business life. Universities, schools, religious institutions, governments, and individuals began to collect manuscripts and printed items for their scholarly or historical value (or for the prestige of having a library).

The Romans wrote on wood and wax slates, which could be hinged together in the form of a book. More flexible media (such as linen) could be sewn together in sheets. The Chinese had introduced paper making to Arabic trading partners before the eighth century A.D., and the first European manufacture of paper can be traced to the 13th century. The Chinese were also early inventors of block printing and moveable type, although it is not clear that their influence was responsible for European developments. In any event, block printing was well known in Europe by the 15th century, and also by this time a relatively large proportion of the business classes could read. The biggest breakthrough in publishing technology was the development of the printing press in the middle of the 15th century, usually attributed to Gutenberg.

It would be unreasonable to expect at this time that printing technologies would be used to create everyday business records, and indeed handwriting continued to be commonly employed until the invention of the typewriter in the 1860s. Similarly, outgoing records were largely hand-copied in bound copy books until the adoption of the letter press in the latter half of the 19th century (Yates, 1989). As has been the case with computer technology in the 20th century, costs of printing decreased and new methods proliferated through the 19th and early 20th centuries.

In 1867, the first practical and affordable typewriter was invented, by Christopher Latham Sholes,[1] followed in the first half of the 20th century by electric and later electronic typewriters. Printing and allied duplicating technologies, as well as developments in photography and micrographics,

---

[1] Vrooman (1923) presents a fascinating history of the typewriter and its impact on business and society.

quickly found commercial application in business records creation and reproduction. Data processing became a viable and then essential tool for modern office (and eventually library) management from the middle of the 20th century. The 1980s saw the widespread adoption of word-processing software and printers for written business communications, and machine-readable storage of not only data and text but also voice and image is now commonplace.

Filing Equipment

Increasingly heavy trading resulted from the age of exploration, and some of the early developments in filing systems date from this period. Libraries were already becoming astute at developing check-in systems, but merchants had different needs. A quick method of filing bills and other records of business appeared with the spindle file, a perpendicular rod affixed to a base (these can still be found in antique shops and the occasional small store). Two spindle files could be used to stack up (for instance) paid bills and unpaid bills. While primitive, this served the purpose at hand and with a minimum of space.

Pigeonhole files, such as still used in mail sorting environments, were a widespread way of filing correspondence. Once individual sections were full, their contents were tied into bundles and stored. In the mid-19th century "flat" files (so called because items were stored flat rather than folded) were also quite common. These took the form of books, boxes, and interchangeable cabinet drawers. Of course, in the case of both pigeonhole and flat files, any unevenness in the filing distribution of records created problems, and interfiling (or retrieval) was not very convenient. One popular variation on the flat file theme was the Shannon file, which fixed items in place by impaling them onto metal clamps, somewhat resembling a ring binder. The logical and much more flexible extension, the vertical file, was devised by the Library Bureau (a supply company founded by Melville Dewey), based on the model of the card catalog (Yates, 1989). In one form or another, the vertical file has remained the storage method of choice for most paper records ever since. As new media were introduced into offices, equipment manufacturers responded with a vast array of cabinetry, stationery, and shelving (covered in depth in Chapter 7).

Administrative Practices

Given the labor intensiveness of creating copies of outgoing documents prior to the development of easy duplication methods, it is not surprising that medieval records collections consisted primarily of incoming documents and internally kept records. In the later Middle Ages the practice of keeping register books (containing copies of outgoing items) began to take hold (Posner, 1967, p. 24). As geographic loci of political power became more settled and paper came into widespread use, codes of practice for archival inventory and preservation were adopted. France appears to have been the first nation to develop the notions of centralized state archives and the public's right to access state records in the 1790s. The former (if not the latter) practice spread gradually to other European nations. Britain, for instance, passed a Public Records Office Act in 1838. In the first part of the 19th century such establishments evolved into repositories of historical manuscripts, managed by scholars trained typically in library practices. By the latter half of the century more attention was being given to the problems of gaining control over current government records, and archival management began to be widely recognized in Europe and North America as an activity requiring specialized training and qualifications.

The 20th century has seen two world wars, a number of other widescale military engagements, accelerated developments in industrial production, increasingly complex structures in public administration, and the "information explosion." Wars (and complex governing bodies) by their nature generate large numbers of documents requiring speedy analysis and efficient storage and retrieval.[2,3] Industry, driven by profit and monitored by government agencies at all levels of jurisdiction, also demands effective records management. At the same time, the information explosion has created an information industry which has brought technological advances to bear on both creating information and on managing it. These influences have contributed to the evolution of the profession of records management, and in the United States as in many other industrialized nations, to efforts to standardize records handling practices and procedures at the national level.

RECORDS MANAGEMENT AND THE U.S. GOVERNMENT

Records Management in the Legislature

While most businesses did not establish formal records management procedures until after the 1950s (Diamond, 1983, p. 1), the U.S. federal

---

[2] Posner (1967, p. 87) describes a conversation between himself and an archivist colleague at the outbreak of the second World War: "in the last analysis, the overwhelming success of the Germans was attributable to the fact that they had entered the war with a better filing system."

[3] In a more recent example of records-keeping systems arising from military conflict, the Department of Veteran Affairs (at the request of the Defense Department) developed the automated VA/DOD Contingency Plan reporting system to handle anticipated heavy casualties during the Gulf War of 1990 (Schwartz, 1991).

government has shown itself to be quite progressive in attempting to cope with the problems of mismanaged paperwork. Most histories of records management practices at the national level begin with the establishment of the United States National Archives in 1934. However, it is worth noting that Congress passed a General Records Disposal Act in 1889 (contained in 25 Stat.), and the Bureau of Efficiency (harbinger of many things to come) was established in 1913 (Penn, Morddel, Pennix, and Smith, 1989, p. 5). During its first four years of existence, the National Archives assessed federal records keeping, and found, not surprisingly, a general state of disorder. This was further compounded by the paperwork generated by World War II and all the emergency agencies operating during the conflict. The National Archives worked on developing records disposal schedules, the use of which was authorized by a 1943 Records Disposal Act, amended in 1945 to authorize the use of a general schedule, and amended again in 1968 with changes in the definition of a record (82 Stat. 1238, 44 USC 3301).

In 1946, President Truman issued an executive order requiring records management programs in federal agencies. This was followed the next year by the signing of the Lodge-Brown Act (61 Stat. 246), which established a Commission on Organization of the Executive Branch of the Government. Herbert Hoover chaired the Commission, and among the materials reviewed was the report of the Task Force on Paperwork, contracted to the National Records Management Council (NAREMCO), and chaired by NAREMCO's Executive Director Emmett J. Leahy. The Hoover Commission made a number of recommendations, among them the passage of a Federal Records Act and the establishment of a Records Management Bureau in the Office of General Services.

In 1949, the Federal Property and Administrative Services Act (63 Stat. 377) established the General Services Administration (GSA), to which was transferred the renamed National Archives and Records Service, which, in turn, included a Records Management Division. The Federal Records Act of 1950 (64 Stat. 578) authorized the GSA to survey government records keeping practices and to recommend improvements. Records disposal programs were also mandated for all federal agencies, and records management programs spread to the ten GSA regional centers. The National Archives and Records Service also established regional records centers (nine of them by 1952). In 1953, the GSA issued the first of many editions of the *Guide to Records Retention Requirements*. By 1954, federal agencies claimed that the vast majority of their records were covered by federal records retention schedules.

The Second Commission on Organization of the Executive Branch, again chaired by Hoover and with assistance from NAREMCO, was established by the Brown-Ferguson Act (P.L. 83-108, 67 Stat. 142) in 1953. In discussing the Commission's mandate, President Eisenhower mentioned the importance of government living "as economically as it can;" there must be more efficiency and economy in government to ensure, in part, that a "domineering bureacuracy does not emerge" ("Annual Message to the Congress...," 1959, p. 22; "The President's News Conference...," 1959, pp. 293-294). The President's comments, and the findings of the Commission, echo what earlier studies had found, and presage what subsequent studies would find in the future: records had been collected from industry for no apparent use or purpose, and sometimes had not even been filed; both industry and the government were shouldering an extensive paperwork burden, with much unnecessary duplication of effort, producing redundant information; and, there was no monitoring of missing or incomplete reports.

The Commission was quite detailed about the deficiencies of current practice and the lack of improvement, and again made a number of recommendations. The gist of these were that a governmentwide records management program was needed, that it should be under the supervision of the GSA, and that each agency should undertake an assessment of how to reduce paperwork.

In 1956, the National Archives and Records Service advanced from the status of division to office, and gained an Office of Records Management concerned specifically with paperwork management.

Various other acts in the next two decades bore a direct relationship to the keeping of federal records. The Freedom of Information Act of 1966 and its amendments (5 USC 552) mandate that any person can request access to any records of the executive branch of the federal government, and that those records (unless they are protected, e.g., by national security or by other statutes) must be released. The Fair Credit Reporting Act of 1970 (84 Stat. 1114) gives individuals the right to amend incorrect credit records. The Privacy Act of 1974 (5 USC 552a), with certain exceptions, grants individuals access to personal files kept by the government, and protects individual privacy by requiring consent before those files might be viewed by other parties. The Buckley Amendments (20 USC 1232g) of the same year give parents and young adults access to school records.

In 1976 the Federal Records Act was supplemented by the Federal Records Management Amendments (90 Stat. 2723), which stress paperwork reduction and documentation of records keeping procedures, and also emphasize the concept of the "life cycle" of a record. The Paperwork Reduction Act of 1980 (P.L. 96-511, 94 Stat. 2812-2826) reaffirmed that concept, formally introduced the allied concept of "information resources management," and emphasized not only reduction in volume but also efficiency in records management.

This act also established the Office of Information and Regulatory Affairs (OIRA) in the Office of Management and Budget (OMB). The policy functions of the Director of OMB's Office of Information and

Regulatory Affairs include (see 44 USC 3503):

(1) Developing and implementing uniform and consistent information resources management policies and overseeing the development of information management principles, standards, and guidelines and promoting their use;

(2) Initiating and reviewing proposals for changes in legislation, regulations, and agency procedures to improve information management practices ...;

(3) Coordinating, through the review of budget proposals and as otherwise provided ... agency information practices;

(4) Promoting ... greater sharing of information by agencies;

(5) Evaluating agency information management practices to determine their adequacy and efficiency, and to determine compliance of such practices with the policies, principles, standards, and guidelines promulgated by the Director; and

(6) Overseeing, planning for, and conduct of research with respect to, Federal collection, processing, storage, transmission, and use of information.

The Current Picture

Governmentwide records and information management activities are loosely coordinated by three federal bodies: the Office of Management and Budget, the General Services Administration, and the National Archives and Records Administration.[4] Many departments and agencies also have offices which handle records and information management for that particular body (for instance, the Department of Agriculture has an Office of Information Resources Management, and Federal Emergency Management Agency (FEMA) records keeping functions are supervised by FEMA's Office of Administrative Support).[5] The National Institute of Science and Technology (NIST, formerly the National Bureau of Standards) also plays

---

[4] In 1985, the National Archives and Records Service became an independent agency, and was renamed the National Archives and Records Administration.

[5] The journal Government Computer News is an excellent source of information on and examples of federal information resources management problems and practices.

an important role in information resources management in that one of its charges is to provide technical services in support of federal information processing activities (Radack, 1990).

The General Services Administration (Figure 2-1) includes among its many subunits the Information Resources Management Service. This body is responsible for

> the coordination and direction of a comprehensive, Governmentwide program for the management, procurement, and utilization of automated data processing and telecommunications equipment and services; planning and directing programs for improving Federal records and information management practices; and managing and operating the Federal Information Centers. (National Archives and Records Administration, Office of the Federal Register, 1990, p. 613)

The Information Resources Management Service operates the Office of Technical Assistance (OTA), which advises federal agencies in information resources management, especially with respect to automation. The Service also publishes a number of practical "how to" guides under the series title *Information Resources Management Handbook*.

The Federal Information Centers, which were recently privatized, serve as referral points for information services and programs provided by the federal government, regionally and nationally.[6]

The National Archives and Records Administration (Figure 2-2) "establishes policies and procedures for managing U.S. Government records" (Ibid., p. 641). NARA advises and assists federal agencies in records and information management, and, of course, maintains the nation's archives. Two NARA units of interest to records managers are the Office of Records Administration and the Office of Federal Records Centers. The former

> develops standards and guidelines for the management and disposition of recorded information ... It appraises Federal records and approves records disposition schedules. It also monitors archival records not in the Agency's custody, inspects agency records and records management practices, develops records management training programs, and provides guidance and assistance with respect to proper records management. (Ibid., p. 643)

---

[6] The Centers accept telephone questions; written inquiries may be addressed to the Federal Information Center, P.O. Box 600, Cumberland, Maryland 21502-8600.

30   Records Management and the Library

Figure 2-1. Organization Chart, General Services Administration.

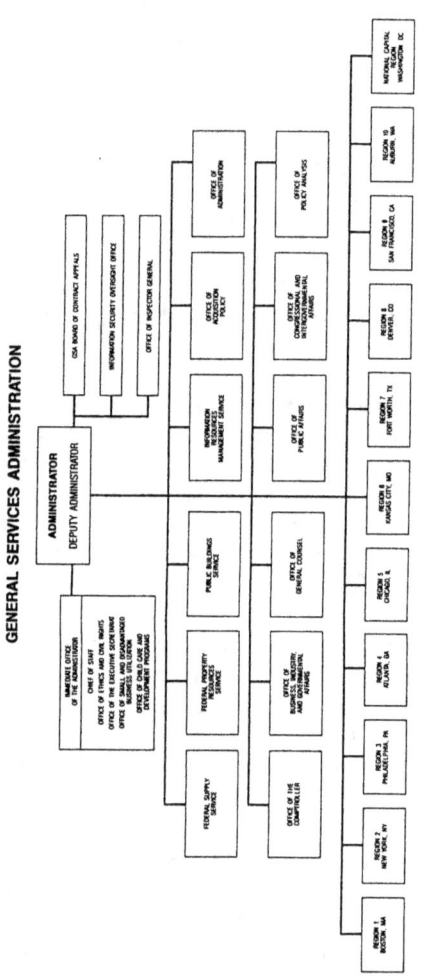

(From National Archives and Records Administration, Office of the Federal Register, *The United States Government Manual, 1991/1992.* Washington, DC: National Archives and Records Administration, Office of the Federal Register, 1991, p. 610.)

Figure 2-2. Organization Chart, National Archives and Records Administration.

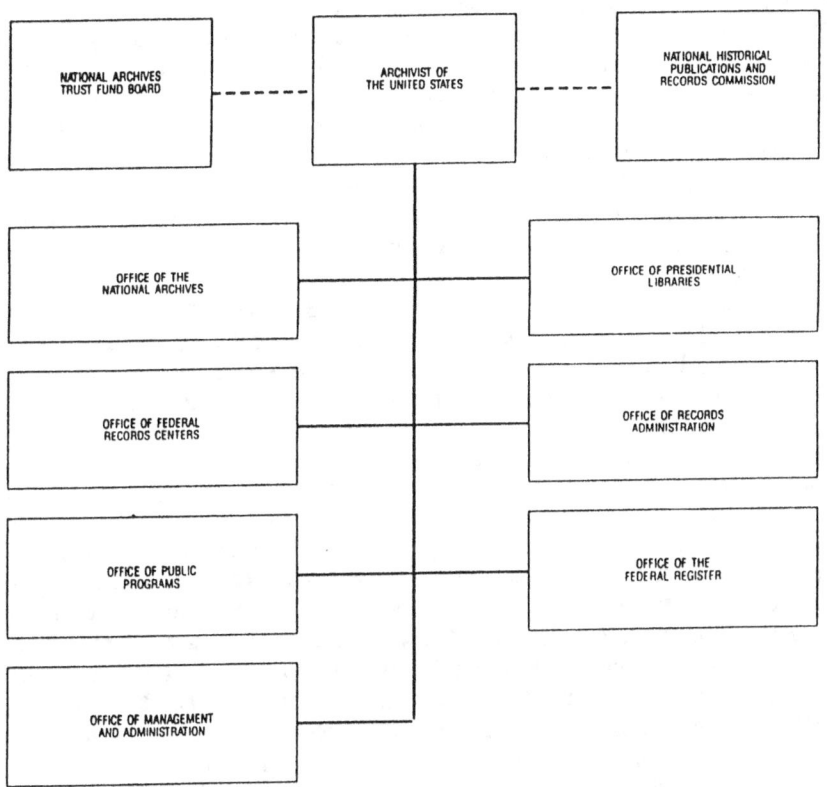

(From National Archives and Records Administration, Office of the Federal Register, *The United States Government Manual, 1991/1992.* Washington, DC: National Archives and Records Administration, Office of the Federal Register, 1991, p. 640.)

The Office of Records Administration publishes a series of *Instructional Guides*, and makes available (for a fee) a number of standard workshops designed for any federal employee responsible for records management. The Office's Records Administration Information Center provides telephone reference service for records management questions, publishes a directory of training programs in the greater Washington area, lends training materials, does some consulting to federal agencies, and arranges for speakers on records management topics. The Office of Federal Records Centers supervises the 14 records storage facilities located throughout the country. These centers provide reference services, prepare copies (including microform) of stored items, supply information, dispose of records, and offer a range of local records management workshops. NARA also maintains the Office of the Federal Register, which publishes (among other things) the daily *Federal Register*, the *United States Statutes at Large*, the annual *Code of Federal Regulations*, and, most important to records managers, the *Guide to Record Retention Requirements in the Code of Federal Regulations*.

At the time of the writing of this chapter (Summer 1992), Congress had reauthorized OMB's Office of Information and Regulatory Affairs, but not the Paperwork Reduction Act. Congress has considered various bills over the past few years to replace and expand the Paperwork Reduction Act with legislation calling for stricter information resources management over the life cycle of government information. Reauthorization has turned into a political contest between the President and competing members of Congress. Agencies, however, still honor the spirit of the 1980 Act and adhere to Circular No. A-130 of the Office of Management and Budget on the management of federal information resources. Revision of this circular proposed for late 1992 will focus on information dissemination as well as the provision of electronic products and services to the public (see Chapter 13).

The need to manage government information in an effective manner has been recognized by almost all recent administrations (and the same is probably true in most developed countries). Ronald Reagan tasked a force of some 161 leading executives to examine the various departments and agencies of the federal government as if they were considering a merger or takeover bid. They found that

> Key information regarding Government services, personnel, facilities, equipment, performance, and cost often was not available, and when available, was frequently out of date, inaccurate or incomplete. ... In addition, it became evident to the private sector executives that critical information was missing not only with respect to making an acquisition decision, but, more importantly,

with respect to running the Government even if it were acquired. (President's Private Sector Survey on Cost Control, 1984, p. i)

Presumably the objective of improving information handling is to improve overall operations and to promote informed planning and decision making. This is true at the federal level, as it is true in the smallest of businesses, and in the case of the federal government a fundamental issue of accountability to the governed is also at stake. Unfortunately in the case of the federal government, the sheer volume of information is overwhelming, even the more so as information is transmitted electronically. Figure 2-3, showing the increase in holdings of the Federal Records Centers alone, is indicative of the enormity of the problem.

The consequences of inefficient government records handling affect all levels of a society in which the state accepts the principle of accountability (and a citizen's right of access) and the burden of gathering information in order to meet that responsibility. These consequences are felt by individuals, and by private and public institutions:

> Almost every adult American fills out at least one Federally-required form, survey, or questionnaire each year. In FY 1988 alone, nearly 100 million citizens and over 5 million business firms and associations will report detailed information on income and finances to the Internal Revenue Service. Over 80 million Americans will provide detailed information demonstrating their eligibility to receive financial benefits from the Federal government. Thousands of businesses, non-profit organizations, and State and local agencies that must comply with Federal regulatory requirements or that receive Federal grants or contracts will file lengthy reports and applications. In all, Americans will spend almost 2 billion hours to meet Federal information collection requirements during FY 1988. (Office of Management and Budget, 1988, unnumbered first page of "Introduction")

CONCLUSION

Throughout history, the key to effective business information management has been the development of systems for organization and access. From rudimentary catalogs on temple walls to complex management information systems on mainframe computers, we have attempted to use the tools at hand to gain control over collections of data. The more that individuals and institutions interact, and the more that they share information with each other, the greater the need for compatibility and standardization in record handling systems.

34   Records Management and the Library

Figure 2-3. Holdings of Federal Records Centers.

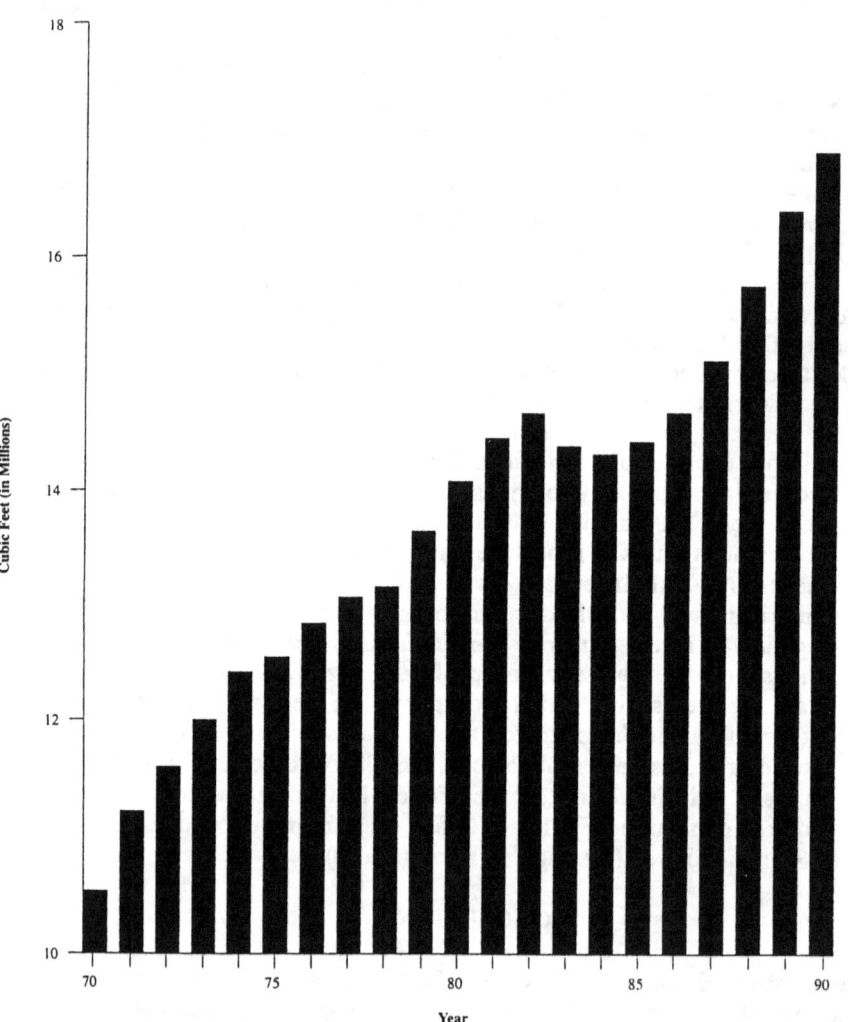

(From National Archives and Records Administration, *Annual Report for the Year Ended September 30, 1990*. Washington, DC: National Archives and Records Administration, Office of the Federal Register, 1990, p. 94.)

The same is true in library and information science. Where once each library carried out its activities using idiosyncratic local practices, we now have generalized principles, international standards, and a body of theory which we look to when developing systems to organize library collections and to promote intersystem cooperation. In the field of management (and also applicable to library management), a body of principles, guidelines, and tools for organizing and evaluating systems have been developed. The concepts of "information resources management" and the "life cycle" of a record are not used uniquely by the federal government; they are also applied in business records management environments, where the need for systematic control over information is just as important. The next chapter looks at systems analysis and the role that it plays in records management.

REFERENCES

"Annual Message to the Congress on the State of the Union, January 6, 1955," *Public Papers of the President: Dwight D. Eisenhower.* Washington, DC: GPO, 1959, pp. 7-30.

Avrin, Leila. *Scribes, Script and Books: The Book Arts from Antiquity to the Renaissance.* Chicago, IL: American Library Association, 1991.

Diamond, Susan Z. *Records Management: A Practical Guide.* New York: AMACOM, 1983.

Dunlap, Leslie W. *Readings in Library History.* New York: R.R. Bowker, 1972.

Johnson, Elmer D. *Communication: An Introduction to the History of Writing, Printing, Books and Libraries.* 4th ed. Metuchen, NJ: Scarecrow Press, 1973.

Johnson, Elmer D. and Michael H. Harris. *History of Libraries in the Western World.* 3d ed. Metuchen, NJ: Scarecrow Press, 1976.

National Archives and Records Administration, Office of the Federal Register. *Annual Report for the Year Ended September 30, 1990.* Washington, DC: National Archives and Records Administration, Office of the Federal Register, 1990.

National Archives and Records Administration, Office of the Federal Register. *The United States Government Manual, 1991/1992.* Washington, DC: National Archives and Records Administration, Office of the Federal Register, 1991.

Office of Management and Budget. *Information Collection Budget of the United States Government, Fiscal Year 1988.* Washington, DC: GPO, 1988 (SuDocs: Pr Ex 2.29:988).

Penn, Ira A., Anne Morddel, Gail Pennix, and Kelvin Smith. *Records Management Handbook.* Brookfield, VT: Gower, 1989.

Posner, Ernst. "Some Aspects of Archival Development Since the French

Revolution." In *Archives and the Public Interest: Selected Essays by Ernst Posner*, edited by Ken Munden. Washington, DC: Public Affairs Press, 1967, pp. 23-35.

"The President's News Conference of February 23, 1955," *Public Papers of the President: Dwight D. Eisenhower*. Washington, DC: GPO, 1959, pp. 282-295.

President's Private Sector Survey on Cost Control. "Information Gap in the Federal Government." In *Report on the Management Office Selected Issues* [popularly known as The Grace Commission Report], v.7, Washington, DC: GPO, 1984 (SuDocs: PR40.8:C83/R22).

Radack, Shirley M. "More Effective Federal Computer Systems: The Role of NIST and Standards," *Government Information Quarterly* 7 (1990): 37-49.

Rider, Alice Damon. *A Story of Books and Libraries*. Metuchen, NJ: Scarecrow Press, 1976.

Schwartz, Karen D. "Gulf War Triggers VA to Automate Casualty System," *Government Computer News* 10 (May 13, 1991): 57.

Vrooman, John Wright. *The Story of the Typewriter, 1873-1923*. Herkimer, NY: A. H. Kellogg Company for the Herkimer County Historical Society, 1923.

Yates, JoAnne. *Control through Communication: The Rise of System in American Management*. Baltimore, MD: The Johns Hopkins University Press, 1989.

READINGS

Bradsher, James Gregory. "A Brief History of the Growth of Federal Government Records, Archives, and Information 1789-1985," *Government Publications Review* 13 (1986): 491-505.

Hay, Denys. "Fiat Lux." In *Reader in the History of Books and Printing*, edited by Paul A. Winckler. Englewood, CO: Information Handling Services, 1978, pp. 5-25.

Lundgren, Carol A. and Terry D. Lundgren. *Records Management in the Computer Age*. Boston, MA: PWS Kent, 1989. Chapter 5: "Legislation Affecting Records Management."

Posner, Ernst. *Archives in the Ancient World*. Cambridge, MA: Harvard University Press, 1972.

Ricks, Betty R. and Kay F. Gow. *Information Resource Management: A Records Systems Approach*. 2d ed. Cincinnati, OH: South-Western Publishing, 1988. Appendix B: "History of Records Management."

Robek, Mary E., Gerald F. Brown, and Wilmer O. Maedke. *Information and Records Management*. 3d ed. Encino, CA: Glencoe, 1987. Chapter 2: "History and Status of Records Management."

Wallace, Patricia E., Jo Ann Lee, and Dexter R. Schubert. *Records Management: Integrated Information Systems.* 3d ed. Englewood Cliffs, NJ: Prentice-Hall, 1992, pp. 18-24.

Yates, JoAnne. *Control through Communication: The Rise of System in American Management.* Baltimore, MD: The Johns Hopkins University Press, 1989. Chapter 2: "Communication Technology and the Growth of Internal Communication."

DISCUSSION POINTS

1. Try to estimate how much time you, as an individual, spend each year filling out local, state, and federal government forms (such as taxes, car registration, etc.). What would be the advantages and disadvantages (*to you as an individual*) of sending this information electronically to a centralized service or to specific agencies (as one may now do with federal tax returns)? What would be the advantages and disadvantages from the service or agencies point of view?

2. Call the nearest Federal Information Center (a list of telephone numbers can be found in the current issue of the *United States Government Manual*). What kinds of services does it provide?

3. How would you go about requesting to examine your past tax records or census records as held by the federal government? Do you think that most citizens know about this right, or know how to exercize it? Do you think the government should make this right more widely publicized, and if so, how?

4. Visit a regional office of the National Archives or one of the Presidential libraries (see the current issue of the *United States Government Manual* for a list). What kinds of records does it have, and what kinds of services does it provide?

Chapter Three

Systems Analysis

General systems thinking emphasizes flexibility, the environment, and the fact that an organization consists of various interdependent parts. Systems analysis is a method for better understanding the relationship among those components and interdependent parts that have an impact on the operation of the organization, more precisely on its effectiveness and efficiency. A system is defined as a group of interrelated parts acting together to accomplish specific goals and objectives. Furthermore, one part affects other parts and the behavior of the entire system; the manner in which the parts affect the system is *more than* their sum. In short, the interaction among the different parts of the system combines to produce an attribute of the system that is not achievable by the individual parts alone.

Simply stated, the primary goal of a records management system is to assist in the effective and efficient management of organizational records, and to provide staff of the organization, as well as the clientele, with relevant information at the right time and at the lowest possible cost. Supporting goals relate to:

o   Retaining those records required by government statute or regulation;

o   Preserving vital records -- those needed for continuation of the operations of the organization in the case of a disaster;

o   Maintaining records reflecting the organization's past;

o   Providing documentation needed in case of litigation;

o   Retaining records needed for management decision making; and

o   Meeting the legitimate information needs of the organization's clientele.

PARTS OF A SYSTEM

Figure 3-1 depicts the basic model for an open system, a system which exchanges resources with the environment. The five parts of this general systems model are:

Figure 3-1. Model for Records Management System.

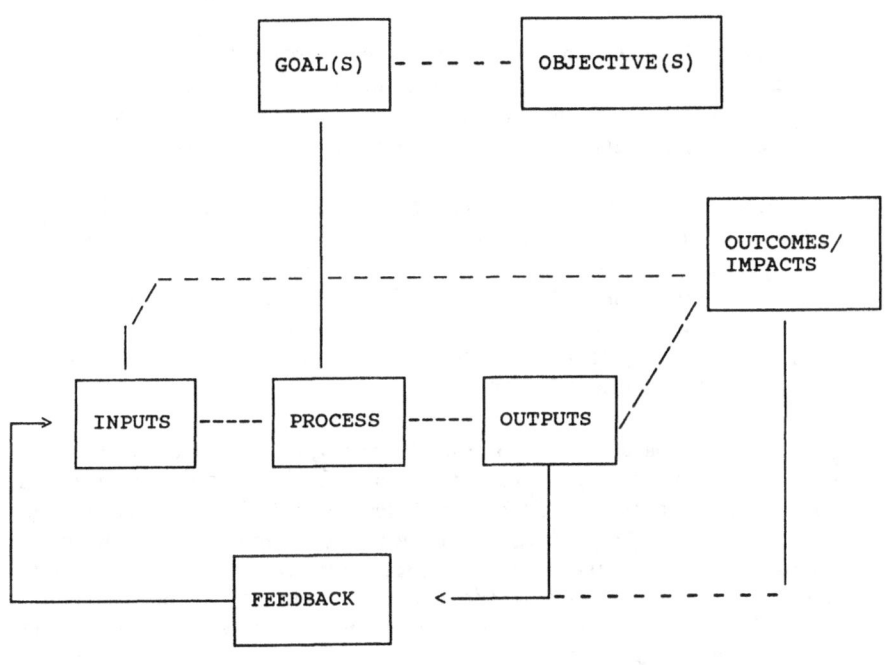

o *Input.* The system deals with internal and external factors from the larger environment:

  - Internal factors include budgeting (money), clientele, equipment, information, legal or regulatory requirements, and staffing; and
  - External factors have economic, physical, political, and social attributes.

o *Process (or Throughput).* The system moves resources through itself and transforms a resource, through some kind of process (program activities have formal and planned functions, and informal and unplanned functions), into a product. Central activities during processing include review and decision making;

o   *Output*. The system sends the transformed resource (a product, service, or other kind of result) back to the environment;

o   *Feedback*. The system obtains information from the environment that assists it in regulating the importation of resources and other system activities. Feedback among various parts of a system can occur without direct intervention through the environment; and

o   *Outcome*. The output has either an internal or external impact on the environment. Internal impacts are likely to occur within a couple of years, whereas external ones take place in five to ten years. External impacts include political, economic, educational, ethical, social, and physical factors. The program or service results might be unitary or multiple, intended or unintended, positive or negative, or short or long term.

Inputs to a records management system include both internal and external factors. The processing portion of the system includes individual records creation, maintenance, and disposition. These records form a product (e.g., information, report, or software), one which the organization can either distribute or disseminate. That product, therefore, is used by various members of the organization and its clientele, assuming that product is not protected -- available to only a few on a need-to-know basis. Outcome centers on the impact of that product on the organization, society, and so forth, while feedback provides evaluative data impacting inputs and the whole system. Records managers must look at the five parts in the context of organizational goals and objectives -- planning and evaluation (see Chapter 11).

The general systems model should serve as a reminder that there is a connection between inputs and outputs and that evaluation examining effectiveness looks at impacts and outcomes within the context of specific inputs, outputs, goals, and objectives. An analysis of organizational activities and operations can lead to the identification of potentially significant problems requiring decision research (see Carroll and Johnson, 1990), the evaluation of services and operations, and the development of plans to ensure that the organization adopts change that will result in *improved* services and operations.

In times of fiscal retrenchment, organizations may reduce their inputs and parts of the process. The results impact both outputs and outcomes. Some agencies of the federal government, for instance, have either privatized part of the records management system (e.g., let the private sector set up and maintain an electronic record-keeping system) or hired lower-level staff (e.g., those with less formal education, training, and knowledge) to carry out and, in some cases, to manage processes and outputs. Clearly, there may be instances in which organizations do not view the five parts within the context of goals and objectives, thereby inhibiting the ability of managers to determine the effectiveness and efficiency of a system (see McClure, 1984; Hernon and McClure, 1990).

Other Characteristics of a System

In addition to the above-mentioned elements of the general systems model, records managers should be aware of other characteristics of an open system. These are as follows (Nadler and Tushman, 1980):

o   *Differentation.* As a system grows, it tends to become more specialized, to add components, and to develop additional transformation processes and feedback loops;

o   *Equifinality.* The organization and processes of different systems may reproduce the same end result;

o   *Negative Entropy.* Ultimate entropy represents the death of the system; thus, negative entropy is obtaining adequate resources for the system to accomplish goals and objectives, to adapt to changing environments, and to support system differentiation; and

o   *Equilibrium Seeking.* The system tends to move toward a state where all elements successfully contribute to the organization's accomplishment of goals and objectives. When changes that result in an imbalance are made, different system components restore the balance both within the system and in terms of the system's relationship with the environment.

These four characteristics of an open system describe the typical organization. Evaluators must recognize and cope with these characteristics as well as with political factors and a bureaucracy that perhaps favors the status quo.

Records managers intending to engage in planning and evaluation and to improve the decision-making process should first identify and describe current services/activities/operations. The general systems model (Figure 3-1) and open systems characteristics are *tools* to force records managers to consider:

o   How the various parts of the organization work (or do not work) together;

o   The impact of specific resources on other areas of the organization;

o   The success with which organizational resources are transformed into products and services; and

o   How well the collection of records responds to the information needs of the organization's clientele.

PROBLEM SOLVING

Overview

Systems analysis provides a framework for viewing organizational activities, as well as visualizing and studying problems relating to effectiveness or efficiency. Systems analysis becomes critical when problems transcend individual departments and encompass multiple activities.

Systems analysis encourages human interaction and group communication. The purpose is to involve different facets of the organization in understanding common problems and seeking their resolution. In other words, individual units of the organization might focus narrowly on a problem; they deal with it within their narrow confines. However, action on the part of one unit might have repercussions on other units. Systems analysis, therefore, stresses the larger picture and knowledge of work flow, space layout, and so forth.

Systems analysis attempts to get members of the organization to accept change. Change is any planned or unplanned alteration in the status quo that affects an organization's structure, services, programs, or allocation of resources. Furthermore, it is assumed that:

o   Change is a normal pattern of growth and development for individuals as well as organizations;

o   Change is neither inherently "good" nor "bad;" and

o   Certain types of management styles and interpersonal techniques best facilitate change.

Thus, records managers must develop strategies to encourage change if they are to be successful in getting the right information to the right person at the right time and at the lowest cost possible.

Systems Analysis 43

Figure 3-2. Overview of the Systems Development Life Cycle.*

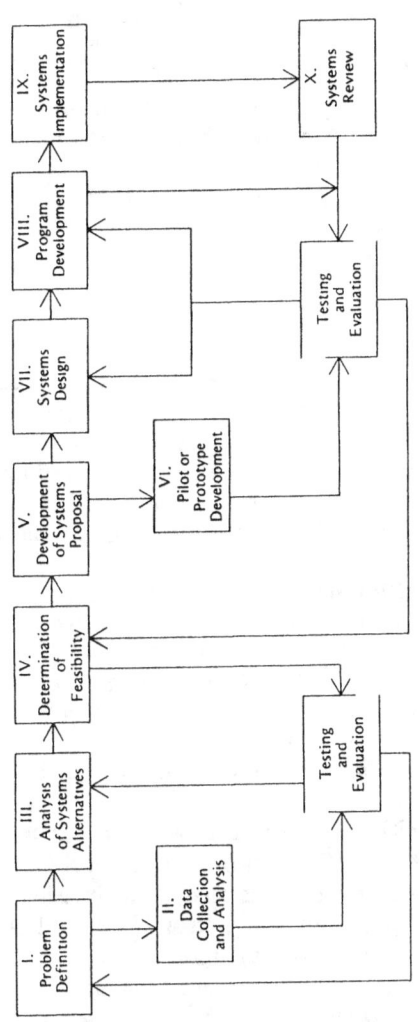

* "Overview of the Systems Development Life Cycle" appears on page 21 of *Systems Analysis: Definitions, Process, and Design*, 2nd edition by Philip C. Semprevivo. Copyright 1982 by Macmillan Publishing Company. Reprinted by permission of the publisher.

Systems analysis might involve the conduct of an evaluation research study and necessitate that the evaluators and records managers know the steps involved in setting up a study (see Hernon and McClure, 1990, Chapters 4 and 5; Hernon, 1991, Chapter 1), statistics, and analytical techniques which produce implementation models. The systems analyst identifies interactions that occur and observes and evaluates their impact. The analyst also offers suggestions for solving problems.

In both systems analysis and evaluation, the organization must be willing to live with the results, however they turn out. According to Robek, Brown, and Maedke (1987, p. 72), "perhaps the most important decision to be made in systems analysis is whether more will be gained by doing the study than will be lost by not doing it."

Steps in Systems Development

As shown in Figure 3-2, systems development encompasses 10 steps, the first of which is problem definition. Evaluation, a type of research, and testing produce data useful in exploring and evaluating alternative sytems, developing and testing a prototype system, and refining that prototype and the resulting system itself. Any system merits periodic review to determine the extent to which it continues to meet the organization's needs, goals, and objectives.

Problem definition demonstrates the presence of a problem -- e.g., a lack of knowledge or conflicting evidence about which system best meets the stated goals and objectives of an organization. Records managers, for instance, may note a backlog in the processing of records or the inadequacy of the filing system. In an evaluation study, they may frame the problem as a question, one in which they want to determine the magnitude of the problem (see Hernon and McClure, 1990, Chapter 4). Is it as serious as they suspect?

Problem definition also suggests why a particular problem rates high priority and merits investigation over other problems. Records managers only selectively conduct a systems analysis addressing some or all the steps specified in Figure 3-2. Depending on staff size and other factors, they may only want to conduct one study at a time.

Step VI, "Pilot or Prototype Development," in Figure 3-2, affords an opportunity to test a new system on a small scale. The purpose is to see whether the system works, what types of adjustments and modifications might be necessary, and what types of problems might emerge in developing and implementing the full system. A pilot or prototype system also enables organizational staff to get used to the new system, without there being a large-scale disruption of their work activities. One would not want records managers to implement a pilot or prototype system, or any system for that matter, in such a way that mass confusion or rapid change suddenly results.

PHASES IN CONDUCTING A SYSTEMS ANALYSIS STUDY

The conduct of a systems analysis project involves three phases: *preparation or planning, research or design,* and *organizational development.* During the preparation phase, records managers review organizational goals and set quantifiable objectives. They define the problem and determine the feasibility of resolving it with present resources and organizational support. If necessary, they train staff (or have them trained) to conduct a study, to analyze systems alternatives, and to assess a system's costs, benefits, effectiveness, and efficiency. They might need to conduct a cost-benefit, cost-effectiveness, or cost-efficiency study (see Rossi and Freeman, 1989).

During the second phase, if they are engaged in systems design, they review systems specifications, the allocation of space, software considerations, testing, documentation, and, if necessary, possible contingency plans. On the other hand, if they intend to conduct an evaluation study and to determine the effectiveness or efficiency of a process, output, or outcome, they develop and implement appropriate research questions, evaluation designs, and data collection methodologies.

During the final phase, records managers review the operation, maintenance, and need for modification of the new system. In the case of an evaluation study, they assess the results of an evaluation study and make value judgments concerning which services or activities should be modified and how these services and activities will be modified. The organization then implements strategies to change those services or activities, and presumably improve organizational performance.

Completion of a successful systems analysis study depends on the ability of records managers and their teams to complete the three phases and provide information useful for organizational planning and decision making.

Figure 3-3 summarizes the relationship among general systems concepts, evaluation research, decision making, and planning. As already noted, where systems analysis focuses on the review and possible implementation of new systems which are technologically based, records managers can replace formal evaluation research with a feasibility assessment, analysis of systems specifications, testing, and review of documentation (see Figure 3-2).

Phase One: Preparation

Successful evaluations *do not* begin with data collection; rather, they rely on the establishment of objectives to accomplish organizational goals, staff training, reviewing available resources, and identifying/reviewing topics for

46 Records Management and the Library

possible investigation. Preparing for successful completion of the study is critical for the success of the systems analysis process and may, in fact, require a number of months before records managers can move into the next phase.

Figure 3-3. Systems Concepts and Related Activities.*

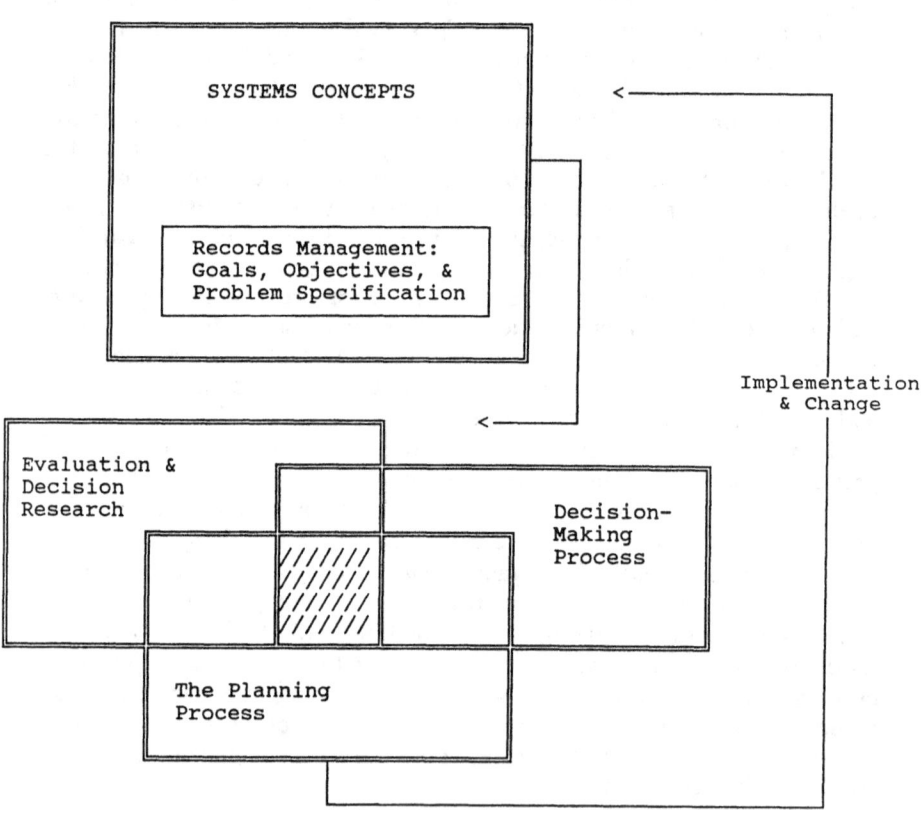

Phase Two: Research or Design

The second phase includes data collection. However, records managers must carefully consider *what* data will be collected, as well as *why* and *how* the data will be collected. In the preparation phase, records managers formulate the problem statement, while in the second phase, they develop research objectives, hypotheses, or research questions. Hypotheses and research questions operationalize research objectives and provide specific guidance about what will be investigated. Hypotheses and questions limit the general area of investigation to specific topics that are manageable. With this framework in place, records managers develop research designs and data collection procedures.

Once records managers know what is to be studied, they then decide how they will conduct the study. The research design is simply a plan that outlines the procedures by which they can address the hypotheses and/or research questions. The design outlines the specific approach that will organize and select the subjects to be studied. As an example, the design might set up an experimental or quasi-experimental study (see Hernon and McClure, 1990, Chapter 5).

The methodology is simply the manner in which systems analysts actually collect data. Data collection might involve the use of questionnaires (see Hernon, 1991, Appendix), interviews (in-person or by telephone), or observation (see Wolchak, 1986). Careful attention must be given to the selection of the research design and method of data collection to ensure that the resulting data will be consistently gathered (reliable) and that they measure what they are supposed to measure (internal validity).

In some cases, records managers do not conduct a research study that conforms to the above-mentioned steps. Once the organization's objectives have been set, they focus on criteria (means for determining the effectiveness of a system and assessing the performance of that system). They will also identify alternative systems and explore their feasibility. Systems studies may focus on the use of space, work flow, personnel performance, the utilization of equipment, scheduling of work and queuing, and the cost of operation. Questions to consider might include:

o How reliable is the system? How does the reliability of a new system compare with that of the old one?

o Is the new system cost-effective? Does the cost justify change?

o How easy is the system to implement and operate?

o What changes in work flow will result?

o   Will organizational personnel accept and *trust* the new system?

o   Is the new system user-friendly?

To identify different alternatives, records managers might form an advisory group from different parts of the organization and rely on their suggestions.

To determine whether particular alternatives meet the study's objectives, records managers might conduct a *feasibility study* to explore the alternatives. Feasibility, simply stated, is a determination of whether the proposed system will meet systems' objectives based on established criteria and available resources. A feasibility study also examines the impact of alternatives on the organization and assesses the cost effectiveness or cost benefit of each alternative. Based on the results of the feasibility study, records managers decide whether or not to proceed with the design of the new system.

The exploration of alternatives might be based on the construction and analysis of different models. A model is defined as a "simplified view of complex phenomena; the model can take many different forms and serve a number of different purposes" (McClure, 1989, p. 278). "The modeling process can be thought of as an effort to depict verbally, mathematically, or graphically a complex set of factors related to the phenomena in a straightforward manner that assists others to better understand that phenomena" (Ibid.). By manipulating a model, records managers determine how making a change in the model affects other aspects of the system.

The final activity during the second phase is the creation of the basic structure of the system and the implementation of a research or feasibility study. The features and capabilities of the new system are identified, and detailed specifications concerning equipment, personnel, and procedures are developed. Furthermore, records managers address space requirements and the processing of data. In the case of a database, they examine the design of the file structure, the nature of the software, the extent to which the system is user-friendly and conforms to the information-gathering behavior of organizational personnel and their clientele, and so forth.

Records managers might validate computer programs and develop a pilot project to test a system or model on a small scale. They must review the pilot project and any programs to ensure that these conform to their expectations. After all, records managers must authorize the purchase of any software or the writing of a computer program. Implementation involves the replacement of the old system with a new or modified one.

The implementation process calls for careful scheduling and planning of the various activities, and may require considerable coordination among different members of the organization, the things to be investigated, and the resources necessary to support the study.

Figure 3-4. Planning Chart.

PROJECT SCHEDULE

Current as of ___/___/___/

Project Name: Proj. No:

Activity	Month	1				2					3				4					5				6					
	Week	01	02	03	04	05	06	07	08	09	10	11	12	13	14	15	16	17	18	19	20	21	22	23	24	25	26	27	->
a:																													
b:																													
c:																													
d:																													
e:																													
f:																													
g:																													
h:																													
i:																													
j:																													
k:																													
l:																													
m:																													

Project Mgr: ________________

Proj. Start Date: ____/___/____ Est. Completion Date: ____/___/____

SYMBOLS: <> Completed ◆ Milestone | Act of Fate / Begin Task \ End Task -+ Slip ? Infinite

Planning/Scheduling Charts. Records managers establish projects and expect staff to complete phases of the project and the project itself by certain dates. They might keep a manual list of tasks and anticipated completion dates. Depending on the complexities of the project and the tasking, it might be advisable to use project management software, such as *Manager* (Culver City: Spectrum International Inc.), which permits the identification and monitoring of project tasks (*Datapro: Directory of Microcomputer Software*, 1991, lists other project managers in section MS38, Management Sciences). As needed, resources (e.g., people and money) can be shifted from one task to another to ensure that deadlines and objectives are met. Further, different tasks can be compared and priorities constantly reevaluated.

Figure 3-4 reproduces a planning chart in which the only constant is time. The scale of the chart is based on future time, with the calendar spread horizontally across the page. Time can be subdivided into months, weeks, or days. The figure was produced by modifying one of the sample charts contained in *FormTool*, a microcomputer software program published by BLOC Development Corp. (Miami Beach, Florida).

Planning charts, such as Gantt charts, the Critical Path Methods (CPM), and the Program Evaluation and Review Technique (PERT), provide a basis for records managers to understand what is to be done, when it is to be done, and how various parts of the investigation relate to each other. Furthermore, planning charts, such as the one represented in Figure 3-4, assist records managers in completion of the investigation.

A Gantt chart "tasks out" or "proceduralizes" the implementation process by indicating (1) the tasks to be completed, (2) who will do each task, and (3) the time frame for the completion of a task. Additionally, such charts include information about the resources that will be necessary for the accomplishment of various tasks and benchmark dates indicating when the tasks will be completed (see Figure 3-5). Careful planning and scheduling of Phase Two make the next phase, organizational development, much easier and more efficient.

Critical Path Analysis (CPA) includes both CPM and PERT. The starting point in CPA is a listing of the activities involved in the project. The related activities of a problem are identified in paths according to the order in which they must be performed if the desired standard of performance is to be achieved. In other words, a critical activity and time chart names and numbers the activity in the order in which it will be completed. Next, there is an identification of the preceding activity (together with related activities) and the number of days that it will take to complete these activities. The times along each path are totaled and the longest path, the project's critical path, is determined. There might be more than one critical path because different paths might yield equal totals.

Figure 3-5. A Gantt Chart.

	1991											
PHASE ONE: PROJECT INITIATION	JA	FE	MA	AP	MAY	JU	JLY	AU	SE	OC	NO	DE
1. Identify records series 2. Review goals and objectives 3. Develop procedures to review records series 4. Decide which series to review	***** ****			********	**********							
PHASE TWO: DATA COLLECTION												
1. Meet with staff and explain procedures 2. Determine if retention period has expired						***********						
PHASE THREE: COMPLETION												
1. Seek permission to dispose of records 2. Disposition of records										- - - - - - - -		

KEY:
  PERSON A = ***
  PERSON B = ...
  PERSON C = - - -

Both CPM and PERT show graphically all the tasks that must be performed to complete a project. They form a network of activities and events that comprise the project and indicate any relationship among activities or events. An activity, a specific task or effort applied over time, is bounded by two events. An event, then, marks the end of one activity and the beginning of another. A PERT diagram represents activities with arrows and events with circles.

The network shows the order in which activities must be performed. A new activity cannot begin unless the scheduled preceding event has occurred. Some activities are dependent on other activities, while others are not.

PERT and CPM differ in the time-estimating procedure. PERT uses a statistical method to approximate the time an activity will take. The expected time is calculated from three estimates: an optimistic or shortest possible time, a pessimistic or the longest time (which assumes everything will go wrong), and a most likely time based on normal progress. CPM, on the other hand, only uses one time estimate, normal time.

After estimating time, by using either PERT or CPM, records managers calculate the total time it will take to complete each path of the network, and they then determine the longest or critical path. The critical path indicates the length of time it will take to complete the project.

By monitoring each activity as it occurs, records managers see whether or not that activity is proceeding on schedule. When delays occur along the critical path, they can divert resources from noncritical activities. An advantage of both PERT and CPM is that they monitor completion of the project and can pinpoint problems and delays that may arise. They also focus attention on the critical activities that are behind schedule. Both methods can determine where extra money must be placed to achieve the desired schedule.

Carlson (1986) provides a useful discussion of flowcharts and illustrates Gantt charts. Penn, Morddel, Pennix, and Smith (1989) offer an example of a Gantt chart (p. 30) and a PERT chart (p. 31), while Robek, Brown, and Maedke (1987) reproduce a Gantt chart (p. 77) and a PERT chart (p. 79). Semprevivo (1982) presents a Gantt chart (p. 373) and CPM (pp. 375, 381). He also indicates how to construct a Critical Path network diagram (pp. 384-386). In their discussion of Graph Theory and Library Networks, Kraft and Boyce (1991, Chapter 5) present both CPM and PERT charts.

Analysis of Data. The data collected in an evaluation study are unintelligible until they are analyzed, summarized in terms of their descriptive and inferential characteristics, and interpreted. Typically, records managers analyze data in terms of descriptive statistics (e.g., frequencies, percentages, and histograms) as a means to simplify, reduce, and report the basic nature of the data collected. On the other hand, inferential statistics (e.g., regression analysis and analysis of variance) enable records managers to predict and infer characteristics of a population from the sample studied (see Hernon, 1991).

Phase Three: Organizational Development

The final phase of systems analysis identifies specific strategies to improve the effectiveness and efficiency of the organization. Those strategies can then be implemented. Reports and other means of communication about the study findings must be specifically tailored for the:

o   Intended audience;

o   Expected level of understanding the audience already has about the topic;

o   Amount of time available to decision makers to consider the content of the report; and

o   Magnitude of change being recommended.

Other more tangible factors, such as the format of the report, the use of clear and easy-to-read graphics, and a readable and pleasing writing style, must also be considered.

CONCLUSION

As this chapter indicates, records managers must be knowledgeable about systems analysis, evaluation and research methods, and statistics. They use these *tools* for organizational planning, for making better decisions, and for maintaining effective and efficiently operated organizations. In other words, organizational management, not the conduct of research for its own sake, guides the application of evaluation research.

Chapter 11, which discusses planning and evaluation, builds on the present chapter. Evaluators often do not make use of general systems thinking. Records managers, however, must. They must know the various parts of the system and how these parts fit together. Again, the parts exceed their sum; the implications of this impact the entire organization and perhaps the organization's relationship to the external environment as well.

REFERENCES

Carlson, David H. "Structured Analysis and the Data Flow Diagram: Tools for Library Analysis," *Information Technology and Libraries* 5 (June 1986): 121-128.

Carroll, John S. and Eric J. Johnson. *Decision Research*. Newbury Park, CA: Sage, 1990.

Datapro: Directory of Microcomputer Software. New York: McGraw-Hill, 1991.

Hernon, Peter. *Statistics: A Component of the Research Process*. Norwood, NJ: Ablex, 1991.

Hernon, Peter and Charles R. McClure. *Evaluation and Library Decision Making*. Norwood, NJ: Ablex, 1990.

Kraft, Donald H. and Bert R. Boyce. *Operations Research in Libraries and*

Information Agencies. San Diego, CA: Academic Press, 1991.
McClure, Charles R. "Management Information for Library Decision Making," In *Advances in Librarianship*, vol. 13, edited by Wesley Simonton. New York: Academic Press, 1984, pp. 1-47.
McClure, Charles R. "Frameworks for Studying Federal Information Policies: The Role of Graphic Modeling," In *United States Government Information Policies*, edited by Charles R. McClure, Peter Hernon, and Harold C. Relyea. Norwood, NJ: Ablex, 1989, pp. 271-295.
Nadler, David A. and Michael L. Tushman. "A Congruence Model for Organizational Assesssment," In *Organizational Assessment*, edited by Edward E. Lawler III, David A. Nadler, and Cortlandt Cammann. New York: Wiley, 1980, pp. 261-278.
Penn, Ira A., Anne Morddel, Gail Pennix, and Kelvin Smith. *Records Management Handbook*. Brookfield, VT: Gower Pub. Co., 1989.
Robek, Mary E., Gerald E. Brown, and Wilmet O. Maedke. *Information and Records Management*. 3d. ed. Encino, CA: Glencoe Publishing Co., 1987.
Rossi, Peter H. and Howard E. Freeman. *Evaluation: A Systematic Approach*. 4th ed. Newbury Park, CA: Sage, 1989.
Semprevivo, Philip C. *Systems Analysis*. 2d ed. Chicago, IL: Science Research Associates, 1982.
Wolchak, William H. "Conducting a Systems Analysis," *Records Management Quarterly* 20 (July 1986): 16-19.

READINGS

Alexander, M. J. *Information Systems Analysis: Theory and Applications*. Chicago, IL: Science Research Associates, 1974.
Hernon, Peter and Charles R. McClure. "Organizational Change," In *Evaluation and Library Decision Making*, edited by Peter Hernon and Charles R. McClure. Norwood, NJ: Ablex, 1991, pp. 224-239.
Kesner, Richard M. *Information Systems: A Strategic Approach to Planning and Implementation*. Chicago, IL: American Library Association, 1988.
McGrath, Joseph, Joanne Martin, and Richard A. Kulka. *Judgment Calls in Research*. Beverly Hills, CA: Sage, 1982.
Palmer, Richard P. and Harvey Varnet. *How to Manage Information*. Phoenix, AZ: Oryx Press, 1990.
Semprevivo, Philip C. *Systems Analysis*. 2d ed. Chicago, IL: Science Research Associates, 1982.

DISCUSSION POINTS

1. Review the indexes and journals mentioned in Chapter 1. Locate and analyze an article reporting the application of systems analysis to records management. Locate and analyze an example of CPM and PERT, as well.

2. Assess your strengths and weaknesses as a systems analyst, evaluator, and researcher. Should you compensate for these weaknesses? Why yes/no? How would you offset the weaknesses?

3. Do you think systems analysis deals exclusively with automated systems or the planning of such systems?

Chapter Four

Records Inventory

The first step in putting a records management program into place (or improving an existing one) is to locate and identify the records. Because this inventory stage may be the first point of an actual working contact between the records manager and other members of the organization, the records manager must be sensitive to a number of political issues. The most obvious of these is that the records manager can be perceived to be taking over control of information, and information is usually (and correctly) viewed as something which carries a certain degree of empowerment in an organization. It is very important that the benefits of records control be made clear to everyone who will be affected by it, and that the records manager establish an environment of mutual cooperation rather than antagonism. Certainly, the records manager must be vested with authority at appropriate management levels, but that must be accompanied by clear messages as to the organizational objectives which records management is helping to accomplish. Considering that records staff may be going into offices, examining files, and perhaps removing records, a wrong step at this point could set the stage for a lack of future cooperation at least, and active hostility at worst.

Another sensitive issue has to do with the idiosyncrasies which develop in an individual office. We are all familiar with the staff person who has been filing materials in his or her own unique manner for years, and in such a way that nothing can be retrieved when this person is not present. Despite the obvious problems inherent to situations like this, it is important not to suggest that things could be handled much more efficiently, at least not at the outset of a program. If information is power, then the methods by which information is controlled for retrieval are power tools, and it does the records manager little good to denigrate an individual's personal work habits.

MAKING THE CASE FOR RECORDS MANAGEMENT

How does a records manager convince an organization (and especially its senior officials) that records management is worth the investment in personnel and facilities? There are many persuasive arguments in favor of records management, and the Association of Records Managers and Administrators (ARMA) and a number of other associations and agencies have even gone so far as to produce videotape and slide-tape presentations

Table 4-1. Audiovisual Presentations on Records Management.

Association of Records Managers and Administrators. *The Inside Track to Disaster Recovery [videotape]*. Prairie Village, KS: ARMA International, 1986. 13 minutes.
> A presentation on the basics of disaster preparedness, accompanied by graphic film footage of the results of actual disasters.

Bennick, Anne. *Active Filing for Paper Records [transparencies]*. Prairie Village, KS: ARMA International, 1989.
> Seventy-seven paper masters or color slides showing filing methods and equipment.

Brathal, Daniel A. and Mark Langemo. *Planning Conversions to Micrographic Systems [transparencies]*. Prairie Village, KS: ARMA International, 1987.
> A 62-page book and 51 paper masters or color slides which provide an overview of the concepts and methods in planning conversion of paper records to microform.

Capture by Video, Inc. *Information and Micrographics Management [videotape]*. Lake Park, FL: Capture by Video, Inc., 1985. 56 minutes.
> An introduction to records management, with a section on cost-benefit analysis and marketing to management.

——————. *Microcomputers in Records Management [videotape]*. Lake Park, FL: Capture by Video, Inc., n.d. 20 minutes.
> An overview of the applications of microcomputers to records control.

Commonwealth Films Inc. *Buried Alive [videotape]*. Boston, MA: Commonwealth Films, Inc., 1989. 25 minutes.

——————. *Under Wraps [videotape]*. Boston, MA: Commonwealth Films Inc., 1990. 19 minutes.

——————. *When Products Harm [videotape]*. Boston, MA: Commonwealth Films, Inc., 1986. 33 minutes.
> All three Commonwealth Film videos offer dramatized accounts of the costs of inadequate records and information security. These videos have been well reviewed in the professional literature. ARMA distributes a "customized" version of Buried Alive.

Kupsch, Joyce and Carol Lundgren. *Records Management [transparencies]*. Huntington Beach, CA: National Instructional Systems, 1985.
> Fifty transparency masters and other instructional materials covering the basics, adaptable to many training needs.

Langemo, Mark and Roger J. Bloomquist. *Overview of Records and Information Management [slide tape]*. Prairie Village, KS: ARMA International, 1985.
> Three cassettes and 73 paper masters or color slides which can be used in modules for training and promotional purposes.

Table 4-1. (Continued)

Langemo, Mark and Daniel A. Brathal. *Managing Business Forms [transparencies]*. Prairie Village, KS: ARMA International, 1988.
> A 30-page book accompanied by 52 transparency masters or color slides illustrating the fundamentals of forms management. The book or the visual aids can each be purchased separately.

Lockheed Missiles and Space Company. *A Look at Records Management [videotape]*. Sunnyvale, CA: Lockheed Missiles and Space Co., n.d. 9 minutes.
> A short introduction to the benefits of records management, supported by some amusing cartoons.

National Information Center for Local Government Records. *The Guardians of the Public Record [videotape]*. American Association for State and Local History, 1985. 13 minutes.
> A well-produced videotape demonstrating the importance of applying records management to state and local records.

Saffady, William. *Optical Disk Systems for Records Management [transparencies]*. Prairie Village, KS: ARMA International, 1988.
> A 56-page book and 61 transparency masters or color slides, prepared by one of the acknowledged experts on the applications of optical disk technology to records control.

Young, Richard F. and David J. Tinsley. *Library and Archival Disaster Preparedness and Recovery [videotape]*. Oakton, VA: BiblioPrep, 1986.
> Twenty-one minutes on the importance of planning for disaster prevention, principally directed to libraries.

---

on the benefits of systematic control of records (see Table 4-1). Many of these are also useful as training tools in records management programs.

Successful tactics of persuasion point to the legal, financial, and historical advantages of records management. All organizations are subject to certain legislative and regulatory requirements, and often these requirements emanate from local, state, and federal authorities. A records manager is in the best position to be aware of such requirements, and to monitor changes as they are enacted in procedural documents governing the making of rules or regulations.[1] In the case of litigation brought against an

---

[1] For example, at the federal government level, Congress, together with the President, enacts statutory law. Such law sets the framework for the Food Stamp and other programs and activities. Executive agencies, such as the Department of Agriculture, adopt rules and regulations to convert statutory law into administrative law, or they implement rules and regulations under which a program will operate.

organization, the lack of a documented systematic records management program can have serious legal consequences. In fact, courts might demand a company's records as evidence, and compliance with these demands might reveal damaging evidence in records which could otherwise have been destroyed in the normal course of retention and destruction schedules developed by a records management program.

Another convincing argument for records management is that it streamlines paperwork, reduces volume,[2] and thereby reduces the costs of records creation, storage, and retrieval. Reduction in the volume and duplication of recorded information also should make it easier to find the individual needle in the proverbial haystack. Although many organizations have looked to new information technologies to solve "information bottlenecks," the solution lies in the effective use of such technologies, not simply in their implementation. A records manager should be in the best position to understand the flow of information through an organization, and can work to ensure that the *right* information gets to the *right* person in a timely manner, and in an appropriate format.

Information is a commodity within an organization--a resource like any other, and one which has costs and attendant benefits.[3] While there are obvious benefits in improved efficiencies in storage and retrieval of internal records, the information represented in those records can also actively contribute to management planning, evaluation, and decision making. A department store chain, for instance, which is planning expansion into a new suburban market, must take demographic and other external realities into account, but must also consider data concerning current sales, inventories, and so on. An academic library planning to install additional terminals or local area network ports for online catalog access can make better decisions in light of the information about current queuing problems, numbers of active users, typical length of a user session, and so on. These data can be drawn from internal records (such as activity logs), but only if the information has been stored and organized effectively.

Finally, records represent the recorded history of an organization, and in that an organization exists in a social context; they may represent social, cultural, and political history as well. While administration is usually only

---

[2] Records management thereby conforms to the Paperwork Reduction Act of 1980 (P.L. 96-511; 94 Stat. 2812), which attempted to "minimize the Federal paperwork burden...; to minimize the cost to the Federal Government of collecting, maintaining, using, and disseminating information."

[3] The U.S. Office of Management and Budget's Circular A-130, "The Management of Federal Information Resources," underscores that information is a commodity with economic value and requires management as does any other resource (see United States, Office of Management and Budget, 1985).

concerned with such historical records as might be needed in a centennial celebration or an annual report, social historians and other scholars may find a wealth of relevant data in company records. This last point is particularly important in settings which do not maintain a formal archives program.

PREPARING FOR RECORDS INVENTORY

Records are usually dealt with in *records series*, groups of like items which are filed together, and considered as units for retention and disposition purposes. The objectives of records inventory are to:

o   Identify individual records series, determine where they originate, how they are used, and how they interrelate;

o   Determine periods of active and inactive life and to establish retention schedules and disposition methods; and

o   Maximize the efficiency of storage methods and locations.

Records inventory requires an understanding of what constitutes a record, and it should be founded on an awareness of the information life cycle within an organization. The concept of the life cycle of a record, or the life cycle of information, provides a framework in which the *total* information flow in an organization may be better understood. The issue of the information life cycle is taken up in detail in Chapter 12, in the broader context of information resources management.

What is a Record?

The ARMA standard glossary states that a record is

> recorded information, regardless of medium or characteristics, made or retrieved by an organization that is useful in the operation of the organization. (Association of Records Managers and Administrators, 1989, p. 16)

Penn, Morddel, Pennix, and Smith (1989, p. 3) are more pragmatic, claiming that a record is "any information captured in reproducible form that is required for conducting business." Emmerson (1989, p. 5) sees records as

> All those documents, in whatever medium, received or created by an organisation in the course of its business, and retained by that organisation as evidence of its activities or because of the

information contained.

Records are intended to carry information, promote communication, contribute to planning and decision making, and preserve the history of an institution.

All of the definitions presented above are appropriately broad, and imply that the form, or medium, of a record is secondary to the role of the information which it carries.[4] This is particularly important in the modern age of electronic records. The advent of duplicating technologies contributed to the paperwork explosion of the past half century, but at least paper copies have the advantage of being visible, and the problems which copying creates (such as overflowing files resulting from storing unnecessary duplicates) demand solutions from records managers. Electronic files are more insidious, being easy to create and duplicate, vulnerable to minute and undetectable change, difficult to "see" with the naked eye, and unlikely to cause visible problems of physical storage. Nonetheless, they are "records," playing a role in the life cycle of information, and as such should be subject to the same controls as paper, microform, and audiovisual media.

Information carrying items, then, can be characterized by form (i.e., medium), status, and function. Records managers, like librarians, must handle written, printed, oral, and visual information, and that information may be captured on paper, microform, audiotape, videotape, film, electronic, and optical media. Records managers may also have to deal with artifacts (medals, trophies, office Christmas decorations, hat samples, and so on).

While form is an important consideration in later stages of records control, status and function are the criteria which determine whether or not a particular item or series of items constitute a "record," from the point of view of the records manager. *Status* pertains to the activity and permanency of a record, and *function* deals with the role that the record plays in the conduct of the business of the institution.

There are a variety of terms used to describe the status of a record. *Non-records* are documents of convenience, which are typically disposed of after use. Examples of these might include routing slips, temporary copies, superseded telephone directories, and so on. The *copy of record* is the one which will be kept for the life span of the record, as opposed to a copy of convenience. It is often, but not always, the original record. For instance, in

---

[4] In some cases form is important, as, for instance, when an original document must be produced to meet some legal requirement. Vulnerability of the medium is a consideration in information preservation (i.e., electronic records are subject to tampering and are less preferable to microform for retention of many types of records).

the case of outgoing correspondence, it is the copy kept by the originator.

Active records are those which are used in everyday operations, and are usually kept close at hand in offices. Manufacturers' catalogs, current personnel files, service contracts, and similar files which might require frequent referral are all examples of active records.

Inactive records are records which are not used everyday, but which might be necessary for occasional referral, for instance, past personnel files and old accounts. The distinction between active and inactive records is useful in maximizing efficiency in records storage. Filing cabinets occupy space, and space in offices tends to be more costly than space in records centers, where inactive records might be stored. Also, the filing methods for active records place an emphasis on quick, and usually systematic (e.g., subject), access; whereas inactive records can be filed using compressed (and therefore less expensive) storage methods, with a tradeoff in the immediacy of access. Finally, the fewer items in an active file, the easier and quicker it is to find a particular item. As we will see, there are a number of published guidelines to help records managers make decisions as to the length of time particular types of records should remain in active storage.

Archival or permanent records are records which must be kept for fiscal, legal, or historical reasons. These might include charters of incorporation, annual reports, internal publications, and so forth. *Vital records* are those which would be needed for the institution to function in the event of a disaster. In libraries, for example, a copy of the shelflist kept in a remote location is in the worst case (for instance, fire) a record of holdings for insurance purposes. The nature of vital records will be explored in more detail in Chapter 8, in the context of disaster management.

These categories are obviously not mutually exclusive. An inactive record may also be a vital record, and many archival records are also vital records. Characterizing records by their status is helpful in making decisions as to filing method, storage location, retention, and disposition. The function of a record within an institution (personnel records, inventories, general ledgers, etc.) also provides guidance in making these decisions. Furthermore, that function is useful in gaining a systematic picture of the information flow (and possible duplication of files and effort) within a setting.

The Preliminary Records Survey

In a large organization, the first step in records inventory is usually a preliminary survey to determine the volume of records, and to gain an idea as to the amount of time and effort which the full inventory will likely take. The preliminary survey may be the first point of personal contact between records staff and office staff, and so it helps if the way has been paved by either a general orientation to the nature of records management, or at the least a memo from management to the effect that a records survey is about to take place, and what its benefits are expected to be. Although it would be possible to send out a form to be completed by office staff, the survey should preferably be conducted by records management personnel through scheduled appointments. This serves the dual purpose of making initial personal contact and ensuring accuracy in collecting information. If the data collection form is carefully designed and the surveying staff are well trained, disruption of normal office procedures can be kept to a minimum.

The survey (and the subsequent detailed inventory) should include all records (other than personal files which are not properly part of the institution's "records"), in whatever medium, and wherever found (filing cabinets, desk drawers, floppy disks and hard disks, and boxes stashed behind doors and under sinks). Some kind of consistent scheme should be devised for identifying location (to avoid entries like "beside the dark brown desk, third drawer down from the top in the right hand filing cabinet"). A typical method is to number locations clockwise or counterclockwise on a map of each room, numbering drawers from top to bottom or bottom to top, identifying each location for the type of equipment it represents, and giving guidelines for calculating volume in cubic feet. Standards for equipment codes and volume calculations are widely available in the literature. Figures 4-1 and 4-2 illustrate a typical coding scheme and calculation guide. Figure 4-3 shows a sample room map and a preliminary survey form filled in for that room.

Figure 4-1. Typical Equipment Codes.

LL	Legal-sized lateral filing cabinet	BC	Bookcase
ll	Letter-ized lateral filing cabinet	RC	Record carton
VL	Legal-sized vertical filing cabinet	C	Card file
vl	Letter-sized vertical filing cabinet	SC	Supply cabinet
D	Desk or tub file	S	Safe
P	Package or bundle		

Numbers are added to these letter codes to indicate the precise location and quantity of a record series. For instance,

$2VL_5$ indicates 2 drawers of a 5-drawer legal-sized vertical filing cabinet, and

$2C_3$ indicates 2 drawers in a 3-drawer card file.

Figure 4-2. Cubic Foot Equivalency Chart.

FILE FOLDER DRAWERS	CU. FT.	MAP OR PLAN DRAWERS	CU.FT
Letter	1.5	2" x 26" x 38" (flat)	1.1
Letter Transfile	2.0	2" x 38" x 50" (flat)	2.2
Legal	2.0	4" x 26" x 38" (flat)	2.3
Legal Transfile	2.5	4" x 38" x 50" (flat)	4.4
Ledger	3.0		
Jumbo	4.0		

SHELF UNITS		MAP OR PLAN TUBES	
Letter 36" long	2.4	2" x 2" x 38" (roll)	0.1
Legal 36" long	3.0	2" x 2" x 50" (roll)	0.1
		4" x 4" x 38" (roll)	0.3
		4" x 4" x 50" (roll)	0.5

CARD FILE DRAWERS		RECORD CENTER CONTAINERS	
3" x 5" x 26" long	0.4	10" x 12" x 15" (Paige)	1.0
3" x 5" x 14" long	0.2	3½" x 8" x 14" (tab)	0.2
3½" x 7½" x 26" long (tab)	0.4	3½" x 8" x 24" (check)	0.4
3½" x 7½" x 14" long (tab)	0.2	6" x 6" x 36" (map)	0.6
4" x 6" x 26" long	0.5	6" x 6" x 48" (map)	0.8
4" x 6" x 14" long	0.2	4" x 4" x 48" (map)	0.3
5" x 8" x 26" long	0.7		
5" x 8" x 14" long	0.4		
6" x 9" x 26" long	1.0	ALL OTHER USE FORMULA	
6" x 9" x 14" long	0.6		
8" x 8" x 26" long	1.2	$\dfrac{L \times W \times H \text{ (inches)}}{1728}$ = cu. ft./unit	
8" x 8" x 14" long	0.6		

(From Connolly, Michael J., *Municipal Records Management Manual*. Boston, MA: Office of the Massachusetts Secretary of State, Division of Archives, n.d., Appendix i.)

Records Inventory 65

Figure 4-3. Sample Preliminary Survey Coding.

```
┌─────────────────────────────────────────────────────────────┐
│                                                             │
│  ┌──────────┐    ┌───┬───┬───┐    ┌──────────┐              │
│  │  Desk    │    │VL₅│VL₅│VL₅│    │  Desk    │              │
│  │          │    │3A │3B │3C │    │          │              │
│  │    2     │    └───┴───┴───┘    │    4     │              │
│  ┌────┬─┐   │    ┌───────────┐                              │
│  │Safe│1│   │    │  Table    │                              │
│  └────┴─┘   │    │    6      │         5      ┌────┐        │
│             │    └───────────┘                │ SC │        │
│  ─Entrance─                                                 │
│                    Room L-101                               │
└─────────────────────────────────────────────────────────────┘
```

The record holding equipment in a room is numbered in a consistent manner, so that the exact location can be found when records are to be transferred. In the room above, for instance, the locations have been numbered clockwise from the entrance, using letters to differentiate the three filing cabinet units. The code for room location is then used in the preliminary survey form, as the example below illustrates.

Record Series *Service Calls*				Form # *A-213*		
Room *L-101*						
PRELIMINARY INVENTORY						
Range	Years	Location	Equipment	Cu. Ft.	Action	
A-Z	1987-1988	5-SC	1P	2	Destroy	
A-Z	1989-1990	3-B-1/2	2VL₅	4	Transfer	
A-Z	1991-	3-C-③	1VL₅	1	Retain	

A circle around a number indicates that only part of the space is taken up by the record series.

One of the immediate benefits of the preliminary survey is an assessment of the overall volume of space consumed by records and an indication of underutilized expensive office space (typically where sneakers, lunches, and purses are stored).

PHYSICAL RECORDS INVENTORY

The preliminary survey results are used to plan and schedule the full physical records inventory. Obsolete records and reference files (such as manufacturers' catalogs) can usually be inventoried in bulk, and will not require gathering much more detailed information from office personnel. Recently created records, however, will have to be examined in depth. The literature contains some guidance as to the time required for physical inventory. Smith (1986, p. 116) suggests that one person can handle 1,000 cubic feet of records a week, and Leahy and Cameron (1965, p. 30) estimate 150 cubic feet a day, assuming a well-trained records analyst. Physical inventory may take more than half of all staff time required for establishing a records management program (Wallace, Lee, and Schubert, 1992, p. 77). Some consultants specialize in records inventory, and for a large organization this route might be worth the possible savings in time and efficiency (traded off against the advantages of establishing that first personal contact with office staff). Other alternatives include hiring temporary staff for the inventory process, or having office staff inventory their own files (although they may be reluctant to admit to perceived deficiencies). In both of these cases, training is of paramount importance. If the inventory is to be done by other than office staff, it should be conducted through scheduled onsite visits.

The Inventory Form

The inventory form, developed by the records manager, should be clear and complete, with separate instructions for elements such as equipment coding schemes. A brief training session for the staff who will be conducting the inventory is wise. A separate copy should be filled in for each different record series, and for the same series if it shows up in different offices. The information gathered in inventory is used for a variety of purposes, including records appraisal, equipment assessment, file management, and weeding. To serve those ends most efficiently, the form should include the elements listed in Table 4-2. Examples of inventory forms are shown in Figures 4-4 and 4-5.

Table 4-2. Elements of the Inventory Form.

Heading Information
    Title of department, unit, agency, etc.
    Name and phone number of person responsible for the record series
    Date of inventory and name of person taking inventory
    Series title
    Alternate titles (for use later in establishing authority control)
    Location (using a mapping system as for the preliminary survey)

Coverage
    Inclusive dates or other range
    Missing segments (missing years, portions of the alphabet, etc.)

Physical Details
    Medium (e.g., paper) and format (e.g., legal-sized)
    Physical extent (e.g., cubic or linear feet, number of items, bytes)
    Annual accumulation (useful information for space planning)
    Description (size, color, types of binders, etc.)
    Equipment (using a standard coding scheme for equipment types)
    Condition of the equipment

Arrangement and Access
    Filing arrangement (include a checklist) and indexes
    Problems of access (have staff experienced difficulties in retrieval?)

Use
    Frequency of use
    Purpose of use
    Circulation and charge-out procedures
    Confidentiality or other restrictions on use

Provenance
    Frequency of creation (daily, weekly, monthly, etc.)
    Is this the copy of record?
    Availability elsewhere (in other locations, and/or other formats)
    Origination (records were used in the creation of these records)

Value
    Description
    Purpose in relation to the operations of the organization
    Audit requirements
    Administrative requirements
    Value for archival purposes
    Is this a vital record?

Retention
    Departmental retention period
    Retention recommendations (and reasons for recommendations)

Figure 4-4. Records Inventory Form.

1) Department	Division	Section

2) Title of Records Series

3) Location of Records

4) Description of Records Series (content, purpose, etc.)

5) Earliest Date Latest Date	6) Records still created? YES ☐ NO ☐	7) Volume ______ cu ft	8) Annual Accumulation ______ cu ft

9) Record Series Characteristics (Check Appropriate Boxes)

TYPE: ☐ PAPER ☐ CARD ☐ BOUND VOLUME ☐ MICROFILM ☐ MACHINE READABLE
☐ OTHER (Specify) ______

SIZE: ☐ LETTER ☐ LEGAL ☐ OTHER (Specify) ______

STATUS: ☐ ORIGINAL ☐ COPY

FORMAT: ☐ TYPEWRITTEN ☐ HANDWRITTEN ☐ OTHER ______

ARRANGEMENT: ☐ CHRONOLOGICAL ☐ ALPHABETICAL BY ______ ☐ NUMERICAL BY ______ ☐ OTHER ______

10) Reference Frequency (check blocks insert numbers, circle appropriate words)

______ Times, daily, weekly, monthly, yearly for ______ months, years Never after ______

11) Information Available Elsewhere? YES ☐ NO ☐ (If yes, where? ______)	12) Microfilmed? YES ☐ NO ☐ (If yes, explain) ______)

13) Are records indexed?

YES ☐ NO ☐ (If yes, identify ______

14) How stored?

☐ Filing Cabinets ☐ Shelves ☐ Boxes ☐ Other ______

15) Condition of Records

___ Poor ___ Fair ___ Good (Explain any problems) ______

16) Records on State Archives' Records Retention and Dispositon Schedule?

YES ☐ NO ☐ If yes Schedule No ______ Item No on Schedule ______

If no, suggested retention period and justification ______

17) Condition of Storage Area (security, fireproof, alarms, environment, etc.)

☐ Good ☐ Poor State any storage problems ______

18) Additional Comments

19) Name of Person Completing Inventory ______ Date ______

20) Action taken

☐ Records disposed of, date ______ ☐ Microfilmed date ______

☐ Sent to inactive records center, date ______ ☐ Retain permanently, sent to archives, date ______

☐ Other (Explain) ______

21) Name of person taking action ______

(From New York, State Education Department, *Managing Local Government Records*. Albany, NY: University of the State of New York, State Education Department, State Archives, 1985, p. 50a-b.)

Records Inventory 69

Figure 4-5. Files Survey Record.

FILES SURVEY RECORD		DATE PREPARED
1. NAME OF OFFICE (Include Division, Branch, Section and Unit)	2. REPORTED BY (Name, extension, and room number)	
	3. LOCATION OF FILES (Room number)	
4. TITLE OF FILES	5. INCLUSIVE DATES	

6. DESCRIPTION OF FILES (Summary of contents, purpose, relation to what program or function ..)

7. NUMBER OF FILE DRAWERS/SHELVES

TYPE	NUMBER	TYPE	NUMBER	TYPE	NUMBER
A. LEGAL		C. LEGAL, LATERAL		E. SHELVES/BOOKCASES	
B. LETTER		D. LETTER, LATERAL			

8. TYPE OF FILES (Check one)
- [ ] A. CASE OR PROJECT FILE
- [ ] B. SUBJECT FILE (Attach list of subject topics)
- [ ] C. TRANSITORY CORRESPONDENCE
- [ ] D. TECHNICAL REFERENCE FILE
- [ ] E. EXTRA COPY CONVENIENCE FILE (Reading, suspense, followup, etc.)
- [ ] F. SPECIAL TYPES (Maps, photographs, tab cards, index cards, etc.)

9. CONTENT OF FILES (If more than one type is maintained, indicate percentages of each)

TYPE OF DOCUMENT	PERCENTAGE	TYPE OF DOCUMENT	PERCENTAGE
A. OFFICIAL		C. NON-RECORD (Such as extra copy or working papers, publications or printed matter, or other non-record material)	
B. PERSONAL (Private papers of office head)			

10. ARRANGEMENT OF FILES
(Check appropriate block. If more than one arrangement pattern, number blocks to show first breakdown, second breakdown, etc.)

- [ ] A. SUBJECT CLASSIFICATION SYSTEM (Attach folder listing)
- [ ] B. ALPHABETICAL (Name) (Attach folder listing)
- [ ] C. ALPHABETICAL (Subject) (Attach folder listing)
- [ ] D. NUMERICAL BY (Specify)
- [ ] E. CHRONOLOGICAL
- [ ] F. GEOGRAPHICAL LOCATION
- [ ] G. OTHER (Specify)

11. ARE COPIES OF DOCUMENTS KEPT IN THESE FILES AVAILABLE ELSEWHERE? (If yes, explain where) [ ] YES [ ] NO

12. ESTIMATED "BUILD-UP RATE" OF FILE	13. FILE DISPOSITION	
[ ] A. 6 INCHES OR LESS PER YEAR	A. CUT-OFF PERIODICALLY	INTERVAL
[ ] B. UP TO ONE FILE DRAWER PER YEAR	B. TRANSFERRED TO FEDERAL RECORDS CENTER	DATE
[ ] C. MORE THAN ONE DRAWER PER YEAR	C. DESTROYED	DATE
[ ] D. NO BUILD-UP, SERIES IS CLOSED	D. RETAINED PERMANENTLY	

14. HOW OFTEN ARE FILES USED?
- [ ] OFTEN (More than once a month per file drawer)
- [ ] SELDOM (Less than once a month per file drawer)
- [ ] RARELY

15. DISPOSITION AUTHORITY (Schedule and item number and disposition instructions, if any)

16. NUMBER OF YEARS FILES NEEDED TO CONDUCT CURRENT BUSINESS
- [ ] 1 YEAR
- [ ] 2 YEARS
- [ ] 5 YEARS
- [ ] OTHER (Specify)

17. REMARKS

GENERAL SERVICES ADMINISTRATION   GSA FORM 3119 (8-78)

(From National Archives and Records Administration, *Disposition of Federal Records*. Washington, DC: GPO, 1981, reprinted 1989 (Records Management Handbook), p. 13).

In the case of component documents (records which are composed of several different types of items filed together), the inventory form should reflect the existence of the component series, realizing that the complete inventory may reveal that the component parts are also filed as individual series in other locations. For instance, a personnel file may contain, for each individual, an interview report, the initial position offered and subsequent letter of acceptance, and a copy of the first contract. There might also be a separate file containing all the contracts, another containing interview reports (as records of the activities of the appointments committee), and so on.

While it may not be possible to gather all of this information at the same time, at least the form will make the entire process as systematic as possible. The inventory record essentially becomes a dynamic document contributing to the record manager's understanding of the interplay between all the pieces of an organization's information resource structure.

WHAT NEXT?

Completed inventory files (either interfiled in hardcopy or entered into a machine-readable database) can yield a number of insights into the state of record keeping in an institution. These include the following points:

o   Duplication of files and records will be readily apparent.

o   Frequency of use, and staff recommendations for retention, can give an indication as to which files might be considered to be inactive, although other factors come into play as well.

o   The costs of current records storage can be calculated from the physical extent portion of the inventory form and a knowledge of the costs per square foot of office space. This can be a very telling argument for moving inactive files to less costly storage locations. Penn, Morddel, Pennix, and Smith (1989, pp. 66-68) provide an excellent breakdown of the costs of file maintenance, including space, materials, and labor.

o   Physical extent information can also be used to assess the amount of space which will be needed as inactive files are identified and relocated, and how much office space will be released as that activity proceeds.

o   Annual accumulation rates will be instrumental in planning for future storage needs.

o   Underutilized and deteriorating or inadequate equipment will be identified, and the total equipment picture might suggest more effective equipment placement.

o   Reported difficulties in retrieval might suggest priorities for filing improvements.

o   Alternate titles for records, and indexes which accompany particular files, will both be helpful in creating references for authority control systems.

o   In the longer term, information about where records come from, and what other records they contribute to, will be valuable in effecting forms control (especially with respect to reducing redundancies).

Moving towards these various activities, and especially those involving space management, the next phase of records management is records appraisal and retention, which are taken up in Chapter 5.

REFERENCES

Association of Records Managers and Administrators. *Glossary of Records Management Terms*. Prairie Village, KS: ARMA International, 1989. (ARMA International Guideline for Records and Information Management)

Connolly, Michael J., *Municipal Records Management Manual*. Boston, MA: Office of the Massachusetts Secretary of State, Division of Archives, n.d.

Emmerson, Peter. "What is Records Management?," In *How to Manage Your Records: A Guide to Effective Practice*, edited by Peter Emmerson. Cambridge, Eng.: ICSA Publishing, 1989, pp. 5-10.

Leahy, Emmett, and Christopher A. Cameron. *Modern Records Management*. New York: McGraw-Hill, 1965.

National Archives and Records Administration, *Disposition of Federal Records*. Washington, DC: GPO, 1981 (reprinted 1989) (Records Management Handbook), p. 13.

New York, State Education Department, *Managing Local Government Records*. Albany, NY: University of the State of New York, State Education Department, State Archives, 1985.

Penn, Ira A., Anne Morddel, Gail Pennix, and Kelvin Smith. *Records Management Handbook*. Brookfield, VT: Gower, 1989.

Smith, Milburn D. *Information and Records Management: A Decision-Maker's Guide to Systems Planning and Documentation*. New York:

Quorum Books, 1986.

United States, Office of Management and Budget. Circular No. A-130, "The Management of Federal Information Resources," *Federal Register* 50 (December 24, 1985): 52730-51.

Wallace, Patricia E., Jo Ann Lee, and Dexter R. Schubert. *Records Management: Integrated Information Systems*. 3d ed. Englewood Cliffs, NJ: Prentice-Hall, 1992.

READINGS

Aschner, Katherine. "How to Do a File Inventory." In *Taking Control of Your Office Records: A Manager's Guide*, edited by Katherine Aschner. White Plains, NY: Knowledge Industry Publications, 1983, pp. 19-27.

Diamond, Susan Z. *Records Management: A Practical Guide*. New York, NY: AMACOM, 1983. Chapter 4: "Records Disposition: What to Keep and How Long to Keep It."

Parker, Elizabeth A. "Developing the Programme." In *How to Manage Your Records: A Guide to Effective Practice*, edited by Peter Emmerson. Cambridge, Eng.: ICSA Publishing, 1989, pp. 24-39.

Penn, Ira A., Anne Morddel, Gail Pennix, and Kelvin Smith. *Records Management Handbook*. Brookfield, VT: Gower, 1989. Chapter 5: "The Information Survey."

Ricks, Betty R. and Kay F. Gow. *Information Resource Management: A Records Systems Approach*. 2d ed. Cincinnati, OH: South-Western Publishing, 1988, pp. 51-59.

Robek, Mary E., Gerald F. Brown, and Wilmer O. Maedke. *Information and Records Management*. 3d ed. Encino, CA: Glencoe, 1987. Chapter 5: "Records Inventory."

Smith, Milburn D. *Information and Records Management: A Decision-Maker's Guide to Systems Planning and Documentation*. New York: Quorum Books, 1986. Chapter 9: "Conducting an Inventory."

Wallace, Patricia E., Jo Ann Lee, and Dexter R. Schubert. *Records Management: Integrated Information Systems*. 3d ed. Englewood Cliffs, NJ: Prentice-Hall, 1992. Chapter 4: "Records Inventory and Analysis."

DISCUSSION POINTS

1. What different types of records would you expect to find in a library office? Make a list, and for each record series, take a guess at how it might be filed. What different formats would you be likely to encounter?

2. Conduct a preliminary records survey of a library office. This may have

to be hypothetical, in which case you will not be able to engage in the complete process. Begin by creating a floor plan and numbering the locations (including individual drawers and shelves). Design a survey form, or copy the one provided in Figure 4-1. Now survey the records and complete the form. How long did it take to complete the survey? How closely did your findings match your expectations from Point 1. Did you find anything unexpected? Was there any unused storage space? How many cubic feet of records did you find?

If you cannot find a real office, then try the same process with your files at home (although these are likely to be much smaller).

3. How do you think a detailed records inventory would be received by the office staff (keep in mind that the survey should include machine-readable business files)? How would you "sell" the idea of records management to them? If you can determine the cost per square foot of office space, calculate how much money is being spent on records storage in the office. How long do you think it would take to conduct a detailed physical inventory?

Chapter Five

Records Appraisal and Retention

Once an organization's records have been inventoried, the next step is to decide what to keep, for how long, and what the appropriate method of disposal is for nonpermanent records. The objectives of establishing retention are to eliminate the storage of unnecessary records (thereby releasing valuable storage space, whether in cabinets or on disks), to promote efficient and timely access to active and inactive records, to comply with legal requirements regarding retention, and to identify and protect vital records. Retention decisions include the amount of time a record series will remain in active files, at what point it will be moved to inactive storage, whether it will be microfilmed, whether it will be archived, whether it will be designated as a vital record and treated in a special way, whether it will be kept permanently or destroyed, and if the record is to be destroyed, when, and in what manner.

Classification of records according to their function, and appraisal or analysis based on their value, are the two steps which lead toward establishing retention schedules. These activities are both based on data obtained during the detailed inventory, although records appraisal also requires input from various other sources, internal and external to the organization.

CLASSIFICATION

Classification involves dividing records series into groups according to their function (for instance, accounting records and personnel records). Classification takes the primary function of a record series into account. When considering function, records can be described as transactional, reference, or housekeeping. Transactional records document routine transactions, such as purchase orders. Reference records document functional activities and include such items as market studies, correspondence files, and project files. Housekeeping records relate to internal day-to-day operations (for instance, work schedules and announcements).

There are several advantages to classifying record series functionally. One advantage is that records which serve the same function may have similar retention periods, or at least the factors which influence retention decisions may be similar, and decision making may be made more efficient by dealing with similar series in a group.

Another advantage is that classifying records by function may reveal duplicate record series which do not fall together in an alphabetized inventory listing because of differences in titles used by different offices in which they are located. Most records are duplicated at some point in their lives (especially in this day and age of easy copying), and most of these duplicates can be disposed of once the purpose of duplication has been served.

APPRAISAL/ANALYSIS

While classification concerns the role a record series plays within an organization, appraisal focuses on the value of that series to the organization. The value of a record series is assessed for different value categories, and is usually expressed in terms of months, years, or some other chronological unit. A series may have different values for different categories. The categories for which records managers consider value can be divided into "primary values" (usually designated as administrative, legal, fiscal, and research or scientific values) and "secondary" values, also known as evidentiary and informational values.

Administrative Value

The administrative value of a record is its value in helping the organization do its job, in the short term and the long term. The short-term value is often called the "operating" value. Administrative value is essentially the length of time a record is needed within the organization, for the organization's functioning. This value is usually set by the head of the department where the record is stored, often in conjunction with other departments. The department head also typically sets the period of active use. For most records, active value is usually not more than two years.

Legal Value

Records with legal value are those which are evidence of the legal rights and obligations of an organization. They are records which might be needed, for instance, in the case of litigation. The retention rate for records with legal value is normally based on government regulations, which are established through federal statutes and administrative rulings, as well as through local statutes. Legal value depends on factors such as the type of record, the type of organization or industry sector, the states and municipalities in which an organization does business, and the government agencies with which an organization may be involved in some relationship.

Certain types of records fall under federal reporting and retention requirements regardless of the nature of the organization or its operations. Mostly these include tax, income, and employment records. By the same token, certain industries are subject to greater regulation (for instance, health services, banks, and utilities), and so are certain processes common to almost all organizations (notably waste disposal). Any organization which contracts with the federal (or other) government can expect its records to be subject to certain regulations which might not otherwise have been imposed.

There are a number of problems in determining legal value, not the least of which is having to pour through the *Code of Federal Regulations* to find the appropriate administrative law and having to monitor changes through the *Federal Register*. These two sources, of course, only cover federal law, and lack comprehensiveness, as well as not providing any information on state, county, or other local codes which might require a longer retention period than federal law mandates.

The obvious answer, "keep everything," is far too costly and potentially damaging, but is the route which many organizations take. The reasons for which organizations keep everything usually have more to do with inertia and a reluctance to make decisions than with any understanding of federal or state laws. In fact, many small organizations have virtually no inkling that laws governing retention periods even exist, much less why compliance with them might be worthwhile.

The cost of "keeping everything" is related to two factors: space and litigation. On a very obvious level, space is expensive (especially office space), and should not be used to store unnecessary records. In a less obvious way, the larger the files, the more difficult it is to find an individual record, with the result that retrieval is inefficient and time-consuming, and productivity suffers. Aside from the space issue, the more damaging cost may be obtained by having to produce (or allow to be found during the discovery process[1]) a piece of damaging evidence which otherwise might have been destroyed at the end of a legal retention period. An established records management program is partial evidence that destruction of a particular record was not deliberate and willful, but rather just part of normal documented procedures.

So, for several telling reasons, it is worth sifting through a morass of sometimes conflicting information to determine the legal value of a record series. Statutes may be vague (apart from being difficult to find), but it is important to be able to demonstrate that the intent of the law was followed

---

[1] Discovery is the stage during litigation when the opposing parties gather relevant information from each other, whether by verbal deposition, written interrogatory, or examination of internal documentation. Each party is responsible for gathering all relevant information. A good discussion of the impact of this process on records management can be found in Betton (1991).

as best as possible. Fortunately, several sources provide some assistance. First and foremost is the Office of the Federal Register's *Guide to Records Retention Requirements in the Code of Federal Regulations* (National Archives and Records Administration, Office of the Federal Register, 1989, unnumbered preliminary page), which is

> a Guide in digest form to the provisions of Federal regulations relating to the keeping of records by the public. It tells the user (1) what records must be kept, (2) who must keep them, and (3) how long they must be kept.

The *Guide*, which is intended to be issued annually (but does not always manage to meet that objective), pulls together the regulations published in the *Code of Federal Regulations*, and includes any amendments found in the daily issues of the *Federal Register*. The regulations are organized by the government departments, agencies, commissions, administrations, and offices which administer and enforce the requirement. The numbering system makes it relatively easy to move between the abridged *Guide* (a sample page is shown in Figure 5-1) and the full statute in the *Code*.

Other aids in determining legal value are available from a variety of sources. Professional associations (for instance, the American Bar Association, or the American Institute of Certified Public Accountants) and special interest groups within ARMA occasionally publish industry specific guidelines (examples of these can be found in the records management textbooks). Commercial records centers will sometimes provide clientele with suggested retention periods, citing federal regulations for legal value. Some local governments and state archives provide guidelines for local agencies. Figure 5-2 shows a page from such a publication. The journal, *Records & Retrieval Report*, has published several issues on retention; one of these lists recommends retention periods for a large list of record types ("Retention Schedules," 1985). There are many other examples, and some list not only total retention time, but suggested length of time in active versus inactive storage.

Fiscal Value

Fiscal value is attached to records which reflect financial transactions, and, in fact, fiscal value is closely related to legal value in that many fiscal records are retained for purposes of compliance with requirements of the Internal Revenue Service or the Securities and Exchange Commission. However, records which have to do with the receipt, transfer, payment, adjustment, or encumbrance of private or public funds may also need to be kept to comply with an organization's own internal audit.

Figure 5-1. Guide to Records Retention Requirements.

FEDERAL COMMUNICATIONS COMMISSION

47 CFR

1.526 Commercial applicants, permittees, and licensees.

See 73.3526.

1.527 Permittees or licensees of stations in the noncommercial educational broadcast services.

See 73.3527.

1.613 Licensees or permittees of AM, FM, noncommercial FM radio, and television stations.

See 73.3613.

2.938 Grantees of FCC equipment authorizations, including registration.

To maintain records of original design drawings and specifications and of the procedures used for production, inspection, and testing.

Retention period: 1 year after manufacture of item is permanently discontinued or until notified of conclusion of any investigation or proceeding.

2.955 Manufacturers (or importers of radio frequency equipment subject to verification).

To maintain records of the original design drawings and specifications and of the procedures used for production, inspection, and testing.

Retention period: 2 years.

5.163 Licensees of radio stations in the experimental services (other than broadcast).

To keep adequate station records of operation; of service or maintenance duties which may affect proper station operation; and of the illumination of antennas or antenna supporting structures.

Retention period: 1 year.

5.165 Experimental Radio Services (other than Broadcast).

To maintain station records.
Retention period: 1 year.

5.410 Licensees of radio stations holding student authorizations for experimental services.

To maintain record of date, time, and frequency of operations and brief description of experimentation being conducted.

Retention period: 1 month after termination of authorization.

15.312 Holders of grants of authorization of perimeter protection systemn.

To maintain a list of all installations and records of measurements.
Retention period: Not specified.

17.49 Licensees of radio stations.

To maintain record of tower light inspections in the station record.
Retention period: Not specified.

18.105 Owners or operators of industrial, scientific, and medical equipment.

To keep a log of inspections of industrial heating equipment.
Retention period: Not specified.

21.201 Licensees of radio stations in the domestic public-fixed radio services.

To maintain at the station the name, address and telephone number of the custodian of the station license if such license or authorization is not maintained at the station.
Retention period: Not specified.

21.208 Licensees of radio stations in the domestic public radio services.

To maintain a technical log of station operations and an operation logbook as indicated in section cited.

Retention period: 1 year, or if records involving communications incident to a disaster or involved in an investigation by the Commission—until written authorization by the Commission to destroy; or if involved in a claim or complaint—until satisfaction of claim or complaint or until barred by statute limiting time for filing a suit upon such claim.

(From National Archives and Records Administration, Office of the Federal Register, *Guide to Records Retention Requirements*. Washington, DC: GPO, 1989 (SuDocs: AE.108:R24), p. 355.)

Figure 5-2. Retention Guidelines for Library System Records.

LIBRARY/LIBRARY SYSTEMS

ITEM	DESCRIPTION OF RECORD	RETENTION
	LIBRARY/LIBRARY SYSTEM	
249.	**Incorporation, chartering and registration records:**	PERMANENT
250.	**Accession records:**	1 year after accessioning procedure becomes obsolete
251.	**Directory of public library system** and member libraries, prepared by public library system	
	a. Official copy of public library system:	PERMANENT
	b. Member library's copy:	0 after superseded
252.	**Borrowing or loaning records**, including interlibrary loan:	0 after obsolete
253.	**Catalog of holdings**	
	a. Official copy of manuscript or printed catalog:	PERMANENT
	b. Continuously updated catalog:	0 after superseded or obsolete
254.	**Individual title purchase requisition** which has been filled or found to be unfillable:	1 year
255.	**Records documenting selection of books** and other library materials:	1 year
256.	**Library material censorship and complaint records**, including evaluations by staff, patrons' complaints and record of final decision:	6 years after last entry
257.	**Patron's registration** for use of rare, valuable or restricted materials:	6 years

(From University of the State of New York, State Education Department, State Archives, *Records Retention and Disposition Schedule CO-1, for Use by County Governments*. Albany, NY: State Archives, 1987, p. 39.)

Research or Scientific Value

Records have research value (or scientific value) if they represent technical data, research results, test results, and so on. These record series represent the intellectual property of the institution, and are a resource as important as human and material resources.

Secondary Values

Various sources, including the National Archives and Records Administration, suggest there are additional "secondary" values (National Archives and Records Administration, 1989; Penn, Morddel, Pennix and Smith, 1989). These include evidential values and informational values. Evidentiary records are those relating to the origin of the institution or to policy and procedure. Examples of evidentiary records might include organization charts, annual reports, audit reports, minutes, executive orders, and statutes.

Informational records are created as a result of institutional activities, and may be important for reference purposes. Informational records may include lists of persons and corporate bodies, plans of buildings and so forth, documents associated with the historical record of certain phenomena (such as natural disasters), field surveys and data collections, case files, and similar materials.

We could also think of these records as having historical value. Records have historical (or archival) value if they have to do with the origin and history of the organization. Items such as superseded organization charts and company directories, blueprints, notebooks, articles of incorporation, old trade catalogs, awards and prizes, photographs of founders and other significant persons, and other materials of little current value, but of significant historical note. In an organization which has an archivist, decisions about this type of value would be made in consultation with that person. Unfortunately, all too many organizations have neither an archivist nor a librarian, and in these cases it is up to the records manager to guard the record of the organization's beginnings and its subsequent development. Apart from the obvious need to have some sense of corporate history (especially as anniversaries and jubilees roll around), these types of records may also serve the interests of social historians.

RETENTION SCHEDULING

The next steps in retention involve setting retention values based on appraisal, developing the retention schedule, putting the program into place, and monitoring compliance.

Retention Value

The retention value is based on the individual values discussed above, and is usually the longest of the values for each record series. For instance, if a record series has an administrative value of two years, but a legal value of five years, then the retention value would be five years. For an individual record series, the data regarding administrative, legal, fiscal, research, and other values will clearly come from a range of sources, including an intimate understanding of the organization.

A retention authorization form sets out the retention decision made for a particular record series, and includes the sources for the decision. Recording decision-making information on a form (which may be a section of the detailed physical inventory form) ensures a systematic and thorough approach. Some of the information to be collected will come from office managers, some from file clerks, some from organization lawyers or accountants, and some from published guidelines or regulations. Recommendations may come from an informed individual (such as the records manager) and be ratified by a committee composed of representatives of the departments involved. Figure 5-3 shows an example of a form used to gather appraisal information and to set down retention decisions.

A number of very useful and practical publications on appraisal and retention by Donald Skupsky are listed in the readings at the end of this chapter. Skupsky could lay claim to being the national expert on retention, and is a frequent speaker as well as a prolific author on the subject.

As is frequently the case in records management activities, sensitivity to the emotional aspects of information control is important. It may be clear to the records manager that budgets from 20 years ago do not need to be kept in active files, but that might not be clear to the "owner" of the file cabinet in question. In most cases, a conservative approach at the beginning works well, and a monitoring of the actual use of a record series can help to make a later case for negotiating revisions to a retention value. The general "rule of thumb" suggests that most records enjoy an active life of one or two years before being retired to inactive storage.

Developing the Retention Schedule

A retention schedule is a comprehensive list of an organization's record series showing their retention periods in active and in inactive storage. The schedule represents an agreement between the creators/users of records and the records manager, and it essentially recognizes the "caretaker" role of a records management operation. The amount of detail included in a retention schedule may vary, but the basics include:

o   Office identification;
o   Date;
o   Official title of the series;

Figure 5-3. Records Appraisal (Attachment to a Records Inventory Form).

```
Record series title:

Location:

Frequency of use:
   [ ] daily        [ ] quarterly    [ ] other: _____
   [ ] monthly      [ ] yearly

Never used after: _____

Is this the copy of record?
   [ ] Yes. Duplicate copies are located _____
   [ ] No. The copy of record is located _____

Relationship to other record series:
```
```
Administrative use of the record:
```
```
Fiscal requirements:
```
```
Legal requirements (cite statues, etc.):
```
```
Research/Scientific value:
```
```
Proposed retention period:
```
```
Final retention:
```
```
Signatures:                                    Date
   Records Manager:    _____   _____
      Legal Services:  _____   _____
  Financial Services:  _____   _____
      Department Head: _____   _____
```

- Brief description;
- Unique report number or form number (if any);
- Office (i.e., active) retention period;
- Storage (i.e., inactive) retention period (for the copy of record);
- Appropriate federal or state statute(s);
- Special instructions (e.g., regarding microfilming);
- Special treatment (in vital records or archival programs); and
- Method of destruction.

A uniform coding system should be developed for specifying retention periods, triggering points (i.e., when a record series is to be designated inactive), and other actions. Examples of such codes include AS (after settlement), CQ (current quarter), CY (current year), OBS (when obsolete), SUP (when superseded), and P (permanent). An example of a retention schedule may be seen in Figure 5-4.

Figure 5-4. Retention Schedule.

Department/Agency: ASSESSORS
Secretary of State/Supervisor of Public Records/Records Management Section
RS-1-77
RECORDS RETENTION SCHEDULE

NUMBER	TITLE	STATUTORY REFERENCE	RETENTION PERIOD
	ABATEMENT, APPLICATION FOR		
1.1	Motor Vehicle Excise Tax (126)	c. 60A, s. 2	Following completion of satisfactory audit or final settlement of levy, whichever is later (if no appeal is pending).
1.2	Motor Vehicles Excise Tax -- Subsequent	c. 60A, s. 1A	Same as above.
1.3	Personal Property Tax (127)	c. 59, s. 59	Same as above.
1.4	Real Estate Tax (127)	c. 59, s. 50	Same as above.
1.5	Sewer, Street, Sidewalk Betterment Tax (129)	c. 80, s. 5	Same as above.
	ABATEMENT, RECORDS OF		
1.6	Copy, Application for (150B)	c. 59, s. 60	After use.
1.7	Motor Vehicle and Trailer Excise Tax (151)	c. 59, s. 60	Permanent.
1.8	Motor Vehicle and Trailer Excise Tax -- Monthly Listing to Accounting Officer (156)	c. 59, s. 70A	Following completion of satisfactory audit.
1.9	Property Tax (150)	c. 59, s. 60	Permanent.
1.10	Property Tax -- Monthly List to Accountant	c. 59, s. 70A	Following completion of satisfactory audit.
	ABATEMENT CERTIFICATES		
1.11	Motor Vehicle Excise Tax (146)	c. 60A, s. 2	Following completion of satisfactory audit.
1.12	Property Tax (147)	c. 59, s. 63	Same as above.
1.13	Water Charges (147W)	c. 59, s. 63	Same as above.

(From Michael J. Connolly, *Municipal Records Management Manual*. Boston, MA: Office of the Massachusetts Secretary of State, Division of Archives, n.d., Appendix i.)

In actual practice, a large organization may have a number of detailed individual schedules (for individual offices or categories of record series) and one general master schedule. Within a retention schedule, record series are usually grouped either by function or by primary user department, and then alphabetically by title. In the case of multiple copies of records, there should be a separate entry for each separate copy which is retained and used somewhere in the organization. If the copy of record (the one which is to be retained beyond active use) is clearly identified, then the other copies will be disposed of appropriately.

Whether large or small, the schedule must go through an approval cycle, so that all parties concerned have agreed to the decisions implied on the schedule. The approval cycle should include the manager of the office(s) where the record series is stored and (to the degree that these are present) the legal department, the administration head of operations, the fiscal audit department, and the archives manager.

Implementing the Retention Schedule

In most cases responsibility for transferring records to inactive storage rests with office staff rather than records center staff, and so one of the first steps in putting a retention schedule into action is to set up a training program for these departmental records coordinators. Training includes orientation to the general goals of records management, as well as specific instructions on things as mundane (but critical) as how to pack a records carton, how to label a carton, how to calculate the cubic feet of materials about to be transferred, and so on. A good records center manual (discussed in Chapter 10) can act both as a training tool and back-up reference guide for records coordinators.

For the records manager, the temptation may be strong to move all inactive files to the records center as soon as the retention schedule is put into effect. The resulting flood of record cartons would be overwhelming. In the early years of a new program, transfer of records should be staggered so as to permit an even workload distribution for records center staff. The same problem holds for ongoing records management programs, since most organizational activities (and the records which capture them) end and begin at the same change of year (be it a fiscal, calendar, administrative, or academic year). One common way to avoid peaks and valleys in records center activity is to close active files at the change of year, but spread the transfer of closed files from various offices over several months.

Records Appraisal and Retention 85

Figure 5-5. Records Transfer Form Used by the Massachusetts State Archives.

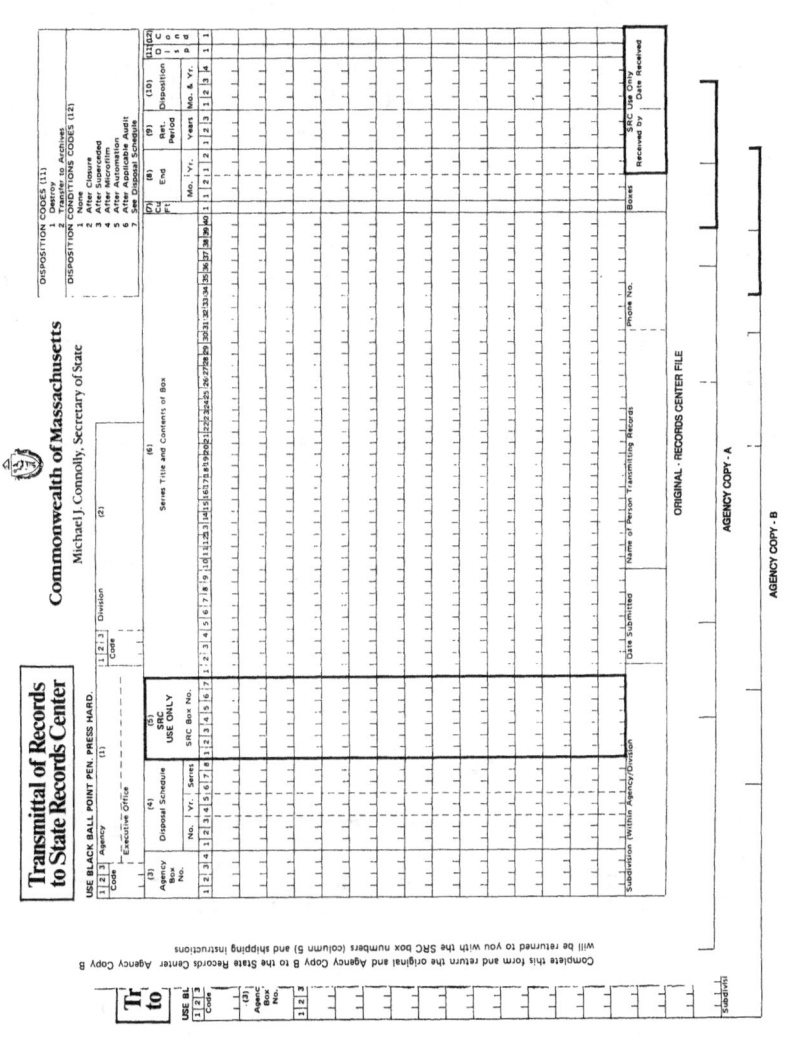

86 Records Management and the Library

The transfer process involves using a standard carton label, packing cartons according to established procedures, and filling in a records transfer document provided by the records center (an example can be seen in Figure 5-5). This form typically has three parts: one for the originating office to keep temporarily until the records center has acknowledged receipt, one for the records center to complete and file on receipt, and one to return to the originating office as evidence of the transfer having been completed. The records center, at the time of receipt, initiates a storage and destruction form for the newly received series, detailing where it is stored and at what time (and how) it should be disposed of.

A records request mechanism must be in place so that individual records or entire series can be easily retrieved. Depending on the particular setting, requests should be able to be sent to the records center in person or by telephone, internal or external mail, fax, or electronic mail, and the records center should be able to service requests in a timely manner using the same delivery mechanisms (including messenger services where appropriate). Figure 5-6 shows an example of a reference request form.

Figure 5-6. Reference Request Form.

(From New York State Education Department, *Managing Local Government Records*. Albany, NY: University of the State of New York, State Education Department, State Archives, 1985, p. 49.)

Like libraries, records centers have developed circulation procedures, including claiming of overdue items. A three-part check-out form allows for one copy to be attached to the item when sent to the requester, one copy to be filed as a place marker in the record series carton, and one copy to be filed by date in what is called a "tickler" file for follow up. The tickler file copy is pulled after check-in. It could also easily be refiled by series title as an ongoing record of activity in a series, which is useful information for revising retention periods. Similarly, a departmental request card, showing the number and type of requests coming from individual departments, can contribute to an overall understanding of information resource activity in an organization. Figure 5-7 shows an example of a simple charge-out form.

Compliance

Backsliding by departmental records coordinators, although usually unintentional, is a large problem. It is exacerbated by high staff turnover. Records managers need to establish close relationships with human resources officers, so that staff changes can be monitored and new coordinators appointed and trained when necessary. For that matter, new managers may have to be oriented to the importance of complying with records transfer procedures. In the beginning years of a new program, annual audits of files can reveal backlogs, filing disorders, new record series, and other problems. Another, perhaps slightly devious, method of dealing with proliferating records (as represented by a need for more cabinetry) is to persuade upper management that as a matter of policy the records manager must approve all equipment requisitions.

In the normal course of operations, all record series and retention schedules should come under annual scrutiny. Legal and fiscal values change under revisions in statutes, and internal fiscal and administrative values may change as well. Statistics as to the number of requests from inactive records storage may suggest changes in active retention periods. New record series may have evolved, and new records management activities may affect, the way information is captured. Even relatively superficial annual audits also have the added benefit of suggesting a level of commitment and continued activity on the part of the records management department.

DISPOSAL

When records are to be destroyed, the originating department must be notified and must approve the destruction in writing (before it happens!). Destruction methods differ according to both the medium and the nature of the record, and destruction may be carried out onsite or offsite. A number of factors influence the decision as to the destruction method, including

Figure 5-7. Charge-Out Form.

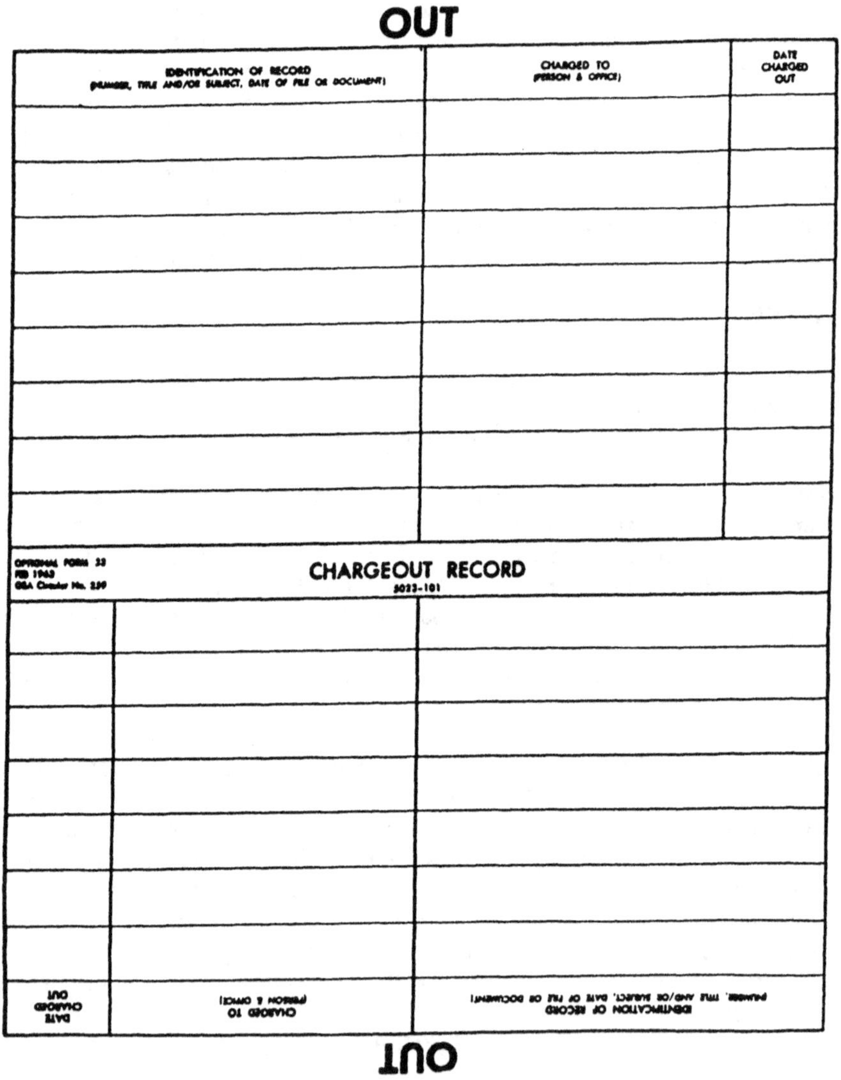
OUT

IDENTIFICATION OF RECORD (NUMBER, TITLE AND/OR SUBJECT, DATE OF FILE OR DOCUMENT)

CHARGED TO (PERSON & OFFICE)

DATE CHARGED OUT

OPTIONAL FORM 23
FEB 1963
GSA Circular No. 259

CHARGEOUT RECORD
5023-101

DATE CHARGED OUT

CHARGED TO (PERSON & OFFICE)

IDENTIFICATION OF RECORD (NUMBER, TITLE AND/OR SUBJECT, DATE OF FILE OR DOCUMENT)

OUT

(From General Services Administration, National Archives and Records Service, Office of Federal Records Centers, *Files Operations*. Washington, DC: GPO, 1981 (Records Management Handbook), p. 53.)

- Volume of records;
- Frequency of destruction;
- Size of records;
- Uniformity of records;
- Confidentiality of records;
- Local and state laws on waste disposal;
- Availability of a reliable salvage company;
- Potential noise problems;
- Amount of preparatory handling necessary;
- Need for skilled operators;
- Cost benefits of sale for scrap;
- Recycling possibilities; and
- Amount of waste left after destruction.

Most modern destruction methods can accommodate paper clips, staples, normal binders, and in some cases, film material. Shredders come in all shapes and sizes, and, of course, do result in a large amount of matter to be removed. Pulverizers and disintegrators go a step further than shredders and reduce records to dust, which again must still be removed. Records can be pulped, but pulpers require large amounts of water. Incinerators are sometimes necessary, but their use is almost always closely restricted by state and local law, and the results must be closely examined, as destruction is not always total. Local salvage and recycling companies may also be helpful. Whatever the method, a representative of the records management department should always witness the destruction, and a storage and destruction form for the record series should be completed and filed.

RESULTS

The literature of records management suggests that after a records retention program has been put into place, a company would find on the average that almost one-half of the office space previously devoted to records storage has been released, and that almost one-fourth of the records which were being kept could be discarded. It is not difficult for a records manager to demonstrate immediate benefits with figures such as these.

Throughout this chapter and the preceding one, it has become clear that much of records management involves creating, completing, filing, and gathering data from forms. A surprisingly large number of records management departments keep these various forms on paper only. Clearly, the activities of records management lend themselves to organization through a database management system, or at the least a simple file management system. The next chapter examines the basic concepts of database management as applied to records management, and will also explore special filing considerations in records management.

REFERENCES

Betton, Vicki L. "Litigation Discovery, Document Production, and Records Management," *Records & Retrieval Report* 7 (June 1991): 1-15.

Connolly, Michael J. *Municipal Records Management Manual.* Boston, MA: Office of the Massachusetts Secretary of State, Division of Archives, n.d.

General Services Administration, National Archives and Records Service, Office of Federal Records Centers, *Files Operations*. Washington, DC: GPO, 1981 (Records Management Handbook).

National Archives and Records Administration. *Disposition of Federal Records*. Washington, DC: GPO, 1981, reprinted 1989 (Records Management Handbook).

National Archives and Records Administration. Office of the Federal Register. *Guide to Records Retention Requirements.* Washington, DC: GPO, 1989 (SuDocs: AE.108:R24).

New York State Education Department, *Managing Local Government Records*. Albany, NY: University of the State of New York, State Education Department, State Archives, 1985.

Penn, Ira A., Anne Morddel, Gail Pennix, and Kelvin Smith. *Records Management Handbook.* Brookfield, VT: Gower, 1989.

"Retention Schedules," *Records & Retrieval Report* 1 (April 1985): 53-72.

University of the State of New York, State Education Department, State Archives, *Records Retention and Disposition Schedule CO-1, for Use by County Governments*. Albany, NY: State Archives, 1987.

READINGS

Aschner, Katherine. "Records Retention Scheduling," In *Taking Control of Your Office Records: A Manager's Guide*, edited by Katherine Aschner. White Plains, NY: Knowledge Industry Publications, 1983, pp. 39-46.

Association of Records Managers and Administrators. *Developing and Operating a Records Retention Program*. Prairie Village, KS: ARMA International, 1986 (ARMA Standards Program Guidelines).

Diamond, Susan Z. *Records Management: A Practical Guide*. New York: AMACOM, 1983. Chapter 4: "Records Disposition: What to Keep and How Long to Keep It."

Parker, Elizabeth A. and Peter Emmerson. "Establishing Retention Control," In *How to Manage Your Records: A Guide to Effective Practice*, edited by Peter Emmerson. Cambridge, Eng.: ICSA Publishing, 1989, pp. 40-59.

Penn, Ira A., Anne Morddel, Gail Pennix, and Kelvin Smith. *Records*

Management Handbook. Brookfield, VT: Gower, 1989. Chapter 12: "Appraisal and Retention Scheduling."

Robek, Mary E., Gerald F. Brown, and Wilmer O. Maedke. *Information and Records Management*. 3d ed. Encino, CA: Glencoe, 1987. Chapter 6: "Retention and Disposition of Records."

Skupsky, Donald. *Legal Requirements for Business Records: Federal Requirements*. Denver, CO: Information Requirements Clearinghouse, 1990. (with annual updates)

Skupsky, Donald. *Legal Requirements for Business Records: State Requirements*. Denver, CO: Information Requirements Clearinghouse, 1990. (with annual supplements)

Skupsky, Donald. *Legal Requirements for Microfilm, Computer and Optical Disk Records*. Denver, CO: Information Requirements Clearinghouse, 1991.

Skupsky, Donald S. *Recordkeeping Requirements*. Denver, CO: Information Resources Clearinghouse, 1988.

Skupsky, Donald S. *Records Retention Procedures*. Denver, CO: Information Resources Clearinghouse, 1990.

Wallace, Patricia E., Jo Ann Lee, and Dexter R. Schubert. *Records Management: Integrated Information Systems*. 3d ed. Englewood Cliffs, NJ: Prentice-Hall, 1992. Chapter 5: "Retention and Disposition of Records."

DISCUSSION POINTS

1. How long is it necessary for you as an individual to keep the documents associated with your tax returns? Cite the federal regulation governing this requirement.

2. You have just been hired by a University as the Archivist/Records Manager (the position had been vacant for several years and has been mismanaged prior to that). There is a large University library with a long history. Among the records which are kept in the Director's office are annual budgets submitted to the University President, personnel records for current and past employees, contracts with vendors such as OCLC, annual reports, promotional literature, service contracts for computer and reprographic equipment, library organization charts, awards and citations given to the current incumbent and past library directors, minutes of staff meetings, statistics on paper and on floppy disk reflecting such data as numbers of items processed and numbers of reference requests serviced, and requests for proposals associated with various automated systems which have been implemented. The files have never been weeded. Prepare a retention schedule for these items

using the suggested guidelines mentioned in this chapter and found in the records management literature.

Chapter Six

Database Management for Records Management

It should be obvious by now that records management relies quite heavily on the use of forms. Not only do records managers handle files *containing* records, they also create records themselves to control operations, to share reports on activities, and to record decisions. So far we have seen records inventory forms, records transfer forms, retention schedules, charge out forms, appraisal forms, and a host of other records created by records managers. Future chapters will refer to yet more of the same. Clearly, much of this information could be efficiently handled through the use of database management software, and, in fact, electronic files can also provide a great deal more flexibility than paper files for records management purposes. Librarians have the advantage of being already familiar (more so than most records managers) with the principles and practices of database management, and so this chapter will present a review focusing on the records management context.

COMMERCIALLY AVAILABLE RECORDS MANAGEMENT SOFTWARE

As might be expected for any activity central to the business world, a number of companies have developed software specifically for records management operations. Directories, such as those in Table 6-1, list close to 100 products designed for use by the records manager. In addition to database management, these products cover computer-assisted retrieval, forms management, optical and digital scanning, networking, computer-output microfilm, and other record-keeping functions. Reviews and advertisements for new software titles appear regularly in the professional journal literature, in vendor product announcements, and in producer catalogs. Software products are available for microcomputers, minis, mainframes, and networked environments.

Some commercially available records management software packages are multifunctional and some concentrate on one particular aspect of records management. BOXTRAX (Image Source, Inc.), for instance, manages inactive records in a records center, while OPTEX (Optex Document Systems, Inc.) handles both active and inactive records and also stores images. Some software is targeted to specific groups (for example, COLLECTION (Vernon Systems Limited) is designed with museum information management in mind). There are several which are compatible with the MARC (machine-readable cataloging) format, for those libraries

Table 6-1. Software Directories for Records Management.

Cox, Lynn and David Bearman. *1990 Directory of Software for Archives & Museums.* Pittsburgh, PA: Archives & Museum Informatics, 1990 (Archives and Museum Informatics Technical Report no. 12).
> Lists over 50 software products of various kinds, many of which include records management functions. Descriptions are detailed, and comparative tables are included for features and functions (including one for records management). Indexed by vendor, hardware and operating system, applications, and utilities.

Cibarelli, Pamela R. and Edward John Kazlauskas. *Directory of Information Management Software for Libraries, Information Centers, Records Centers, 1989-1990.* Studio City, CA: Pacific Information, Inc., 1990.
> Lists a large number of products, principally for library applications, with detailed descriptions. Includes by vendor, hardware, and function.

Phillips, John T. and Albin Wagner. *Software Directory for Automated Records Management Systems.* Prairie Village, KS: ARMA International, 1990.
> Lists almost 50 products, with very rich descriptions, including "life cycle costs". Comparative charts are provided for records management functions, life cycle costs, and data processing architecture. Indexed by vendor.

Virando, Jacqueline. *AIIM Resource Report: Software for Information and Image Management.* Silver Spring, MD: Association for Information and Image Management, 1988.
> Lists more than 100 entries divided up among 8 functional categories, one of which (and the largest) is document/ records management. Descriptions are short, and there are no indexes.

Note: Many general software directories include records management software, to some degree. These include both printed directories and directories which are available as online databases from services such as DIALOG and BRS.

---

which would prefer to integrate records management (and archives) information into general library operations. MINARET (Cactus Software) is one example of a MARC-based archives and records management package.

The chief advantage of purchasing ready-made software for records management is a savings in development costs. Writing the program code for a records management utility from scratch (or contracting internally or externally with a data processing service to have it done) would be very expensive. The more common route, using a general purpose database management product such as DBASE (Aston-Tate) or PARADOX (Borland International), still takes both planning and implementation time in database design and creation. A commercial product already tailored to records management would, in most cases, allow for much quicker start up, and (presuming that the company is reputable, and that the product has been thoroughly tested) would include all necessary records management functions. Of course, no prepackaged product can ever satisfy every possible need in an individual setting, but if the product's customer experience is reasonably extensive and the records manager's needs are typical, then it is likely that use of a commercial software package will be satisfactory.

Costs of such software vary widely depending on the size of the installation, what hardware is already available on site, the number of users, and a number of other factors. The ARMA directory (Phillips and Wagner, 1990) shows life-cycle costs ranging from $595 (for a turnkey system running on a single microcomputer) to $200,000 for a mainframe system which is customized by the vendor for the site. In addition to purchase (or lease) costs, there are also costs associated with training, service, data conversion, special input media (such as barcode) options, telephone assistance, and so on.

The records manager who is considering purchasing commercially available software for records management would do well to use Phillips and Wagner's checklist as a guide in evaluating products. Skillman and Dmytrenko (1989) compared 24 different software products for records management, and their checklist would also be a valuable aid. One of the ARMA guidelines discussed criteria to be considered in developing and evaluating software (Association of Records Managers and Administrators, 1990). It is important to keep in mind that successful evaluation and selection of records management software begins with a thorough analysis of the purposes to be served by automation, the types of data to be stored, the products which will be needed, the current and future size of the database, and the technological constraints in place.

USING A DATABASE MANAGEMENT PACKAGE

It is more than likely that any library considering automating the records management process would already be in possession of a microcomputer and one or more file management or database management packages. File management software, such as INMAGIC (Inmagic, Inc.), PFS PROFESSIONAL FILE (Software Publishing Corporation), and PC-FILE (ButtonWare), and database management software such as DBASE and PARADOX, have been widely applied in library settings, and could equally as well be used for records management. Lundeen and Tenopir's (1988) text, while geared to the library world, is a good practical guide to database management in a microcomputer environment. The basic tasks in database creation and maintenance are the same whatever the application:

o   Needs assessment;
o   Data dictionary compilation;
o   Software selection;
o   Data structure design;
o   Data collection and input;
o   Report generation;
o   Database maintenance; and
o   Documentation.

Needs Assessment

The principles and techniques of systems analysis, as discussed in Chapter 3, should be applied to planning and implementing database management as to any other activity in an organization. It would not be wise to select software, or design a database, without a thorough understanding of exactly what the new system is intended to do, what institutional objectives it will serve, and how it will be different from whatever may be currently in place. The most important initial considerations specific to database management are what the information needs of the organization are, and how the records management automation can better serve those needs. More specific questions are discussed in the various sections that follow.

Data Dictionary Compilation

A data dictionary is a document (or a machine-readable file) which describes all the significant data elements which will compose the database. In a microcomputer environment this is usually a document rather than an integrated element of the database system (although data structure design necessarily automates some aspects of the data dictionary). In a larger environment, or with sophisticated microcomputer software, the data dictionary is a fully integrated part of the database system. To use library jargon, the data dictionary represents a complete listing of all the fields (and subfields) which will make up the records in the database. Common elements of a data dictionary include, for each field,

o   The name of the field;
o   The field code or number;
o   The field name abbreviation;
o   Which data structure(s) the field appears in;
o   A narrative description of the contents;

- An example of an entry;
- The authority or authorized dictionary for data entry;
- Whether the field may have more than one value
    (such as several different subjects for one record);
- The data type
    (numeric, alphanumeric, logical, date, currency, graphics, etc.);
- The case (upper case, lower case, mixed);
- Whether the field is fixed or variable in length;
- Maximum field length in characters;
- The range of the field;
- Whether the contents are unique for each record;
- Whether the field is required for each record;
- Whether there is a default value for the field;
- Whether the value is calculated from other fields;
- Whether the value should be expanded to a text equivalent
    (e.g., entered as "AC", but displayed as "Accounts");
- Whether data should be validated during entry;
- Whether data should be converted to specified formats
    (e.g., from "10/29/92" to "Oct. 29, 1992");
- Whether the field is to be indexed
    (and in some cases *how* it is to be indexed);
- How the field is to be sorted;
- Whether the field is to be searched;
- What reports the field will appear in;
- Whether the field is subject to calculation in report generation;
- Whether the contents should be secured against view by unauthorized users; and
- Date of creation of data dictionary entry.

A document such as this is clearly invaluable in developing the criteria by which to judge the capabilities of one software package against another for a particular application. Furthermore, the act of compiling the data dictionary leads to an in-depth familiarity with the structure of the data. Finally, the data dictionary forms the basis of the input manual which will be created to promote consistency and accuracy of data entry. If the data dictionary is an integrated component of the database software, it also allows for automatic data formatting, entry validation, and error checking. Figure 6-1 shows an example of a data dictionary entry for a "Department" field in a hypothetical records management database.

Figure 6-1. Data Dictionary Entry.

Field Name: Department
Field Code: 003
Field Name Abbreviation: DEPT
Data Structure(s): INVTRY, DEPTMT
Description: Name of department
Example: ACCT
Authority: List of Department Codes, Input Manual, Appendix 2
Single or Multiple Values: single
Data Type: alphanumeric
Case: upper
Fixed or Variable: fixed
Maximum Length: 4
Range: 4
Unique (Y/N): N in INVTRY, Y in DEPTMT
Required (Y/N): N in INVTRY, Y in DEPTMT
Default Value: none
Calculated Value: none
Expanded Value: expand to text from DEPTNAME dictionary
Validate During Entry (Y/N): Y, from DEPTCODES file
Conversion Format: all upper case
Indexed (Y/N): Y
Sort Method: alpha, a to z
Searchable (Y/N): Y
Reports: RETEN1, RETEN2, TRANSFER, DISPOS, ACTIVITY
Use in Calculations: no
Security Protection: no
Date: 1/10/92

Software Selection

The common case in setting up a database in a library or information center is "make do with what hardware and software you already have." If given the luxury of selecting either hardware or software, the records manager must establish a list of criteria to use in product evaluation. There may be overall institutional policies or existing technological commitments with respect to particular companies or operating systems. Compatibility with other institutional technologies is crucial, especially in the case of a microcomputer system which might potentially navigate to an in-house mainframe as growth is experienced.

Database Management for Records Management

Figure 6-2. Database Management Software Evaluation Criteria.

Product: _____ Version: _____

Vendor: _____ PubDate: _____

Machine Requirements
 Kb of RAM required
 Mb on hard drive required
 Program size (Mb)
 Operating system(s)
 Optical drive compatibility
 Printer compatibility
 Color/monochrome monitors
  CGA, VGA, EGA, Hercules
 Mouse/non-mouse compatibility
 Other software required
 Other hardware required
 Cost

Vendor/Producer
 Years in business
 Principal product line
 Date of product introduction
 Other (related) products
 Vendor will customize
 Knowledge of this environment
 User group and/or newsletter
 Telephone support
 Licensing arrangements
 Warranty
 Demo or trial period

Overall Ease of Use
 General help/tutorials
 Context-sensitive help
 Use of function keys
 Use of windows
 Error messages clear
 Prompts/menus clear
 Screen displays easy to read
 Typographic error in display
 Effective use of highlighting
 Ease of installation
 Options during installation

Documentation
 Types
 Legibility
 Indexed

System Overview
 Flat file or DBMS
 Supports multiple users
 Security features
  overall password
  specific field suppression
  read-only passwords
 Procedural language
  number of operations
  number of functions
  number of variables
  editing, compiling, debugging
  run-time version
  compatibility with other languages
 Macros
  number of definable macros
 Supports optical files
 Image handling capabilities
 New version upgrades
 Reports usage statistics
 Amount of training needed
  by installer, end-user groups
 Integration with other products

File Creation Characteristics
 Size restrictions
  number and length of fields
  number and length of records
  number of files per database
 Data structure
  ease of creation
  types of fields
   fixed
   variable
   numeric
   character
   date
   time
   logical
   "memo" (long text)
  default values
  calculated values
  data formats
  multiple valued fields
 Indexing
  on how many characters
  number of active indexes
  phrase indexing
  keyword indexing
  size of overhead taken by indexes

Figure 6-2 (Continued).

File Creation Characteristics (cont'd)
Sorting
  sort defaults
  alphabetic
  numeric
  ascending/descending
  ignores initial articles
  translates number to characters
  sorts dates
Ease of modification of
  structure
  indexing
  fieldnames
  sorting
  defaults
Addition, deletion of fields
Changing fixed field length
Handles unusual characters

Data Entry and Modification
Ease of entry/modification
User-defined input screen
Interactive input
  immediate updating
Batch input
  log of accepted/rejected records
  imports ASCII files
  imports other formats
Bar code/scanning input
Editing
  character by character
  normal editing functions
    (insert, delete, cut and paste)
Global change
Validation/error checking
Expansion from abbreviated entry
Look up to authority files
  cut and paste from above

Reports
Ease of report creation
Columnar reports
Record reports ("bibliographic")
Crosstab reports
Saving report formats
One-time user-defined reports
Report to screen, printer, disc
Report selected records/entire file

Report selected fields
Rearrange fields in report
Modifiable field labels
Numeric data manipulation
  averages, sums, counts
  subaverages, subsums, subcounts
  calculated fields
Page layout capabilities
Exports ASCII files
Exports to other formats

Search capability
Command-driven
  command stacking
Menu-driven
Query by example
Search multiple fields simultaneously
  upper limit
String search
"Soundex" search
Browsing
  through file
  through field values
Truncation/masking
  terminal, internal, initial
Boolean operators
Proximity searching
Range searching
Numeric search (=, >, <, < =, > =, /)
Search unindexed fields
Upper- and lower-case distinction
Windows to entered data, authority lists
  abbreviated entry of search terms
  cut and paste to search
Response time

Search results
Moving between records
  forward and backwards
  to specific record
Moving within long record
Default results format
User-defined formats
Moving between formats
Default sort
User specified sort
Subsort capabilities
Output to screen, printer, disc
Print options

Possible hardware configurations for records management range from a single microcomputer workstation to shared time on a mainframe to workstations connected through a local area network. In addition to basic data processing equipment, records management might make use of such additional hardware devices as optical scanners, barcode readers, sophisticated computer-based fax technologies, and optical, magneto-optical, or video disk systems. If capabilities demanding these types of technologies are planned for records management, then they will have to be taken into account in developing criteria for software selection.

Beyond these considerations, the data dictionary serves as a good starting point for drawing up an evaluation checklist, since it describes what types of data must be accommodated, and what data handling techniques are required. With input from the data dictionary, tempered with an understanding of the current and future directions of the institution's records management activities, a checklist such as the one that appears in Figure 6-2 can be developed. This particular example was created with microcomputer software in mind, but the considerations with respect to database management software are not extremely different in a mainframe environment.

In Figure 6-2, under the heading *System Overview*, the first line reads "Flat file or DBMS." In point of fact, this decision will probably have been made before the criteria list is created, and it distinguishes between the two major categories of commercially available microcomputer database software. Flat file software, or file management software, handles one file at a time, while database management software is based on exploiting relationships among many files that work together. The terms file management and database management are often used interchangeably, especially in the library world, but there is a real distinction. Most of the database management software available for microcomputers is based on the relational model (although there are others).[1]

The difference is most easily explained with an example. Figure 6-3 illustrates the flat file approach for a few of the fields in a simple records inventory (obviously a real application would have many more fields). In this example, each record series held in Department X would have its own entry in the database, and in each case the department name, room number, contact person, and telephone number would have to be repeated. Every change in, for instance, telephone number or contact name necessitates a change in as many records as that department holds.

---

[1] For a discussion of the different types of database management systems, see O'Brien (1988), pp. 246-281.

Figure 6-3. Records Management – Flat File Approach.

```
                                      Record #: A003
Dept: Human Resources
      Room: Madison 274
   Contact: M. McCrumb              Telephone: x6565

Record Series Title: Personnel
   Alternate Titles: Employees
           Location: 2-B-3

       Coverage: 1968-
        Missing: 1972
    Ongoing(Y/N): Y
         Volume: 10        Annual Accumulation: .5
    Microfilmed: N
             Storage Medium: v1

      Medium/Format: P1
 Filing Arrangement: alpha            Indexes: N
        Description: personnel records, past and current
```

Figure 6-4 shows the same data parceled out among two different files using a relational database manager.[2] With relational database software, links of various kinds can be established between records in different files. The method by which the links are established differs, but one common way is that files which will interact share at least one field in common. In the example, the "Records" file and the "Departments" file share the field "Dept" in common. In this scenario, a change in contact name or telephone number requires only a revision to one entry in the "Departments" file. Each file can be used on its own, as a flat file, and the relationships are exploited when needed. In general, this second model makes for less redundancy, it minimizes the likelihood of error in entry, and it grants much more flexibility and sophistication in data handling. Using database management software also tends to be more complex, and requires more careful preplanning in developing useful separate files and allowing for appropriate linkages.

---

[2] In Figures 6-3 and 6-4, the illustrations show screens designed for the database user. The underlying database structures (in which fields and file relationships are established) would look very different.

Database Management for Records Management   103

Figure 6-4. Records Management – Relational Database Approach.

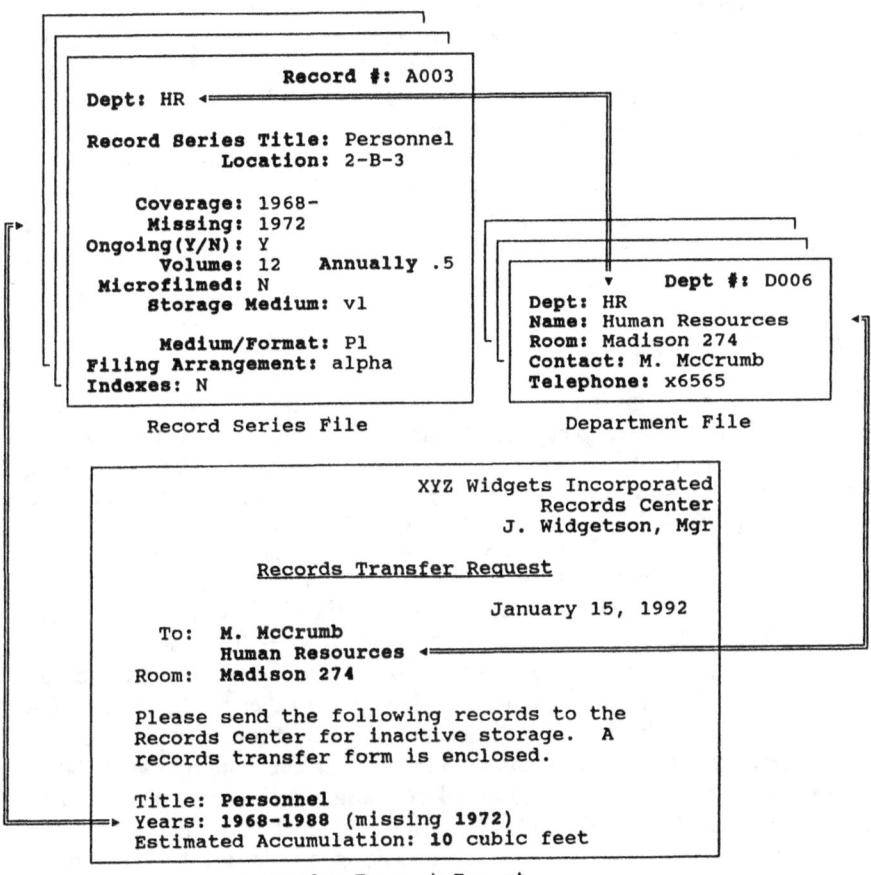

Armed with this basic decision as to type, and with a checklist, the next step involves narrowing down the candidate list to four or five top choices to be evaluated in depth. Candidates can be found in a variety of sources. Apart from software directories, the professional literature of library and information science and the popular computing literature are both good resources for database software surveys and evaluations. Such journals as *Library Software Reviews*, *CD-ROM Professional*, *Computers in Libraries*, *Database*, *The Electronic Library*, and *Library Hi Tech* frequently carry reviews or product comparisons. *PC Week, PC Magazine, PC Sources*, and *DBMS* regularly feature buyer's guides and surveys which compare the most popular file or database management packages. Once the candidate list has been narrowed down, trial periods or fully featured demonstration disks (as opposed to demonstration disk which are simply machine-readable sales presentation) are the best way to test the limits of a software product. While no one product will meet all needs, at least informed decision making can achieve the best collection of desired features for the best price.

Data Structure Design

Data structure design is the actualization of the data dictionary. In this phase of database development the fields are defined to the system. At the least this means entering field names, and it usually also entails describing various characteristics of each field. Figure 6-5 shows several steps involved in setting up a simple data structure using PFS PROFESSIONAL FILE, a flat file management package. In Screen A the field names are entered (and their placement defines field length). Screen B shows identification of which field is the unique identifier for each record in the file, and which fields are to be indexed. Screen C shows entry of default values for some fields, and Screen D shows formatting information. Other possibilities include designating that field values will be calculated from other fields, or that field values must fall within certain numeric ranges or must display certain characteristics (allowing for some degree of error checking and validation). The case study found in Chapter 14 contains an illustration of a data structure for an INMAGIC database. In the case of a relational database manager, a separate data structure must be designed for each file, keeping in mind what linkages are to be established between files.

Database Management for Records Management 105

Figure 6-5. PFS PROFESSIONAL FILE Data Structure.

```
RECMAN               Design the form by typing field names.    Page 1 of 1
 F1-Help  F2-Print  F3-Edit                                     F-10 Continue
                                                    Record #:
             Department:

   Record Series Title:
               Location:

               Coverage:
                Missing:
          Ongoing (Y/N):    Volume:       Annual Cumulation:
            Microfilmed:

         Storage Medium:

          Medium/Format:
     Filing Arrangement:
                Indexes:

            Description:


                            Initials:           Date:
.........1.........2.........3.........4.........5.........6.........7.........8
```

A. Designing the Basic Data Structure

```
RECMAN                    Type or edit indexes                 Page 1 of 1
 F1-Help  F2-Attributes  F3-Edit                                F-10 Continue
                                                   Record #: u
             Department: i

   Record Series Title: i
               Location: i

               Coverage:
                Missing:
          Ongoing (Y/N): i    Volume:       Annual Cumulation:
            Microfilmed: i

         Storage Medium:

          Medium/Format: i
     Filing Arrangement:
                Indexes:

            Description:


                            Initials:           Date: i
.........1.........2.........3.........4.........5.........6.........7.........8
```

B. Designating Indexed Fields ("u" = unique, "i" = indexed)

B. Designating Indexed Fields ("u" = unique, "i" = indexed)

106   Records Management and the Library

Figure 6-5 (Continued).

```
RECMAN                    Type or edit defaults              Page 1 of 1
F1-Help   F2-Attributes  F3-Edit                            F-10 Continue
                                                    Record #:
               Department:
     Record Series Title:
               Location:
               Coverage:
                Missing:
         Ongoing (Y/N): Y      Volume:          Annual Cumulation:
             Microfilmed: N
         Storage Medium: v1  [filing cabinet, letter sized]
          Medium/Format: P1  [paper, letter sized]
     Filing Arrangement:
                Indexes:
             Description:
                                                 [= TODAY is actually
                                                  a "formula", and pulls
                                                  in the cuurent date]
                         Initials: css           Date: = TODAY
.........1.........2.........3.........4.........5.........6.........7.........8
```

C. Setting Defaults

```
RECMAN                Type or edit data formats              Page 1 of 1
F1-Help   F2-Attributes  F3-Edit                            F-10 Continue
                                            Record #: XNNN
          Department: AAAA  [4 uppercase letters]  [1 letter, 3 numbers]
 Record Series Title:
            Location:
            Coverage: [1 uppercase
             Missing:  letter]
       Ongoing (Y/N): A     Volume: ###.##    Annual Cumulation: ###.##
         Microfilmed:              [numbers in this pattern]
      Storage Medium:
       Medium/Format:
  Filing Arrangement:
             Indexes:
         Description:
                         [3 uppercase letters]   [dates in this pattern]
                         Initials: AAA           Date: Jan. dd, yyyy
.........1.........2.........3.........4.........5.........6.........7.........8
```

D. Setting Formats

Data Collection and Input

Data collection and input involve transferring existing information to the database, and creating mechanisms for the capture of new information. Transferring existing manual files will be straightforward (albeit tedious) if these files contain all the information required by the database. To the degree that they do not, there may be a need for some retrospective information gathering. If the files already exist in machine-readable form (i.e., if the new database is an improvement over an old system rather than the first automation project), it may be possible to transfer the information in batch rather than having to reenter each record. Most database software packages accept ASCII files as input, although some expertise will be needed in massaging the data so that it will be "read into" the new database appropriately. For a large project it might be worthwhile to investigate the use of a commercial conversion service. Eddison (1991) provides a good survey of data conversion software and services. One of the problems in converting from one filing system to another is the potential for interruption in service brought about by the need to "close" a file (or a portion of a file) while it is being converted.

The use of paper forms is not completely eliminated by the introduction of database management for records management. For one thing, data capture forms are needed so that information can be gathered remotely from the records center. Data capture sheets should be designed so as to promote accuracy and consistency in recording information, and they should also facilitate entry from the data capture sheet into the database. The forms which illustrate various records management activities throughout this book could easily be modified into data capture sheets. Additionally, many records management forms are signed documents signifying an agreement to a retention period, or a destruction notice, or a similar process, and these must be kept in their original form, although the information will certainly become part of the database management system.

To be effective, data entry must follow conventions and authorities as specified in the data dictionary. A data input manual, a well-designed data capture sheet, and any error checking routines allowed by the software can help to ensure consistent and complete data entry. More sophisticated database management systems usually allow the database manager to design screens for input, which may reduce some of the training time needed by input staff. Data input tends to be done by the least expensive personnel, and this is where staff turnover tends to be high.

Report Generation

Report generation involves determining what information is needed from the database, and designing the printed or machine-readable products which meet those needs. Report formats are the report generating instructions saved as part of the database management system. Most file and database management software systems (especially for the business world) excel at producing columnar reports, such as seen in Figure 6-6, and most allow for sophisticated calculations for numeric data in reports. In addition to columnar reports, the software should also allow for producing reports which display selected fields in label (or what might be called "bibliographic") format (see Figure 6-7). Report production in a relational database environment exploits the links among files, so that fields from different files may appear in one report.

Database Maintenance, Documentation, and Evaluation

Database usage should be monitored, and an active updating and weeding program set into place. Some software can generate usage statistics, such as how many entries were created or revised, how many reports printed, and how much searching was done, using which fields. These figures can be useful in evaluation, and in preparing for growth. Input conventions, code lists, and authority files (especially headings for subject files) should be reassessed periodically. Password assignments must be kept up to date as personnel come and go. The database must be backed up regularly (and back-up copies stored off site) so that operations can be resumed quickly in the event of mechanical failure.

Figure 6-6. Columnar Report.

Total Volume, Inventory Sample

Record Series Title	Department	Coverage	Volume
Annual Audits (External)	Financial Services	1967-1979	06.00
Annual Audits (External)	President	1980-1990	05.00
Annual Audits (Internal)	Financial Services	1967-1979	04.00
Annual Audits (Internal)	President	1980-1990	05.00
Past Employees	Human Resources	1958-1991	10.00
Personnel	Human Resources	1989-	01.50
Requests for Proposals	Library	1988-1989	03.00
Service Contracts	Human Resources	CY	00.50
Service Contracts (Microcomputer)	Library	CY	00.50
		Total:	<u>35.50</u>

Figure 6-7. Label or "Bibliographic" Report.

Preliminary Listing, Inventory Sample

Record #: A103
Record Series Title: Personnel
Department: Human Resources
Location: 2-B-3 Coverage: 1989- Missing:
Volume: 1.50 Annual Cumulation: .50 Microfilmed: N
Description: Employees from 1989-.

Record #: A233
Record Series Title: Past Employees
Department: Human Resources
Location: 7-C-1/5 Coverage: 1958-1991 Missing:
Volume: 10.00 Annual Cumulation: .25 Microfilmed: N
Description: Past employee files

Record #: A298
Record Series Title: Service Contracts
Department: Human Resources
Location: 3-C-2 Coverage: CY Missing:
Volume: .50 Annual Cumulation: .50 Microfilmed: N
Description: Service contracts for all HR equipment

Record #: M298
Record Series Title: Service Contracts (Microcomputer)
Department: Library
Location: 1-B-5 Coverage: CY Missing:
Volume: .50 Annual Cumulation: .50 Microfilmed: N
Description: Service contracts for library microcomputers

Many of these are policy issues, and should be set out in writing. A database management manual or collection of several separate manuals document policies and procedures. In addition to policy statements addressing the issues presented above (back up, password assignment, authority maintenance, usage monitoring, and evaluation), the manual should also include the data dictionary documentation, input instructions, details as to when regular and special reports are printed, examples of reports and data capture sheets, and policies as to which personnel are involved in various database management activities.

IMPLEMENTATION AND COSTS

Given that a new automation project will be likely to alter working procedures, it is wise to plan carefully for implementation. The records manager should develop a timeline, set up training plans, and make sure that all staff involved or affected are fully aware of the value of the new system and its potential impact on their jobs. The new system should be thoroughly tested so as to detect any unforeseen snags before disturbing the normal flow of work, and materials to be entered into the database should be organized so as not to interrupt use. Organizational structures and job descriptions may have to be adjusted to reflect new reporting lines or new job content.

As with any information center activity, there are costs associated with bringing about records management automation. Start-up costs include equipment purchase or lease, software purchase or lease, supplies, physical site preparation (wiring, lighting, and furniture), preparation of documentation (including the data dictionary, authority lists, and entry conventions), training time, collection preparation, and data conversion or input. Ongoing labor and materials costs are associated with supplies, continued data input, charges for mainframe use, service charges, authority list maintenance, software and hardware upgrades, new staff training, report generation, statistics keeping, and regular database back up.

On the surface, automating records management may not be cost effective when simply compared with performing the same task manually. The benefits of automation usually lie not so much in doing the same work at a lower cost, but rather in providing a much more flexible base of information. In addition to merely filing forms, a well-designed database reduces input error and promotes rapid information retrieval. Perhaps most importantly, superior reporting capabilities and usage statistics allow for more well-informed decision making and planning. For example, an automated records management systems should be able to provide data on the total volume and annual accumulation of inactive records (for space planning), number of requests for inactive records in particular series (for fine-tuning retention periods), or chronological listings by retention date (for destruction scheduling).

CONCLUSION

The advantages of managing records in an electronic database make the effort well worth it. In most libraries, this effort would largely be limited to the creation of a machine-readable database, or to the inclusion of records information in an existing online catalog. In more technologically advanced business settings the possibilities for records automation are virtually unlimited. In any setting where a substantial portion of institutional data is machine-readable, the potential exists for records management to be an integrated part of the information flow. Phillips (1991) points out that records managers and data processing managers have much in common, and should work together in automation planning and design. Apart from conventional digital files, developments in text handling software and in optical and other image-handling technologies have meant that in many cases the records themselves are stored in computer-accessible formats. Integration of these formats with the records management database, while challenging, is clearly a direction to consider, and the professional literature of records management is replete with examples of just such projects. Saffady (1989) gives a good overview of the marriage of personal computers and document handling, and d'Alleyrand (1989) covers a wide range of microcomputer and mainframe technologies for records management.

This chapter focused on using database management as a tool for handling record-keeping information. The next chapter focuses on the records themselves (including electronic records), examining in particular the characteristics of different formats in which records appear, and filing and storage considerations.

REFERENCES

Association of Records Managers and Administrators. *Criteria for Developing/Evaluating Records Management Software*. Prairie Village, KS: ARMA International, 1990. (ARMA International Guideline for Records and Information Management).

D'Alleyrand, Marc R. *Image Storage and Retrieval Systems: A New Approach to Records Management*. New York: McGraw-Hill, 1989.

Eddison, Elizabeth B. "Moving Information: A Conversion Project Toolbox," *Database* 14 (June 1991): 15-22.

Lundeen, Gerald and Carol Tenopir. *Managing Your Information: Design and Creation of Textual Databases on a Microcomputer*. New York: Neal-Schuman, 1988.

O'Brien, James A. *Information Systems in Business Management*. 5th ed. Homewood, IL: Irwin, 1988.

Phillips, John T., Jr. "Records Management and Data Processing - A Good Strategic Alliance," *ARMA Records Management Quarterly* 25 (April 1991): 44-48.

Phillips, John T. and Albin Wagner. *Software Directory for Automated Records Management Systems*. Prairie Village, KS: ARMA International, 1990.

Saffady, William. *Personal Computer Systems for Automated Document Storage and Retrieval*. Silver Spring, MD: Association for Information and Image Management, 1989.

Skillman, Juanita and April Dmytrenko. "A Comparison of PC Based Records Management Software," *ARMA Records Management Quarterly* 23 (April 1989): 21-33

READINGS

Association of Records Managers and Administrators. *Criteria for Developing/Evaluating Records Management Software.* Prairie Village, KS: ARMA International, 1990. (ARMA International Guideline for Records and Information Management).

Johnson, Mina M. and Norman F. Kallaus. *Records Management.* 4th ed. Cincinnati, OH: South-Western Publishing, 1987. Chapter 14: "Mechanized and Automated Records Systems."

Robek, Mary E., Gerald F. Brown, and Wilmer O. Maedke. *Information and Records Management.* 3d ed. Encino, CA: Glencoe, 1987. Chapter 9: "Electronic Information Management Systems."

Saffady, William. *Personal Computer Systems for Automated Document Storage and Retrieval.* Silver Spring, MD: Association for Information and Image Management, 1989.

DISCUSSION POINTS

1. Find two recent articles in the records management journal literature which describe automating records management (or an aspect thereof). Compare the approaches and comment on whether one seemed to be more effective than the other. If you could speak with the authors, what questions would you ask? Do the articles discuss costs?

2. Assume that you are the manager of archives and records for a large university. Discuss the advantages and disadvantages of integrating records information into the online catalog (using, for instance, the MARC AMC format for archives and manuscripts).

3. Mock up a sample relational database system for a modest records management automation project. Without developing a full data dictionary, what fields would you have in your database, and in which files would they appear? Illustrate one sample record in each file, and discuss what reports you would expect to generate.

Chapter Seven

Filing and Storage

This chapter covers the activities that come to mind when the layperson thinks about records management, in the same way that stamping books out seems to form the public image of library work. In both cases, the perceptions are inaccurate, but they do reflect the tasks which characterize the main components of the interface between the public and the professional. The public does not *see* planning, decision making, systems analysis, personnel management, disaster prevention, database design, and the other managerial and intellectual activities which drive a records keeping operation. What they *do* observe are filing systems and storage facilities, and those are the topics discussed in this chapter.

There are any number of printed resources which focus on filing and storage. The National Archives and Records Administration publishes a series of free *Instructional Guide* pamphlets on managing certain types of records (Gilmore, 1989; Gilmore and Leary, 1990; Oglesby and Leary, 1990; Young and Miller, 1989). The Office of Federal Records Centers' *Records Management Handbook* series details filing practices and procedures for government records keepers (National Archives and Records Service, Office of Federal Records Centers, 1981a, 1981b, 1983a, 1983b). Texts by Gill (1988) and Goodman, Fosegan, and Bassett (1987) are good sources for detailed examples of filing methods and procedures, and Waegemann (1983) emphasizes space management aspects of record storage. Finally, ARMA International has issued a guideline for general procedures covering all types of media, and guidelines for different types of filing methods (Association of Records Managers and Administrators, 1986a, 1988, 1989a, 1989b).

Since the physical nature of a record generally dictates its storage method, an examination of the characteristics of various formats is a good place to begin.

FORMATS AND MATERIALS

Records, as noted in Chapter 1, are records regardless of the information carrying medium in which they appear. Records managers have been known to handle everything from bond paper and optical disks to shoe samples and Christmas tree ornaments. Some media require specialized equipment for handling and storage, most are vulnerable to deterioration under certain conditions, and all occupy varying amounts of physical space. Each type has certain requirements with respect to climate control, and the longer the retention period, the more important it is to explore those requirements beyond the broad overview given in this discussion.

Function also plays a role when considering the problems of housing active records. Correspondence (usually organized by subject) or other alphabetical files (and subscription services) have a pattern of growth throughout the file, as new correspondence is interfiled with existing material. Files containing forms and chronologically organized items, on the other hand, tend to grow at the end of the file. This difference requires attention when planning cabinet space, just as anticipating shelving needs for serials and printed indexes is different from allowing for growth in the book collection.

Paper

In addition to the more familiar formats, paper also encompasses blueprints, computer printouts, cards of all sizes and shapes, check stubs and similar irregular sizes, and insubstantial tissue-like products, such as plans and patterns. Paper is subject to damage from pests, fire, heat, dampness, and light (although some forms are more durable than one might think). Most types of paper (with the exception of bond) have a relatively short life span.

In terms of space consumption, paper is bulky and heavy, and its use requires facilities with adequate light and space. On the other hand, paper is easily handled and readily reproducible, and requires no special equipment, and everyone is comfortable using it with no special training. Flimsy or odd-sized items, such as bills of lading, clippings, and invoices, may require special handling (such as attachment to a sturdy backing).

Microforms

Microfilm formats include roll microfilm (the starting point for all other formats), microfiches, ultramicrofiches, aperture cards, and several other rarer formats. The film itself comes in different widths (16 mm, 35 mm, and 105 mm) and lengths (100 feet and 215 feet are common), and may be positive image or negative image (from the point of view of the first generation). Negative image film includes silver halide (or silver) film and dry silver film, as is used for Computer Output Microform (COM) applications. Negative image film is more stable, with a better life span than positive image film, which includes diazo film, vesicular film, and silver print film. Diazo film is sensitive to light and has been known to fade even in total darkness, and vesicular film suffers under light and heat. However, positive image film is cheaper and may be used extensively for records which are not expected to be permanently retained. Negative image film has a very long life span and is used widely for permanent records archiving.

Roll, or serialized, microfilm can be held on open reels, in cartridges or magazines, or in cassettes. These formats are advantageous from a storage point of view, as the film itself is unlikely to be handled, the containers can be labeled easily, and misfilings are readily apparent. Unitized microfilm includes aperture cards, microfilm jackets into which strips of film are inserted, and microfiches in many different types and reduction ratios. Labels are usually typed or handwritten on the top line in print large enough to be read by the naked eye. While unitized formats are generally more attractive to users, they collect fingerprints, and are easily lost, misfiled, or removed. Both roll and unitized microfilm formats require special storage cabinets and supplies, as well as microform readers and printers.

Magnetic and Optical Media

Magnetic and optical media include audiotapes, videotapes, computer tapes and disks, videodiscs, CD-ROM and other optical disks, and some of the new magneto-optical formats just now being developed for the recording industry. These media, especially when they contain machine-readable data files, are very dense and compact, but the life span of magnetic media is limited, and the life span of optical media is a matter for conjecture. Tape format magnetic media must be recycled periodically to avoiding "print through" (bleeding of information between layers of closely packed tape). Magnetic media must be kept clean and dust-free, and, of course, must be kept away from magnetic fields (such as might be generated by motors, telephone equipment, and bulk erasers).

Accessing information stored on any magnetic or optical medium requires special equipment, and the older the format, the greater the possibility that it will require equally old equipment for access (consider the Beta format videotape, the 8-track cassette, and a data file created on a computer 20 years ago). Any records facility with a substantial collection of magnetic and optical media will also be required to have the technical expertise to support it.

Other Formats

While paper, microfilm, and magnetic media are the principal formats handled by records managers, there are other media which require special handling. Photographs, slides, films, and filmstrips may form part of the records collection, especially in the absence of an archives. Care and preservation of these formats demand technical expertise, particularly if their retention is based on their importance in representing the history of the institution. The professional literature of archives management and preservation technology is the best source for more information.

In certain types of institutions, managing realia may be a central issue for the records department. A household products company, for instance, may keep samples of its own products as well as those of competitors. These products could contain corrosive and sometimes hazardous materials, and deterioration of containers can cause problems as the products age. Immediate documentation and proper care are crucial in instances such as these. A shoe company may keep a sample of each model. Any organization which has undergone a major construction project might have not only architectural plans, but also models of proposed buildings. Almost every organization has some oddities which make for complications in storage.

FILING EQUIPMENT

A filing system should be efficient, economical, and simple to use and maintain, and should make the most cost-effective use of equipment, personnel, time, and space. It should also promote accurate filing and reliable retrieval. Once methods and equipment have been selected, accuracy can be supported by the adoption of filing procedures manuals, and reliability of retrieval is enhanced with appropriate check-out and recall procedures. Factors which play a role in selecting filing equipment include:

o   Format of the materials;
o   Volume of file;
o   Nature of access;
o   Space availability;
o   Structural considerations;
o   Security demands;
o   Physical protection needs; and
o   Mobility requirements.

Obviously equipment must be compatible in dimensions and capacity with the materials it will have to hold. Legal-size paper is particularly troublesome to records managers as the presence of just a few legal-size folders in a file composed primarily of letter-size materials requires a legal-size file cabinet, which takes up considerably more space (and hence, is more costly). Various records management groups, and notably ARMA International, have been spearheading a movement called E.L.F. (Eliminate Legal Files) in the past decade (Association of Records Managers and Administrators, 1991).

The nature of the way people will be using the materials is also an important consideration. Does everything have to be immediately physically accessible, and is speed of retrieval (i.e., during a telephone conversation) an issue? What will typically be removed -- single items or entire folders or groups? Will the people using the file be trained in the filing method, or will it need to be a very simple, self-evident system? Will files need to be moved frequently (i.e., does office space shift, or are any major moves in the offing)?

Filing Cabinets

The most common method of storing active paper files is the filing cabinet, which can be vertical or lateral, and typically has from one to five drawers. Vertical files need considerable aisle space, whereas lateral files use wall space, and both can be used creatively as room dividers. Taller cabinets should be bolted to the wall, but apart from removing the bolts, one of the advantages of filing cabinets is that they can be shifted without having to remove the contents. Only one person at a time can work comfortably at a filing cabinet, and cabinets can be locked for security purposes. File cabinets are not good in fire, despite claims to the contrary by sales pitches. While cabinet walls may be flame resistant, the heat build up inside the drawer can lead to spontaneous combustion upon opening. Differences among filing cabinet models usually have to do with insulation, dampening devices to reduce noise, drawer handles and locks, and exterior finish.

Open Files

Open files are basically filing cabinets without drawer fronts. They are space efficient, since they can be taller than closed files (as one does not have to peer over the top of the drawer), and do not require as much working room. A lateral file with retractable doors rather than pull-out drawers is a variation on the open file, and is space efficient for the same reasons. Open files can accommodate several people working simultaneously, and retrieval can be more rapid than with closed files. Of course, most open files cannot be locked, and offer no security against theft or damage.

Compactable Files

Compactable (or mobile) filing systems are very expensive, and come in a number of different design models. They operate on tracking systems, and are only undertaken with the advice of a structural engineer. The configuration will depend on floor load, available space, and the number of people who need to be accommodated at any one time. Some compactable shelving is moved by hand (either by pushing tiers or by mechanical cranks), and some models use electric motors (a problem during power failures).

Compactable shelving is attractive for its space saving and security-enhancing features, but the expense (and the permanency of the construction) is usually not justifiable. Truly automated files bring items to users through a series of tracks, but these are prohibitively expensive and rare.

Safes and Vaults

Vital records (see Chapter 8) which need special protection on site may need to be stored in a safe or vault. The National Fire Protection Association (NFPA) has developed codes and standards for three methods of protecting records from fire:

o   Separate fire resistive buildings;
o   Fire resistive file rooms; and
o   Safes and vaults.

The distinction between a safe and a vault is that the latter is a room or compartment permitting entrance, and hence, requires construction. Vaults may be ground-supported or structure-supported. Safes are free-standing units. Good quality vaults and safes will be rated according to national standards for fire resistance and burglary resistance. Fire resistance has to do with interior temperature limit and the time in hours for which that temperature will not be exceeded during a fire (safes are also rated for the effects of impact and explosion). Burglary resistance describes how long the vault or safe will last against attack by different categories of devices (everything from hand tools to nitroglycerine). As might be expected, the higher the ratings the more expensive the equipment.

Specialized Equipment and Supplies

There is probably an equipment type for any file storage need. Vendor catalogs (either for offices or for libraries) list card files, flat files and other map and plan filing equipment, computer tape racks, microfilm cabinets, kardex and other visible files, and wheel and rotary files. The same supply companies will also provide all the necessary (acid-free) folders, envelopes, boxes, cases, tags and labels, hanging files, and other stationery materials.

FILING METHODS

Active files can be organized alphabetically by name, geographically, phonetically, numerically, and by subject (either alphabetically or using a classification system). The method will depend on the nature and purpose of the record series, the need for security, and the level of staff who will be working with the file. Alphabetical systems are direct, that is, no indexes (except for cross-references) are required to access the file. Direct access has the advantage of being easy and quick, but it is cumbersome for large files (this is why libraries developed divided card catalogs), and is also prone to filing error (although errors are relatively easy to spot). Geographic, phonetic, numeric, and classified systems are indirect, as some alphabetical index (whether manual or automated) has to be provided as a guide for the coding device. The resulting two-step retrieval process is good for security and for large volume files, and leads to greater accuracy in filing (but misfilings are difficult to find).

In libraries, we are familiar with name filing and subject arrangements, but even those are slightly different in records management environments.

Alphabetical Name Filing

Alphabetical filing by name is typical for personnel files, customer files, company files, and other files where the principal point of interest is a person or corporation. Depending on the size of the file, folders may represent individual entities or portions of the alphabet. ARMA, like the American Library Association, recommends word-by-word over letter-by-letter filing. As with library filing, conventions have to be established for symbols in names (such as ampersands), prefixed and hyphenated surnames, nicknames, titles and honorifics, acronyms and initialisms, foreign names, numbers as parts of names, choice of entry for complex corporate names, and all those other cases which occupy the time of catalogers and the pages of cataloging tools. Figure 7-1 shows a sample page of alphabetical filing rules. In addition, records management filing practices sometimes choose to leave out "insignificant" words within names (so that "Rib 'n Reef", for instance, files under "Rib Reef"). This makes sense in certain cases (taking the "Rib 'n Reef" example, it avoids the problem of having to look under "Rib and ...", "Rib 'n ...", or "Rib & ..."), but great care must be taken to ensure that treatment is consistent.

As with library files, a database application for records files management may cause problems, since machine filing may differ in order from manual filing conventions. However, a database is an ideal tool for controlling the "see" and "see also" references which are as much a part of records management files as library catalogs.

Figure 7-1. Alphabetical Filing Rules.

RULES FOR ALPHABETIC FILING

Rules	Examples
1. Personal names.	
a. NAMES of individuals are transposed for filing purposes: Last name (surname); first name (given name) or initial; middle name or initial.	Arthur B Anglin—filed *Anglin* Arthur B
b. PREFIXES on surnames (Bel, Bon, D', d', de, del, Des, di, du, El, Ger, L', La, Le, M', Mac, Mc, O', St (Saint), Ten, Ter, Van, Vander, Von, Vonder, and others) are considered inseparable parts of the surname and will be filed as though written as one. M', Mac, and Mc are filed in strict alphabetic sequence.	David de Valera—filed *de Valera* David.
c. HYPHENATED surnames of individuals are filed as one complete surname.	Blanche Duff-Gordon—filed *Duff-Gordon* Blanche.
d. UNDETERMINED surnames. When it is not possible to determine the surnames of individuals, they will be filed as they are written.	*Black* Thunder *Henry* George.
e. MARRIED WOMEN'S names. The legal name will be used and the husband's name, if known, will be cross-referenced. (The legal name consists of the first name, maiden surname, and the husband's surname (Josephine *Adams* Laurens) or her first name, middle name and the husband's surname (Josephine Mary Laurens).	Laurens Josephine Mary (Mrs) (Mrs William A).
	Cross-reference: Laurens William A (Mrs)—filed Laurens Josephine Mary.
f. ABBREVIATED first names are filed as though they were spelled in full.	Chas. Brown—filed *Brown* Charles
g. NICKNAMES followed by recognizable surnames are filed under the surname and the nickname used as the first name. Nicknames with no recognizable surnames are filed as they are written.	Red Larson—filed *Larson* Red Boston Jimmie
h. TITLES or degrees of individuals, whether preceding or following the surnames, are placed in parentheses following the name and disregarded in filing (Courtesy titles, Mr., Madam; military titles, Col , Major; professional title, Dr., Prof.; official titles, governor, mayor, titles of respect, Rev., Hon.; foreign titles, Lord; degrees, LL.D., Ph.D). Titles followed by one or more names not recognizable as surnames are filed in order as written.	Dr Charles C Brown—filed *Brown* Charles C (Dr.). Father Pierre—filed *Father* Pierre
i. ABBREVIATED DESIGNATIONS, such as Sr , Jr., 2d, 3d, appearing as part of a name are disregarded in filing but are shown in parentheses following the name.	C Albert Brown, Jr —filed *Brown* C Albert (Jr).
2. Firms, corporations, companies, associations, institutions, governments, and geographic names	
a. COINED names of firms, including trade names composed of separate letters or a single word, are filed as written, except when they embody the full names of individuals.	A A A Chemical Co.—filed *A A A* Chemical Company. Aunt Jemima's Pancake Flour— filed *Aunt* Jemima's Pancake Flour.
b. SURNAMES are used for filing when the full name of an individual is embodied in a firm or organization name; surname first, with the first name or initial immediately following and the balance of the name as written. Rules for personal names apply.	Charles Brown & Company—filed *Brown* Charles (&) Company
c. PREFIXES on firm and geographic names, such as Co-, D', d', de, des, Di, El, L', la, le, los, Mac, Mc, O', San, Ten, Ter, Van, Von, are considered inseparable parts of the name and will be filed as though written as one word.	De la Verne Co —filed *De la Verne* Company. Los Angeles, Calif —filed *Los Angeles*, California.
d. HYPHENATED firm names are filed as one complete name.	Air-E-Ator Ventilating Co —filed *Air-E Ator* Ventilating Company.
e. COMPOUND names of firms that may be spelled either as one or two words are filed as one word This rule must be restricted to a few frequently occurring words, such as Inter State; Mid West; South Eastern; South Side; North East.	Inter State Warehousing Co —filed *Inter State* Warehousing Company
f. COMPOUND GEOGRAPHIC firm names are filed as written Abbreviations are filed as though spelled in full.	Ft Wayne Paper Co —filed *Fort* Wayne Paper Company N.J Coal & Coke Co —filed *New Jersey* Coal (&) Coke Company

(From National Archives and Records Service, Office of Federal Records Centers, *Files Operations*. Washington, DC: GPO, 1983b (Records Management Handbook), p. 60.)

Filing and Storage   121

Geographic Filing

Geographic filing is useful for obviously geographic materials (such as maps and real estate materials) and for geographically divided activities, such as market reports and sales files. Geographic files could use any geographic level as the principle organizing feature, from continent and country to state, city, street, or sales territory. Organizing materials by place allows for quick reference to useful groupings, shows volume in those groupings very visibly (for instance, volume of sales reports), and is relatively easy to rearrange if the groupings change. It is, however, more complex than filing by name (and may require cross-reference indexing by name), and problems arise when geographical names or units change (consider the former Soviet Union) or in the case of cross-jurisdictional files.

Phonetic Filing

Phonetic filing is basically filing by the way things sound rather than how they are written. It is useful when correct spelling may be obscure (for instance, in police files), or when spelling deliberately departs from the expected, and is unpredictable (as in trademarks). Phonetic search capabilities are a feature of some database management products (for instance, a search for "telephone" would retrieve "tell-a-fone", "tel-e-fon", and so on). Phonetic filing must be based on a scheme which translates sounds into letter/number combinations, and a number of such devices are available.

Numeric Filing

Many record series are associated with numbers (social security numbers, client numbers, requisition or purchase order numbers, contract numbers, report numbers, etc.), and although some of these could equally well be alphabetized by name, numeric filing is often an attractive option. Numeric filing implies that each item (or group of items) to be filed has a unique number or number/letter combination. Since the filing method is indirect, one or more indexes must also be present (and clearly a database would be useful here).

The simplest form of numeric filing is consecutive, and this method would be typical for checks, purchase orders, and similar items. Chronological filing (by date, or even by minute and second) is a variation on consecutive numeric filing, and is useful for follow-up files (such as charge-out records). In consecutive numeric filing, input and retrieval activity tends to concentrate at the end of the file, which is a problem if the file is very active. Consecutive filing is also prone to error (especially for items being refiled), and long numbers can be difficult to commit to short-term memory in a quick hunt.

Terminal- or middle-digit filing is another common way of handling numeric files, especially for record series which are very active (such as client files). The principle is to file by the last digit in the number, reading groups of digits from right to left. Figure 7-2 shows two simple examples of terminal digit arrangement. The advantage to this method is that filing and retrieval activity is evenly distributed across the file, and more people can work in the file at one time. Filing errors tend to be reduced, and security is enhanced, as successful access will be limited to those who are trained in the system. Of course, problems arise when a series of consecutive records needs to be pulled.

Subject Filing

Subject filing is usually used for correspondence, policies and procedures, administrative files, and historical files. These are active files, and many of them are critical to decision making and daily operations. Subject files are also the most difficult, time-consuming, and expensive to develop and administer. They tend to exhibit the eccentricities of the current and past keepers, and are very difficult to revise or weed for retention (since they do not reflect chronological order). On the positive side, librarians are more familiar with the principles of subject filing through working with vertical files.

As with vertical files, indexing is typically done at the folder level, rather than for each item. Subject headings must be sufficiently specific to divide the file into useful topical groupings, but not so specific that each item ends up in its own narrowly defined folder. It is important to aim for consistency, conciseness, and unambiguity. The actual subject scheme used for filing might take the form of an alphabetical subject headings list or a numeric classification scheme. A subject authority file, controlling headings and references, is crucial to the success of subject filing. While the authority file information is best managed as a database, printed indexes should be produced for those who will be working with the file. Figure 7-3 shows a portion of a subject classification scheme, and an example of an index can be seen in Figure 7-4.

Inspiration for subject arrangements can usually be found in organization manuals, industry handbooks, and existing subject headings or classification schemes used or recommended by professional associations, government agencies, or producers of indexing services and online databases. For instance, Figure 7-5 shows a breakdown recommended by the Office of Federal Records Centers.

Filing and Storage   123

Figure 7-2. Terminal Digit Filing.

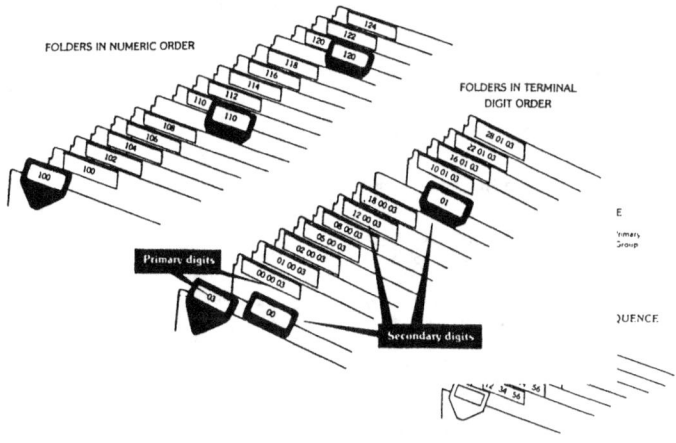

(From National Archives and Records Service, Office of Federal Records Centers, *Case Filing*. Washington, DC: GPO, 1983a (Records Management Handbook), p. 10.)

DOUBLE DIGIT SEQUENCE

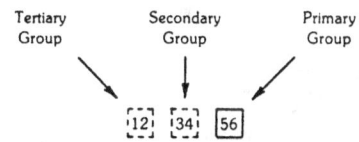

EXAMPLE OF CASE FOLDER SEQUENCE

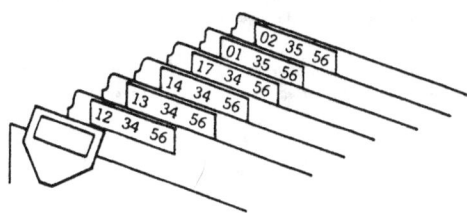

(From National Archives and Records Service, Office of Federal Records Centers, *Files Operations*. Washington, DC: GPO, 1983b (Records Management Handbook), p. 38.)

Figure 7-3. Subject Classification Scheme.

```
4000 — RANGE MANAGEMENT

4100 — GRAZING ADMINISTRATION

4110 — Grazing Administration (Inside Grazing Districts)

4111 — Awards of Grazing Privileges
       .1 Qualifications of Applicants
          11 Qualifications
          12 Effect of Transfer Arising Through Operation of Law
       .2 Base Property Qualifications and Classification
          21 Minimum Requirements; Classification of Base Properties
        3 Adjudication and Apportionment of Grazing Privileges
          31 Mandatory Requirements; Rating and Classification of Federal Range
          32 Procedures
        4 Adjustments of Grazing Privileges
          41 (Reserved)
          42 Increases
          43 Reductions

4112 — Management Practices
        1 Management Considerations
          11 Multiple-Use Objectives
          12 Requirements
          13 Allotments
         .14 Range Improvements
          15 Allotment Management Plans
          16 Grazing Management System
          17 Management of Rehabilitated Areas
        2 Designation of Ranges for Particular Kinds of Livestock
        3 General Rules of the Range
         .31 Acts Prohibited
          32 Rules of Fair Range Practice
        4 Subletting of Grazing Privileges
        5 Southwest Desert Range
        6 Cheatgrass Ranges
        7 Mediterranean Annual Ranges

4113 — Supervision and Inspection
       .1 Procedure for Enforcement of Rules and Regulations
```

(From National Archives and Records Service, Office of Federal Records Centers, *Subject Filing*. Washington, DC: GPO, 1981b. (SuDocs GS4.6/2:Su 1) (Records Management Handbook), p. 35.)

Figure 7-4. Index to Subject Classification.

A

Subject	Filed Under
Accounting	See ACCOUNTING
Administrative issuances	RECORDS MANAGEMENT 1
Allotments	APPROPRIATIONS—BUDGET
Annual leave	PERSONNEL 4-1
Appointing authority	PERSONNEL
Appointments (Committee members)	COMMITTEES—MEETINGS
Appointments (personnel)	PERSONNEL 3
Appropriations	See APPROPRIATIONS—BUDGET
Audits	ACCOUNTING
Authorizations (legal)	LEGISLATION—LEGAL

(From National Archives and Records Service, Office of Federal Records Centers, *Files Operations*. Washington, DC: GPO, 1983b (Records Management Handbook), p. 24.)

Figure 7-5. Subject Arrangement.

Model Subject File Classification System for Administrative Records Common to Most Federal Agencies

The Office of Federal Records Centers (NARS) has developed this subject file classification system for use by Federal agencies that lack a satisfactory system for arranging general correspondence on administrative subjects. Agencies may adopt this system in whole or in part. Some modification may be necessary to tailor this model system to the needs of a particular agency. The following is a list of the primary subjects and appropriate codes appearing in this appendix:

Primary Subject	Code
Automated Data Processing	ADP
Administrative Services	ADS
Audits and Investigations	AUD
Budget	BUD
Committees, Meetings, and Conferences	CMC
Equal Employment Opportunity	EEO
Financial Management	FIN
Grant Management	GMT
Information Services and Public Relations	INF
Legal and Legislative	LEG
Organization, Planning, and Management	OPM
Personnel	PER
Procurement and Contracting	PRC
Records Management	REM
Travel and Transportation	TRV

Figure 7-5 (Continued).

AUTOMATED DATA PROCESSING (ADP)

Use these subject categories for general correspondence and related papers pertaining to automated and electronic data processing equipment, systems, management, and operations. Do NOT use this outline for documentation that is appropriate for filing in specific case files.

CODE	TITLE	
ADP	AUTOMATED DATA PROCESSING	Information pertaining to general policies and procedures that cannot be put under specific subjects of this outline
1	REPORTS AND STATISTICS	General reports, studies, surveys (within agency), progress reports, and reports of significant accomplishments.
2	LAWS AND REGULATIONS	Proposed laws and regulations, and revisions thereto, relating to agency programs.
3	AUTOMATED SYSTEMS	General material regarding systems initiation, development, documentation, operation, and maintenance Subdivide by name of system Includes information and statistics systems and computer simulation systems.
4	DATA PROCESSING FACILITIES	
4–1	Assessories–Auxiliary Equipment	
4–2	Machine Utilization	
4–3	Maintenance and Repair	
5	EQUIPMENT SELECTION	
5–1	Requirements, Specifications and Standards	
5–2	Equipment Studies	
6	FEASIBILITY STUDIES	General correspondence relating to feasibility studies. For specific study projects, create a separate case file
7	LIAISON AND INFORMATION EXCHANGE	General material regarding liaison with computer facilities and programs of other internal agency components and other Federal agencies.
8	STANDARDIZATION	General correspondence regarding data processing standards and standards development

(From National Archives and Records Service, Office of Federal Records Centers, *Files Operations.* **Washington, DC: GPO, 1983b (Records Management Handbook), pp. 42-43.)**

Color Coding

Color coding is usually used in connection with another filing method, and is especially useful in designating something special (e.g., items which have been charged out, items needing follow up, or items of a special type within the series). The coding usually appears on the labels or tabs which carry filing information, and may be single color bars or bar combinations. Effective use of color in conjunction with alphabetic, geographic, or numeric characteristics (for instance, all Massachusetts folders carry green stripes on their labels, with different secondary colors designating cities in the state) can be very useful in minimizing filing error, since misfiled items stand out readily. Too much complexity in color use detracts from effectiveness. Barber and Langemo (1987) demonstrate the usefulness of color-coded filing with ample illustrations (in full color, of course).

Filing Procedures

Systematic controls applied to filing can go a long way toward minimizing filing inconsistency and error. Some of these controls must be applied by the office staff handling incoming materials, which implies that filing manuals and training programs should be instituted by the records management department. Incoming materials, for instance, should be date-stamped. Filing and cross-reference information might be noted on the item at this point as well. When items are "released for filing," paper clips should be removed, any necessary mending should be done to maintain the integrity of the item, and some form of coding for retention and transfer to inactive files should be stamped or written on the item. The person who does the filing (a file clerk in a large operation, but usually the secretary in a small office) should establish any cross-references and create needed labels and folders.

A number of steps can be taken to minimize filing error. Torn paper should be mended, and odd-sized items should be attached to standard paper. Staples are preferable to paper clips. Items are usually stored in reverse chronological order in a folder, and folders should not be more than an inch thick. Unnecessary duplicates should be avoided. File drawers should be labeled with beginning and ending range indicators. Any folder marked "Miscellaneous" should be monitored regularly to see whether new subject headings are warranted.

When something cannot be found in its expected folder, the charge-out index should be checked first, and then any material waiting to be filed. Beyond that, it is wise to look through the entire folder piece by piece, folders in front and behind the correct folder, and underneath the folder. Other predictable filing errors include transpositions in letters or numbers, and filing under similar sounding names or similar letter shapes. If the item really cannot be found, then a "dummy" item should be placed in the folder to avoid going through the whole process all over again.

RECORDS CENTERS

Inactive records are usually stored in the records center, which might be anything from a designated room to a separate floor or building, to the facilities of a commercial records center. The purpose of having a separate records center is to provide for efficient storage of little-used records and to promote standardized controls. Since accessibility is not a great concern with inactive records, they can be packed more densely than active records, thereby gaining the most value out of the space.

Selecting a facility demands an understanding of the estimated volume and space requirements for inactive records, and will involve consideration of floor loads, climate control needs, and security issues. In addition to shelving and housing for records, records centers usually include a loading dock, administrative office space, processing areas for incoming records, a reference area for servicing requests, and such equipment as tabletop carts, telephones, copying machines, microform reader/printers, facsimile machines, and workstations for access to automated records management systems. A large records center with very high shelving might also have catwalks, trucks, and hydraulic lifts.

Paper records are usually stored on open shelves in cartons with lids or flaps and hand-hold slots. The standard box measures 12" x 15" x 10" and is made of heavyweight-treated cardboard or fibreboard. Boxes should have a tensile strength sufficient to avoid buckling (especially as they will be stacked), and should be acid-free. The labeling area should be on the end, and should be large. It is advisable to send boxes to offices, with instructions as to how to pack active files ready for transfer. This avoids having to rebox materials once they arrive. Special boxes are available for rolled papers, x-rays, and similar nonstandard items.

Records Center Activities

When materials are received they should arrive with a transfer list showing the series title, time span, number of cartons, and sending department. After review, a copy of this is returned to the department as evidence of receipt. Space is assigned, using either the records management database (which should be able to automatically assign space) or a manual chart indicating what space is available. The ARMA guideline for records center operations shows a variety of methods for designating shelf location (Association of Records Managers and Administrators, 1986b). The location should be entered into a control file, whether automated or manual. As discussed in Chapter 5, charge-out procedures should be developed for servicing reference requests, and should include an active follow-up mechanism. Analysis of reference requests can be useful in renegotiating retention periods and in studying information resource use across the organization. Records destruction was also covered in Chapter 5, and care should be taken to keep control files up to date as records leave the records center.

Commercial Records Centers

A commercial records center can provide a cost-effective alternative to storing inactive records on site. Commercial records centers are usually located in low-rent districts (often in the suburbs), with professionally trained staff and well-designed facilities. It is important to look for a center which specializes in records handling, especially with respect to fire and theft protection, and climate control. If special formats (such as machine-readable data files) are to be stored, then the center should have experience in handling and caring for those formats. The center should be insured, and employees should be bonded.

A good commercial records center will have 24-hour retrieval service, with capabilities for duplication and telefacsimile, and a messenger service. Commercial records centers often distribute guidelines for retention, and will work with records managers to develop retention schedules. Charges are usually based on a minimum lease rate, costs per unit (with decreasing costs per unit as volume increases), and varying charges for different types of retrievals. Frequent retrievals from commercial centers will be costly.

CONCLUSION

This chapter dealt with the handling and storage of active and inactive records, and touched upon some of the characteristics of different record formats. Chapter 8 returns to some of these issues in the context of developing a vital records program and a disaster management plan.

REFERENCES

Association of Records Managers and Administrators. *Alphabetic Filing Rules*. Prairie Village, KS: ARMA International, 1986a. (ARMA Standards Program. Guidelines).
Association of Records Managers and Administrators. *E.L.F. = Eliminate Legal-size Files*. Prairie Village, KS: ARMA International, 1991. (ARMA International Guideline for Records and Information

Management).
Association of Records Managers and Administrators. *Filing Procedures*. Prairie Village, KS: ARMA International, 1989a. (ARMA International Guideline for Records and Information Management).
Association of Records Managers and Administrators. *Numeric Filing*. Prairie Village, KS: ARMA International, 1989b. (ARMA International Guideline for Records and Information Management).
Association of Records Managers and Administrators. *Records Center Operations*. 3d ed. Prairie Village, KS: ARMA International, 1986b. (ARMA International Guideline for Records and Information Management).
Association of Records Managers and Administrators. *Subject Filing*. Prairie Village, KS: ARMA International, 1988. (ARMA International Guideline for Records and Information Management).
Barber, Donald T. and Mark Langemo. *Filing Dynamics*. Emereyville, CA: Marsdale, 1987.
Gill, Suzanne L. *File Management and Information Retrieval Systems: A Manual for Managers and Technicians*. 2d ed. Littleton, CO: Libraries Unlimited, 1988.
Gilmore, Valita K. *Managing the Records of Temporary Commissions*. Washington, DC: National Archives and Records Administration, Office of Records Administration, 1989. (National Archives and Records Administration Instructional Guide Series).
Gilmore, Valita and William H. Leary. *Managing Audiovisual Records*. Washington, DC: National Archives and Records Administration, Office of Records Administration, 1990. (National Archives and Records Administration Instructional Guide Series).
Goodman, David G., Joseph S. Fosegan, and Ernest D. Bassett. *Business Records Control*. 6th ed. Cincinnati, OH: South-Western Publishing, 1987.
National Archives and Records Service. Office of Federal Records Centers. *Case Filing*. Washington, DC: GPO, 1983a. (Records Management Handbook).
National Archives and Records Service. Office of Federal Records Centers. *File Stations*. Washington, DC: GPO, 1981a. (Records Management Handbook).
National Archives and Records Service. Office of Federal Records Centers. *Files Operations*. Washington, DC: GPO, 1983b. (Records Management Handbook).
National Archives and Records Service. Office of Federal Records Centers. *Subject Filing*. Washington, DC: GPO, 1981b. (SuDocs GS 4.6/2:Su 1) (Records Management Handbook).
Oglesby, Thomas R. and William H. Leary. *Managing Electronic Records*.

Washington, DC: National Archives and Records Administration, Office of Records Administration, 1990. (National Archives and Records Administration Instructional Guide Series).

Waegemann, C. Peter. *Handbook of Record Storage and Space Management*. Westport, CT: Quorum Books, 1983.

Young, Jeanne and Nancy G. Miller. *Managing Cartographic and Architectural Records*. Washington, DC: National Archives and Records Administration, Office of Records Administration, 1989. (National Archives and Records Administration Instructional Guide Series).

READINGS

Aschner, Katherine. "From Inventory to Filing System." In Katherine Aschner, ed., *Taking Control of Your Office Records: A Manager's Guide*. White Plains, NY: Knowledge Industry Publications, 1983, pp.29-38.

Diamond, Susan Z. *Records Management: A Practical Guide*. New York: AMACOM, 1983. Chapter 5: "The Records Center," and Chapter 7: "Managing the Organization's Files."

Hardcastle, Shelley. "Providing Storage Facilities." In Peter Emmerson, ed., *How to Manage Your Records: A Guide to Effective Practice*. Cambridge, Eng.: ICSA Publishing, 1989, pp.60-92.

Johnson, Mina M. and Norman F. Kallaus. *Records Management*. 4th ed. Cincinnati, OH: South-Western Pub, 1987. Part Two: "Alphabetic Storage and Retrieval," and Part Three: "Adaptations of Alphabetic Storage and Retrieval."

Murphy, Terence. "Records Centers." In Katherine Aschner, ed., *Taking Control of Your Office Records: A Manager's Guide*. White Plains, NY: Knowledge Industry Publications, 1983, pp.153-182.

Penn, Ira A., Anne Morddel, Gail Pennix, and Kelvin Smith. *Records Management Handbook*. Brookfield, VT: Gower, 1989. Chapter 9: "Management of Files," and Chapter 13: "Records Storage."

Place, Irene and David J. Hyslop. *Records Management: Controlling Business Information*. 2d ed. Reston, VA: Reston Publishing, 1987. Part II: "Classification Systems."

Ricks, Betty R. and Kay F. Gow. *Information Resource Management: A Records Systems Approach*. 2d ed. Cincinnati, OH: South-Western Publishing, 1988. Chapter 5: "Classification System Selection," and Chapter 6: "Storage Equipment and Supplies."

Robek, Mary E., Gerald F. Brown, and Wilmer O. Maedke. *Information and Records Management*. 3d ed. Encino, CA: Glencoe, 1987. Chapter 8: "Standard Filing Systems," and Part 4: "Inactive Records Maintenance."

Wallace, Patricia E., Jo Ann Lee, and Dexter R. Schubert. *Records Management: Integrated Information Systems*. 3d ed. Englewood Cliffs, NJ: Prentice-Hall, 1992. Chapter 6: "Records Storage and Retrieval Systems," and Chapter 7: "Records Classification Systems."

DISCUSSION POINTS

1. Returning to the files mentioned in Discussion Point 2 of Chapter 5, how would you file each of the record series mentioned in that list?

2. What vendors can you find in your local area from whom you could buy records management equipment? Assume that you are about to buy filing cabinets and supplies from these vendors. Prepare a list of the equipment and supplies you need, and for each, create a checklist of features you would look for. Finally, compare the prices.

3. What commercial records centers exist in your area? Collect promotional literature, and try to visit at least one. What kinds of storage facilities do they have? What formats can they handle? What types of retrieval services do they offer? Try to get a sense of costs (this will probably be difficult).

Chapter Eight

Vital Records and Disaster Management

In this chapter the focus turns to the records manager as guardian of the organization's future well-being. The most effective promotional films and videotapes on the importance of records management use vivid footage of records loss by fire, flood, or other natural disasters, to make the point that a good records management program would enable the organization to rise like a phoenix from the ashes, and flourish once again (or, to put it less dramatically, at least resume normal operations with a minimum of disruption). The first step in fulfilling this commitment is to identify the vital records of an organization -- those records which merit special attention beyond the normal safeguards for preservation and protection. The overall framework of plans and tactics for coping with likely calamities and preserving or restoring vital (and other) records is known as disaster management, or disaster preparedness.

VITAL RECORDS

Vital records are those an organization would need to start up or continue operations if everything were lost in a disaster. They are records which preserve the financial and legal standing of the organization, or which pertain to the rights of employees, clients, stockholders, and external organizations with which there is a relationship. In many cases vital records also include those which would permit the organization to reestablish data processing operations. The ARMA vital records guideline suggests that 3 to 5 percent of an organization's total records might normally be considered vital (Association of Records Managers and Administrators, 1984). As a general rule, the longer you have to retain a record, the more likely it is to be vital. Vital records could include both active and inactive records.

Examples of vital records include constitutions, bylaws, franchises, contracts, leases, accounts payable and especially receivable, intellectual property records (copyrights, licenses, patents, formulae, and research and development files), tax returns, insurance policies, and fixed assets. A vital records program takes time and labor, and should be restricted to those records which really *are* crucial to start-up. Vital records are distinguished from *important* records, which are those whose loss would be troublesome but not ruinous. Important records contribute to smooth operations, but could be reconstructed, even though the reconstruction might take some time and effort.

Implementing a Vital Records Program

Once management approval and support for a vital records program have been gained, records liaisons should be charged with identifying potentially vital records in each department. A committee which includes data processing, human resources, security, and legal services representatives should review the recommendations, assess potential risks, and consider possible storage sites and methods. The records manager can then draw up a vital records schedule detailing the series titles and numbers, media, copy to be protected, methods of protection, frequency of deposit (some vital records change on a daily basis), and retention period in the vital records center or storage area. A vital records manual (or a vital records section of the records management manual) should identify vital records, detail storage methods and locations, and provide instructions on transfer and disposition of vital records.

Evaluation and testing is an ongoing component of a vital records program. For testing, a designated start-up team could be charged with determining what information might be needed in the event of a simulated problem, which could be anything from a fire in the data processing center to theft of an important formula by a disgruntled employee. The vital records schedule should be reassessed annually, as the organization enters into new relationships or engages in new activities.

Methods of Protection

Vital records may already be protected by existing dispersal. That is, copies may be distributed off site in the normal course of business, either to branches or to external (and mutually cooperative) organizations. In this case the protection exists, and the task of the records manager is to monitor the routine dispersal and to ensure that retention periods for dispersed copies are satisfactory. For vital records which are not normally dispersed, planned dispersal of copies to an offsite records center, or to a special vital records center would be appropriate. Another (but less satisfactory) approach is to protect originals or copies on site in a vital records center.

Special attention is paid to the longevity of the media on which vital records are captured. Paper records may last upwards of several hundred years (if the paper is bond), but they are relatively easily destroyed and are bulky. Computer tapes and disks last from one to seven years and need regular recycling. These media are also vulnerable to climatic and electrical influences, and equipment upgrades can render old data formats unreadable. Optical media, generally more robust than magnetic media, are improving with respect to longevity and flexibility. Microfilm has the advantage of being very compact, durable (depending on the type), and inexpensive to duplicate.

Discussion of the facilities and equipment for storing vital records brings up the larger context of disaster management. Certainly storage facilities for vital records should be planned with protection in mind, but this is true of records center facilities in general. In addition to normal criteria for safeguarding records (taken up in the next section), vital records might demand the use of vaulted rooms, safes, or insulated cabinets, all of which should be certified for the medium which they will contain.

DISASTER MANAGEMENT

Properly speaking, a vital records program is one component of an overall disaster management program. Disaster management, also known as disaster planning or disaster preparedness, refers to developing a set of strategies to avoid disasters, and to cope with them should they occur. Libraries and archives are very much concerned with instituting disaster management. Although the historical focus of these fields has been books and documents, recent expansion of library collections into other formats, as well as the growth of automated systems, has resulted in the publication of manuals and texts which are applicable to records management settings. Practical handbooks published by the Canadian and American Library Associations provide a wealth of detail and readings for further reference (England and Evans, 1988; Morris, 1986). Barton and Wellheiser (1985) addresses records centers as well as libraries and archives, and ARMA has issued a planning guide directed specifically to records managers (Bulgawicz and Nolan, 1988). The *Disaster Plan Workbook* prepared by the Preservation Committee of the New York University Libraries (1984) is especially useful for its numerous checklists and blank charts suitable for adaptation to any setting.

Causes of Disaster

One of the first steps in disaster management is to conduct a risk analysis by evaluating possible disasters and assessing their likelihoods and possible consequences. Disasters can be organized according to their severity, ranging from nuclear holocaust to vandalism in one file drawer. Each one has a potential impact on an organization, although clearly a national calamity, such as war, entails a very different set of considerations when compared with the loss of one document, however vital. Disasters of the severe kind, including natural disasters which affect a local area (floods, tornadoes, and earthquakes), are of special concern to institutions which contribute to social welfare. Police and fire authorities, hospitals, public utilities, and some government agencies must be able to resume operations as quickly as possible.

The destruction of an entire building may occur during a severe disaster, or may result from a localized event (a fire, accidental or otherwise). Catastrophe on this scale, if it occurs during working hours, may have the additional unfortunate effect of reducing the numbers of the disaster team. More common, and less catastrophic, disasters include building destruction during nonworking hours, damage affecting one or more major functions (such as a flood in the data processing center), and events affecting a few minor activities (e.g., vandalism in an office).

Damage to records as a result of disaster may be indirect. Certainly, flames can consume printed and other matter, and can melt film materials, but damage is also caused by the heat generated during a fire. Magnetic media, for instance, may appear unharmed on the surface, but the data may have been partially or completely destroyed by exposure to intense heat. Exposure to smoke may leave residue and particles, again a particular problem for magnetic tapes and disks. Fire is also usually accompanied by water damage. Water by itself is principally detrimental to paper, but water which has been used to douse a fire carries contaminants and particles. Water also causes mold, which can remain even after apparent record recovery.

Implementing a Disaster Management Program

With a vital records program in place, and following a risk analysis, a disaster team should be established. The team should include members from inside the company as well as representatives of external organizations important to records recovery (such as data processing and micrographics services). At least the team leader and an alternate should have the authorization to make decisions on the spot, and to draw on financial resources if needed. Recovery priorities should be established for all records series, by media and by series title. Recovery priorities detail initial and long-term salvage procedures, and guide the team in taking quick effective action. Eulenberg (1983) provides an excellent chart of recovery priorities and procedures for different records media. ARMA has published several guidelines for recovery of specific media (Association of Records Managers and Administrators, 1987; Eulenberg, 1986), and similar information can be found in the texts mentioned earlier.

The disaster team should be thoroughly trained and drilled in all steps taken when dealing with a disaster. These include assessing the extent of the damage, calling the team into action and notifying department heads and local service organizations, packing out the damaged items, and instituting recovery. The team leader is responsible for coordinating the whole process, including personnel, supplies, and communication. Disaster plans should be tested with simulated disasters (also a good opportunity to promote an appreciation of the importance of the program). In the event of a real disaster, a complete record of events should be preserved. The demonstrated strengths and weaknesses of the disaster plan can be analyzed once normal working life has resumed, and any deficiencies can then be remedied.

The Disaster Kit

The disaster team should have accessible a well-stocked "disaster kit" containing equipment and supplies necessary for records recovery. The kit should obviously be located away from potential disaster sites, or should be replicated in several places. Figure 8-1 is a list of possible disaster kit components, culled from a variety of sources. Since some of the contents decay over time (notably batteries and certain chemicals), the kit should be inventoried and replenished regularly.

Preventing Disaster

As the adage goes, "an ounce of prevention is worth a pound of cure." Sound facilities management can go a long way in diminishing the risk of disaster, and in minimizing the effects of disasters which do occur.

Protection against theft can be achieved to some degree by installing burglar alarms, and by laying out floor plans so as to reduce traffic in the vital records area. Secure areas should have few or no windows,[1] and access to facilities can be controlled by limiting entry to authorized personnel. Numeric filing and numeric identification on carton labels can also lessen the likelihood of theft, or at least make it more difficult. Environmental and pest controls should be established against dust, mildew, humidity, vermin, and insects. Lighting should be appropriate for the medium (especially where microfilm is concerned).

---

[1] Windowless buildings must be designed with alternative methods of dispersing heat and smoke in case power loss causes the mechanical venting system to fail.

Figure 8-1. The Disaster Kit.

For crating
    Plastic crates (milk cartons)
    Plastic trays
    Cardboard cartons
    Plastic garbage cans

For packing and bagging
    Plastic garbage bags and twists
    Freezer paper
    Plastic sheeting
    Blotting paper
    Paper towels (uncolored)
    Unprinted newsprint
    Nylon rope, Fishing line
    Duct tape
    Toothpicks

For access
    Sharp knives
    Screwdrivers and wrenches
    Crowbars
    Ladders
    Flashlights and batteries
    Spot lights

For moving
    Wooden pallets
    Forklifts
    Dollies
    Book trucks

For personal safety
    Identifying arm bands
    First aid kit
    Eye wash
    Work gloves
    Rubber gloves
    Safety clothing
        Overalls, aprons
        Hard hats
        Hospital masks
    Respirators
    Safety glasses

For communication and recording
    Flash camera, film
    Calculators
    Pagers
    AM/FM radios
    Batteries for all of these

For treatment
    Chemicals
        Fungicides
            Mold inhibitors
    Mops, sponges, buckets
    Fire extinguishers
    Dehumidifiers, Fans
    Pumps, Wet/dry vacuums
    Generators
    Heavy duty extension cords

For inventory and identification
    Note pads
    Ball-point pens
    Pencils
    Waterproof markers
    Colored chalk
    Tags (string or wire fastenings)
    Tape
    Scissors
    Hole punches
    Rustproof paper clips
    Staplers
    Rustproof staples
    String
    Acid-free file folders
    Plastic letter openers

For reference (encased in plastic):
    Disaster team list, Disaster plan
    Recovery guidelines
    Floor plans
    Access to financial resources
    Insurance information
    Designated working area off site
    Supply companies (including chemical)
    Salvage and recovery services
        Data processing
        Micrographics
        Paper and books
        Film
    Emergency services
        Police
        Fire
        Utilities
        Medical
    Portable communications
    Food services
    Locksmiths, plumbers, electricians
    Transport firms

An adequate supply of portable fire extinguishers should be dispersed throughout records areas. Carefully placed smoke detectors and sprinkler systems are recommended by the National Fire Protection Association (NFPA) standards for records protection (National Fire Protection Association, 1986 and 1991), which go into lengthy (but easily understood) detail on fire resistive characteristics of buildings, rooms, vaults, shelving, cartons, and cabinets. The NFPA makes a good case for sprinkler systems over high-expansion foam and gaseous extinguishing systems, but these are also covered in the standards.

One drawback to the windowless office building is that climate control is maintained by water piped through the entire building, and basement flooding is a common occurrence (and might go unnoticed for some time). This is one good reason not to store records in basements. Another is that a collapsing building will collapse onto the basement, and water from fire hoses will eventually seep through to the basement as well, along with contaminants picked up on the way.

All of these safeguards will be wasted unless policies are enacted to provide for regular inspection and maintenance of burglary and fire prevention equipment, and ongoing revision of staff lists, emergency telephone numbers, and disaster supply inventories. Rules regarding prohibitions against food, drink, and smoking in records areas should be enforced. Insurance policies must be kept up to date, and local police and fire authorities should be advised as to the types of fire extinguishing systems which have been installed. Although the disaster team can be expected to have received special training, all records management staff should be well versed in procedures for coping with emergencies.[2]

CONCLUSION

At this point we have taken the records management from its starting point (the physical inventory) to being fully operational, with functional filing systems, retention schedules, and facilities, and with an active disaster management program. The remainder of the book deals with topics related to consolidating and enlarging the role of records management in the organization. This begins in the Chapter 9 with forms management, that is, exerting control over records at the stage of their creation, and continues with correspondence and reports management. Chapter 9 also looks at the wide range of information technologies which are part of the modern

---

[2] Both staff and local authorities, for instance, should know that cabinets containing records must be allowed to cool before opening, otherwise the contents may explode on exposure to the open air.

records management scenario. Subsequent chapters focus on management issues, including the relationship of records management to the overall information structure in an organization, and the significance of information resources management and information policy.

REFERENCES

Association of Records Managers and Administrators. *Magnetic Diskettes--Recovery Procedures*. Prairie Village, KS: ARMA International, 1987. (ARMA International Guideline for Records and Information Management).

Association of Records Managers and Administrators. *Vital Records*. Prairie Village, KS: ARMA International, 1984. (ARMA Standards Program. Guidelines).

Barton, John P. and Johanna G. Wellheiser, eds. *An Ounce of Prevention: A Handbook on Disaster Planning for Archives, Libraries, and Records Centers*. Toronto, Ont.: Toronto Area Archives Group Education Foundation, 1985.

Bulgawicz, Susan L. and Charles E. Nolan. *Disaster Prevention and Recovery: A Planned Approach*. Prairie Village, KS: ARMA International, 1988.

England, Claire and Karen Evans. *Disaster Management for Libraries: Planning and Process*. Ottawa, Ont.: Canadian Library Association, 1988.

Eulenberg, Julia Niebuhr. "Disaster: Planning for Recovery." In Katherine Aschner, ed., *Taking Control of Your Office Records: A Manager's Guide*. White Plains, NY: Knowledge Industry Publications, 1983, pp.129-151.

Eulenberg, Julia Niebuhr. *Handbook for the Recovery of Water Damaged Records*. Prairie Village, KS: ARMA International, 1986.

Morris, John. *The Library Disaster Preparedness Handbook*. Chicago, IL: American Library Association, 1986.

National Fire Protection Association. *Manual for Fire Protection for Archives and Record Centers*. 1991 ed. Quincy, MA: NFPA, 1991 (ANSI/NFPA 232AM-1991).

National Fire Protection Association. *Protection of Records*. 1986 ed. Quincy, MA: NFPA, 1986 (ANSI/NFPA 232-1986).

New York University Libraries, Preservation Committee. *Disaster Plan Workbook*. New York: New York University, Elmer Holmes Bobst Library, 1984.

READINGS

Diamond, Susan Z. *Records Management: A Practical Guide.* New York, NY: AMACOM, 1983. Chapter 6: "Vital Records: Your Organization's Lifeblood."

Eulenberg, Julia Niebuhr. "Disaster: Planning for Recovery." In Katherine Aschner, ed., *Taking Control of Your Office Records: A Manager's Guide.* White Plains, NY: Knowledge Industry Publications, 1983, pp.129-151.

Murphy, Terence. "Records Centers." In Katherine Aschner, ed., *Taking Control of Your Office Records: A Manager's Guide.* White Plains, NY: Knowledge Industry Publications, 1983, pp.153-182.

Penn, Ira A., Anne Morddel, Gail Pennix, and Kelvin Smith. *Records Management Handbook.* Brookfield, VT: Gower, 1989. Chapter 10: "Vital Records," and Chapter 11: "Disaster Planning and Recovery."

Ricks, Betty R. and Kay F. Gow. *Information Resource Management: A Records Systems Approach.* 2d ed. Cincinnati, OH: South-Western Publishing, 1988. Chapter 20: "Records Safety and Security."

Robek, Mary E., Gerald F. Brown, and Wilmer O. Maedke. *Information and Records Management.* 3d ed. Encino, CA: Glencoe, 1987. Chapter 7: "Vital Records Protection Program."

Wallace, Patricia E., Jo Ann Lee, and Dexter R. Schubert. *Records Management: Integrated Information Systems.* 3d ed. Englewood Cliffs, NJ: Prentice-Hall, 1992. Chapter 10: "Managing Vital Records and Disaster Recovery."

DISCUSSION POINTS

1. Examine the National Fire Protection Association standards for records centers. To what degree does your library (or a library you are familiar with) conform to these standards? If you had to store vital records on site, what measures would you take? You might also want to examine other NFPA standards directed specifically to library collections.

2. Make a list of the vital records you think a small public library would have? For each item on the list, how should the library protect these records? Alternatively, if you work in a library, make a list of its vital records, and describe how they should be protected.

3. What records recovery services are available in your local area for microforms, data processing products, and paper documents?

Chapter Nine

Expanding the Role of Records Control

As a profession, records management is relatively young, certainly when compared with librarianship or archives management. Nor has it experienced the same rate of growth and specialization as another new field, data processing. This actually may be to the advantage of records managers, as the territory is not quite clearly delineated, and there is room for new definitions of what tasks and responsibilities fall under the records manager's domain. Neither job titles, nor career paths, are fixed and predictable. A librarian accepting a new position knows in general what the job is likely to entail; a records manager has unlimited possibilities, especially in an organization open to innovation. The processes examined in preceding chapters lay the foundations for achieving systematic control over information throughout its entire life cycle. The ultimate mission is to contribute to an organization's productivity and well-being by managing information resources in the most cost-effective manner. This perspective views information as a commodity with as much importance as materials, labor, and financial resources.

To move in this direction requires a closer look at information and records generating processes and technologies. Activities such as reports creation, correspondence management, and forms design are all organizational functions concerned with producing or dispersing information resources. Technologies applied to creating and administering information include reprography, micrographics, and electronic data processing. In the new model of records management, these functions and technologies are very much components of the job.

REPORTS, DIRECTIVES, AND CORRESPONDENCE

Reports and Directives

Reports and directives are used to communicate among the members of an organization and to satisfy internal or external information recording requirements. Reports flow upward in an organizational reporting chain, and often provide intelligence which contributes to managerial decision making. For instance, branch libraries in a large university library system might report monthly reference statistics to the library director. Reports can be narrative, statistical, graphic, or a combination of all of these, may be issued one time only, or be generated every quarter, week, month, year, or other period of time. Directives flow downward from management, and are used to establish responsibility and accountability. A common, if unfortunate, example of a directive might be a mandate from the library director that each unit cut its budget by a certain percentage.

Reports are expensive, especially as they can be quite lengthy (consider the reports which must be prepared when a graduate program in library and information science is seeking accreditation). They consume salaried time and overhead in research and data gathering, writing and associated data processing, typing, printing and duplication, reading, and filing. Some of the problems records managers face in reports management are that there is a certain amount of status involved in being on the receiving end of a report, that needless reports may be created and disseminated solely for the purposes of documenting activity on the part of the creator, and that reports are all too easy to create in this era of machine-readable information.

The goals of reports management are to inhibit the production of unnecessary reports and to simplify and standardize reports design. The results of a reports management program are the elimination of redundancy (often by consolidation of several reports into one), the limitation of report distribution, development of standards and instructions for report preparation, and continual evaluation of the need for current and proposed reports.

The first step in gaining control over reports is, of course, a reports inventory. The inventory form should include report number and title, requesting departments, report frequency, the report distribution list, and the costs of preparation, printing, and dissemination. The inventory form should also detail the reason for the report. Once reports are inventoried they can be sorted in order of decreasing cost so that the most expensive reports receive attention first. Report recipients might have to be interviewed to assess the strength of their stated need for the report. Separate reports files are established for regular reports. If a copy of a report is always accessible on file, then the case can be made for limiting the distribution list.

In a large organization, one member of records management staff may be designated to be the reports manager. In any size setting a reports manual, or a reports section of a general records manual, should detail standard practices and procedures, including writing style and data presentation guidelines. The manual should include a checklist for evaluating newly proposed reports. Close ties with data processing operations can reveal new reports and bring them under control (and possible preemption) by the reports management program early in the creation process.

Correspondence

Correspondence is expensive. A typical business letter might cost an organization upwards of $6.00. The cost of a letter can be assessed in terms of the personnel and equipment involved in all stages of correspondence production, including composition, dictation, typing, copying, mailing, and filing. The most expensive type of correspondence is a personalized letter, but even form letters incur considerable charges. Correspondence files are principally organized by subject, which is the most difficult and costly filing method, and a large proportion of correspondence can be disposed of within a month or two of creation.

Correspondence management at the least involves selecting or creating standards and manuals for letter styles and formats, and establishing uniform filing methods for correspondence files. Beyond these steps, correspondence management may also encompass mail management. This involves controlling the flow of incoming and outgoing mail. Mail management includes making decisions as to where mail stations should be located, and how mail should be distributed. It also entails monitoring outgoing mail, not only for statistical reporting and cost containment, but also so that the mail meets organizational standards and postal specifications.

In the past decade mail delivery methods have become considerably more complex in several ways. Many commercial services now compete for the express and messenger mail market, and alternative delivery mechanisms have been presented by electronic mail, voice messaging systems, and telefacsimile. These last three pose special challenges for the records manager not only as methods of conveying correspondence, but as records creation and storage technologies in general.

FORMS MANAGEMENT

Records managers are in the business of controlling organizational information, from its creation through to its disposition. That information is largely collected and disseminated on forms. Correspondence, for instance, is generated using a form we call letterhead. Financial information is represented in order forms, bills, invoices, checks and check stubs, budget reports, travel vouchers, and the like. Personnel information is gathered on standardized forms. Materials are transferred from one location to another with packing slips. Federal, state, and local governments provide innumerable forms for reporting purposes.

If the intention of records management is to manage information from the creation stage onwards, then it behooves the records manager to exercise control over forms. Forms are expensive to create, print, and file, and the more difficult or time-consuming they are to complete, the more they cost the organization. The more efficiently information is gathered, the more proficiently it can be managed. Forms management, then, involves eliminating unnecessary forms, consolidating forms which serve different purposes, standardizing forms, controlling the creation of new forms, designing and monitoring forms so that they are used effectively, and managing forms reproduction, stocking, and distribution.

In a large records management setting, one staff member may serve as the forms manager. Gaining control over forms first requires a forms survey, collecting a copy of and information about each form used in the organization. One copy of each form is kept in a numeric file, in which forms are filed by their form number. This file contains a complete history of the form, including any correspondence or directives which were responsible for its creation, ordering and requisitions history, other pertinent data gathered during the survey, specifications data, and a copy of the request form for new supplies. A second copy is kept in a functional file, which groups forms by the purpose which they serve. This grouping makes duplication and redundancy apparent, provides information for microforms analysis, and promotes forms consolidation. This file is also used to evaluate new form requests. A third copy of each form is filed in a specifications file, which is organized by the physical characteristics of the form (for instance, all forms which are printed on 3 x 5 card stock would be grouped together). The specification file is referred to when new supplies are needed, and when information for microfilming is needed. The specification file also makes it possible to reduce costs by printing, for example, two half-page-sized forms in one run. Procurement procedures might include in-house printing, but more typically supplies are ordered from commercial printing services through centralized purchasing and blanket orders. Controlling forms inventory requires monitoring current stock, anticipating future needs, and supervising storage and distribution.

Good forms design is a crucial aspect of forms management. Texts by Myers and Joyce (1978), Nygren (1980), Osteen (1969) and others provide insights into the elements of design that make a form an effective information gathering tool. More recently, automated forms management has been explored as a way of cost effectively controlling design and distribution. Software such as F3 PRO DESIGNER and FORMTOOL (both from Bloc Development Corporation) or PERFORM (Delrina Technology Inc.) facilitate computerized forms design and revision, as well as distribution over telecommunications lines for on-demand printing or for electronic forms completion, and hence, automated information gathering. Sophisticated forms software can produce camera-ready copy with separated art-form color printing, and with manufacturer's specifications for placement of holes, perforations, adhesives, and other form elements.

REPROGRAPHICS

Strictly speaking, reprographics is facsimile reproduction of graphic material. In the context of records management, reprographics refers to all forms of reproduction, including copying and printing. The ease of reproduction afforded by modern office copiers has contributed substantially to the volume of records which consume office space. Copying machines are inexpensive, easy to operate, and able to accommodate varieties of sizes. This, combined with increased government regulation and reporting, and the "make an extra copy just in case" mentality, have put large paper barriers in the way of effective information management.

Reprographics management attempts to reduce these effects by establishing controls over equipment and its use. Reprographics management involves evaluating and selecting copying methods and services, establishing guidelines for operations, making decisions as to placement of equipment, managing supplies, training staff, and monitoring usage, costs, and service. Decisions must be made as to whether to purchase or lease equipment, and the recent surge in commercial copying and printing services throws another possibility into the problem of choosing cost-effective practices.

The familiar office copy machine, an example of the electrostatic duplication method, is but one of a myriad of copying processes. Crix (1975) offers a fascinating history and survey of reprographics technology. These include fluid and stencil duplication, printing methods (e.g., engraving, silk screen, letterpress, and gravure), wet process copying (for translucent materials such as plans, plates, and patterns), and dry process copying, which includes the typical office machine. What processes are in use in a particular organization will depend on the nature of that organization's activities.

A number of criteria come into consideration when selecting office copying or printing equipment:

o   What is the largest size of paper which needs to be accommodated?
o   What is the minimally acceptable quality?
o   Is color a requirement?
o   What type of paper stock will be used?
o   Is there a need for reduction or enlargement?
o   What is the expected volume?
o   What special features are critical
      (automatic feed, collation, double-sided copying, masking, etc.)?

Apart from selecting equipment, reprographics managers also decide where copying is to be done. Copying at point of need, i.e., in the office, may be appropriate for purposes of confidentiality and convenience, but it is difficult to control costs or ensure that volume guidelines are being followed. Centralized copying means that those controls can be maintained. Fewer staff need to be familiarized with operations, and a mix of machinery can be provided to satisfy varied needs. Centralized copying does mean establishing routines for pick up and delivery, and managing schedules and traffic.

MICROGRAPHICS

Although most business records are still stored in hardcopy (Jenkins, 1991), the most popular alternative is microfilm. Records managers frequently become involved in converting paper records to microfilm, using either in house facilities or commercial services. Even if performed by external services, undertaking micrographics projects means that records managers be able to choose among formats, evaluate microfilming quality, prepare collections for conversion, select appropriate reading and printing equipment, and single out the right company for the job. In house micrographics conversion additionally requires evaluating and purchasing microfilming equipment, training staff, and monitoring quality control. The records manager contemplating a micrographics project of any scale would do well to turn to Brathal and Langemo (1987) for an introductory overview and Saffady (1990) for an in-depth discussion.

The most obvious advantage of microfilming records is the savings in space -- a potential reduction of about 98 percent in physical volume, in fact. However, space savings is not the only factor which has made microfilm such a popular record-keeping alternative. Microfilmed records are less susceptible to climate problems than their paper equivalents (assuming that correct storage conditions are maintained), and offer increased security. Microfilming protects the integrity of a file and removes the possibility of filing error at the single-item level (although microfiche sheets can certainly be lost). Rapid retrieval is promoted, as one item in a huge file can be isolated in a matter of seconds (assuming the presence of manual or machine-aided indexes). Another advantage of microfilm is that it can be digitized and integrated into office automation systems. For records which are to be duplicated and disseminated, microfilm offers savings both in reproduction and mailing costs. Lastly, and importantly for the records manager, a microfilm copy of a record meets legal requirements in most cases under the Uniform Photographic Copies of Business and Public Records in Evidence Act (Title 28, Section 1732 of the *U.S. Code*) and the Uniform Rules of Evidence Act (Title 28, Rule 1003 of the *U.S. Code*).

The general physical properties of microfilm were discussed in Chapter 7. Some types of film are suitable for making microfilm masters, while others are more appropriate for copies. The foremost consideration when choosing film types is the length of time the film is to be kept. Archival film, for permanent retention, is expensive, but under proper storage conditions less costly film which does not meet archival standards may still have sufficient longevity to serve the purpose at hand. Apart from its life span, microfilm is evaluated for its density (which affects contrast) and resolution (i.e., sharpness of lines). There are well over 50 American National Standards Institution guidelines (many of them developed with the Association for Information and Image Management) covering these and other matters relating to micrographics.

Microfilm Formats

Roll, or serialized, microfilm includes open reel, cartridge, and cassette. Open reel film would be best in a low reference environment, as it is vulnerable to tearing and can be difficult to thread into a reader. Film contained in cartridges or cassettes is bulkier, but less susceptible to damage from handling. Cassette film does not have to be rewound before removal from the reader, which means that the film can be left on a particular frame for the next use.

Retrieval from any serial form is slower than retrieval from unitized formats, since it involves sequential scanning. Serial film is not useful for high distribution environments, as the containers are not convenient for mailing. On the other hand, roll microfilm cartons or cases offer large labeling areas for easy filing. Only one person can use a roll at a time, which makes roll film unsuitable for high reference situations (a record series which fits onto one roll of film might occupy a number of different fiches).

Unitized formats include aperture cards, microfilm inserted into jackets, and microfiches. Unitized formats are convenient in high reference situations, although they are cumbersome when long runs must be searched. Visible filing and finding information can be typed on the top edges. Unitized microforms do collect fingerprints, and are easily removed, misfiled, and lost.

Aperture cards devote only a portion of their surface to one or more frames or strips of microfilm, leaving the rest free for annotations readable to the human eye. Some aperture cards are notched around the edges for use in key-punched sorting and retrieval systems. Aperture cards allow individual items to be separated, one to each card, which is advantageous for filing and weeding, but costly in space and labor. Microfilm jackets are cards containing rows of plastic sleeves into which strips of microfilm are placed. Like aperture cards, these permit some flexibility in updating and therearrangement of film strips, and they imply similar sacrifices in space savings and labor reduction. Microfiches are the most common form of unitized microfilm, and certainly the most familiar in libraries.

Microfilm Readers and Reader/Printers

Microfilm readers use either front projection (in which case the screen will be at an angle away from the user, and under a hood) or rear projection (so that the screen is upright). They may be outfitted with a stand, able to fit on a desk top, or even portable (including miniature flashlight-sized readers which can be moved over individual frames). Roll film readers use spindles and fiche readers use glass trays, usually with marked grids for location. Some readers can handle both roll and serialized formats through interchangeable carriages.

Features which come into consideration when evaluating microform readers for purchase include:

o Types and sizes of microforms;
o Screen size
    (100% blowback means the image is the same size as the original document);
o Screen angle preference;
o Background color preference;
o Glare;
o Sharpness of image uniformly across the screen;
o Ability to rotate the image;
o Zooming capabilities;
o Ease of use (for right- *and* left-handed personnel);
o Adequate heat dissipation, and consequent noise level;
o General sturdiness; and
o Ease of cleaning and maintenance.

For retrieval purposes, some print or computer-based content indexing is required so that individual frames may be retrieved when needed. Finding the right frame on a unitized format, such as a microfiche, is a relatively easy task, since most fiche carriages are marked with grids, and indexes give frame locations in vertical and horizontal placement indicators. However, anyone who has worked with *reel* film in libraries can attest to the difficulty of finding a particular image. Most library readers move film from spindle to spindle with hand cranks, or perhaps motorized film winders, and finding a desired series of frames is a matter of visual scanning. In some cases target frames, with large print, are interspersed to signal specific locations (such as the end of one series and the beginning of the next), but this still requires visual scanning as the film passes by the screen.

Fortunately, there are other, more pleasant, techniques for retrieving frames from reel microfilm. In the photo-optical method, bar codes or some other visual cue are added during the filming process. The index gives locations using these codes, the user punches the code into a number pad connected to the reader, and the reader scans through the reel searching for that particular code. Another method is based on the principle of an odometer. Blips are added during the filming process, and can then be counted to find a frame which is at a certain distance from the beginning of the reel. Both of these methods can be used in automated environments, in CAR (Computer-Assisted Retrieval) workstations, where the user searches the index (i.e., the database) on a microprocessor and the reader goes automatically to the correct frame, using the location information derived from the database. Regardless of retrieval method or the degree to which readers and computers are connected together, a machine-readable database is certainly a more effective means of indexing microfilm contents than a paper index.

At least one reader/printer will be necessary for producing paper copies of filmed images. Reader printers use electrostatic or photographic technology to produce hardcopies, and since they essentially take a snapshot of the screen, the quality and size of the copy will depend on the quality and size of the image on the screen. Obviously, reader printers are more expensive than readers alone. In most records management environments, a large volume of microfilm printing usually indicates that the record series should have been retained in hardcopy for a longer period of time.

Microfilm Production

Hardcopy documents are microfilmed using either rotary, planetary, or step-and-repeat cameras. Rotary cameras pass paper to the camera on rotating belts using automatic feeders, and are designed for high-speed applications where the material to be copied is relatively regular in size and capable of standing up to machine handling. Planetary cameras take shots one at a time, and are good for drawings, books, and so on. Often a vacuum or an electrostatic charge is used to hold the item stationary. Step and repeat cameras are specialized for direct production of microfiche, exposing images on separate areas of film (i.e., in row and column grids) in a series of position changes. In any camera type, the images may be accompanied by hand typed or machine stamped information. Title frames detailing contents and including an official notice that this record series was filmed in the normal course of records management procedures and policies are added at the beginning. Following filming, the film must be processed, developed, and inspected for density, sharpness, and undesirable chemical residues. Original film can then be duplicated as desired.

Table 9-1. Factors Affecting a Microfilming Project.

Record characteristics
    Size, weight
    Color
    Single-or double-sided
    Brittleness
    Presence of paper clips or staples

File characteristics
    Volume
    Retention period
    Need for archival quality film
    Update frequency
    Access frequency
    Number of copies
    Hard-copy requirements
    Filing order
    Indexing needs

Administrative Issues
    Turn-around time
    Equipment compatability issues
    Available physical space for production
    Need for (additional) equipment and/or staff

Personnel Costs
    Collection preparation
        Retrieval, sorting, coding, removing staples, etc.
    Refiling
    Filming and processing
    Indexing
    Training

Materials Costs
    Supplies
        Film, cartridges, jackets, processing chemicals, etc.
    Equipment
        Cameras, readers, reader/printers
        Housing
        Processing equipment, duplicating equipment
        Testing equipment (densitometers, microscopes)

Computer Output Microfilm (COM) describes the capture of electronic data directly onto microfilm, either by photographic techniques or by using laser technology. COM recorders are extremely fast, and the results can be of very high quality. Data display controls must be included in the data stream to govern the appearance of the output, and camera controls must be included as well.

The first step in a micrographics project is a feasibility study. Table 9-1 provides an outline of some of the factors which affect microfilming decisions. Microfilming in house does have the advantage of security, and provides continual access to the records during the filming process. While initially high, costs will be lowered over the long run, especially if there is a substantial amount of microfilming activity. On the other hand, service bureaus can offer trained staff a range of equipment types and the possibility of a quick start up. Many companies offer onsite filming for certain types of materials, and will provide estimates or bids for projects. Micrographics service companies well attuned to the needs of records managers will be found in almost any urban area.

NEW INFORMATION TECHNOLOGIES

Microfilm has certain qualities that will ensure its survival as a storage method of choice for many types of records. For a long time it was the only reasonable alternative to paper, and for even longer paper was virtually the only original format on which information was captured. Electronic data storage became a widespread possibility in the late 1950s, the appearance and rapid dispersion of microcomputers and telecommunications technology in the 1980s supported that transition, and in the 1990s it has become possible to create optical disks on site with drives that cost little more than household CD players.

Management of Machine-Readable Records

Machine-readable files in organizations can result from word processing, electronic mail, business graphics software, computer-aided design and manufacturing installations, digitized telefacsimile and voice message machines, and numeric data processing. As a method of carrying information, a machine-readable record should be subject to the same inventory, retention, and disposition decisions as any other format. Realistically, however, it may be very difficult to determine what exists in an organization in optical or electronic form, since many files appear only as entries on disk directories and do not occupy visible space. Files can be undetectably altered at a moment's notice, and can be reproduced and transmitted with no effort and no record. Changes in hardware or software, including system upgrades, can render existing files unreadable. Management of machine-readable records, therefore, does require some extra precautions and steps on the part of the records manager.

A complete inventory of software and hardware, with copies of manuals, is a good place to start. It is preferable, but not always possible, to standardize the software titles (and versions) used across an organization. At the least, standards must be created for naming files, creating backups, and protecting against data loss. Each staff member involved in creating or using machine-readable records must then be acquainted with the standards and with procedures for maintaining file integrity and security (many computer users labor under the mistaken belief that erasing a file really deletes it, despite the fact any number of software products for "unerasing" files are on the market). Machine-readable files should be indexed as part of the records management database, and special purpose text management software might be used for retrieval from large collections.

Environmental controls for computer work areas are largely based on common sense. Excessive heat, cold, or static can be damaging, and protection against the effects of electromagnetic influences, blackouts, and power surges are essential. Component theft can be a problem, as can unauthorized use of microcomputers or networks. In an organization which relies heavily on machine-readable information, data processing services will probably have developed controls for data security. These might include file encryption and various forms of user identification and authorization.

Chapter XII of Title 36 of the *Code of Federal Regulations*, on "Electronic Records Management," discusses the legal admissibility of electronic records. In general, they may be admitted as evidence as long as the record-keeping system has been thoroughly documented, and that documentation substantiates that appropriate security measures have been taken to prevent unauthorized alteration. Both the National Archives and Records Administration and the Information Resources Management Service have published guidelines on handling electronic records (Oglesby and Leary, 1990; U.S. General Services Administration, Information Resources Management Service, 1989).

Information Technologies

Apart from having to cope with machine-readable files, records managers also have to understand the potential of computer-based technologies for storage and retrieval. Where it used to be the case that data tapes stored collections of text and numbers, we now face a world where images can be captured in analog or digitized form on magnetic media, video disks, optical disks, or hybrids of all of these. Computer workstations can be complex combinations of hardware and software from different manufacturers, and can be linked through local and wide area networks to remote sites anywhere on the globe (or, for that matter, in space, *vide* the NASA probes).

National and international standards organizations have begun to address the need for compatible data transmission formats, but selecting equipment and methods for handling one organization's information storage and retrieval requirements has to be done with little guidance apart from vendor and consultant advice, and case studies reported in the professional literature. Even recent texts such as Waegemann (1990) may soon be out of date. The Association for Information and Image Management creates and promotes national standards for all aspects of record-keeping technologies (micrographic as well as machine-readable), and distributes an excellent collection of technical reports and texts on these subject.

CONCLUSION

Of course, there are large differences between the one records manager in a small office with only paper files, and the head of a large 20- or 30-person strong records management department working with the latest technologies to control the entire spectrum of information resource creation and use. Mostly these differences are in practical know-how and experience and in the opportunities afforded in a given workplace. With appropriate training and education, any reasonably intelligent individual can master a new technological application, and can evaluate its feasibility for solving a particular problem. Creating the opportunities (and acquiring the resources) to extend records control, on the other hand, requires skill in organizational politics. The next chapter deals with the *management* aspects of records management, and discusses strategies for becoming an effective administrator of human, physical, and financial resources.

REFERENCES

Brathal, Daniel A. and Mark Langemo. *Planning Conversions to Micrographic Systems*. Prairie Village, KS: ARMA International, 1987.

Crix, F. C. *Reprographic Management Handbook*. London, Eng.: Business Books [for the] Institute of Reprographic Technology, 1975.

Jenkins, Tom. "Records Management Means Good Business," *Office Systems* 8 (April 1991): 44-49.

Myers, Gibbs and James M. Joyce. *Forms Design and Management*. Cleveland, OH: Association for Systems Management, 1978.

Nygren, William. *Business Forms Management*. New York: AMACOM, 1980.

Oglesby, Thomas R. and William H. Leary. *Managing Electronic Records*. Washington, DC: National Archives and Records Administration, Office of Records Administration, 1990. (National Archives and Records Administration Instructional Guide Series).

Osteen, Carl E. *Forms Analysis: A Management Tool for Design and Control.* Stamford, CT: Office Publications, 1969.

Saffady, William. *Micrographic Systems.* 3d ed. Silver Spring, MD: Association for Information and Image Management, 1990.

U S. General Services Administration. Information Resources Management Service. *Electronic Recordkeeping.* Washington, DC: GPO, 1989. (Information Resources Management Handbook).

Waegemann, C. Peter. *The Handbook of Optical Memory Systems.* 2d ed. Newton, MA: Optical Disk Institute, 1990.

READINGS

Diamond, Susan Z. *Records Management: A Practical Guide.* New York: AMACOM, 1983. Chapter 8: "Forms Management: An Integral Part of the Records Program," Chapter 9: "Reports Management: Controlling the Latest Paperwork Explosion," and Chapter 10: "Micrographics and Records Management."

Johnson, Mina M. and Norman F. Kallaus. *Records Management.* 4th ed. Cincinnati, OH: South-Western Publishing, 1987. Chapter 13: "Microrecords."

Klunder, Frederick. "Managing a Microfilm Program." In Katherine Aschner, ed., *Taking Control of Your Office Records: A Manager's Guide.* White Plains, NY: Knowledge Industry Publications, 1983, pp. 85-99.

Penn, Ira A., Anne Morddel, Gail Pennix, and Kelvin Smith. *Records Management Handbook.* Brookfield, VT: Gower, 1989. Chapter 6: "Reports Management," Chapter 7: "Directives Management," and Chapter 8: "Forms Management."

Place, Irene and David J. Hyslop. *Records Management: Controlling Business Information.* 2d ed. Reston, VA: Reston Publishing, 1987. Chapter 11: "Forms Management," and Chapter 13: "Micrographics."

Ricks, Betty R. and Kay F. Gow. *Information Resource Management: A Records Systems Approach.* 2d ed. Cincinnati, OH: South-Western Publishing, 1988. Part 4: "Controlling the System."

Robek, Mary E., Gerald F. Brown, and Wilmer O. Maedke. *Information and Records Management.* 3d ed. Encino, CA: Glencoe, 1987. Part 5: "Records Creation."

Smith, Milburn D. *Information and Records Management: A Decision-Maker's Guide to Systems Planning and Documentation.* New York: Quorum Books, 1986. Chapter 5: "Imaging Systems," and Chapter 6: "Computer Literacy and Office Automation for Records Managers."

Tapper, Garry. "Alternatives to Paper: Micrographics and Magnetic Media."

In Peter Emmerson, ed., *How to Manage Your Records: A Guide to Effective Practice*. Cambridge, Eng.: ICSA Publishing, 1989, pp. 93-127.

Wallace, Patricia E., Jo Ann Lee, and Dexter R. Schubert. *Records Management: Integrated Information Systems*. 3d ed. Englewood Cliffs, NJ: Prentice-Hall, 1992. Chapter 13: "Correspondence and Reports Control," Chapter 14: "Forms Design, Control and Management," Chapter 15: "Reprographics Management and Control," and Chapter 15: "Micrographics."

DISCUSSION POINTS

1. Choose a form that employees have to fill in at your place of work (or at your school if you are a student) and redesign it. You should first read some of the chapters and texts on forms design. What features did you change, and why? Ask co-workers or fellow students to use and evaluate your form.

2. Prepare a one-page summary of how each of the technologies listed below works. For each, discuss what its impact is (or will be) on records management.

    o   Voice digitization
    o   Telefacsimile
    o   Electronic mail
    o   Magneto-optical disks
    o   Image digitization

Chapter Ten

Administrative Considerations[1]

Administrative considerations coordinate both human and material resources and ensure that the records management program meets the organization's mission, goals, and objectives. In addition to accomplishing goals and objectives, administration includes: (1) obtaining the full productivity of each organizational member, (2) developing and implementing specific administrative strategies to fulfill goals and objectives, and (3) ensuring that information services and resources meet and resolve the needs of the organization and the users of its resources. Administration is not an end unto itself, but seeks to increase the effectiveness and efficiency of information resources, including records and information services. Records managers must possess skills and competencies related to administration, information resources management, information policy, systems analysis, research, decision making, planning and evaluation, budgeting, personnel and staffing management, and so forth.

As administrators, records managers must devise strategies for accomplishing organizational goals and objectives and for improving organizational and user access to internal records and other resources. Administrative strategies, or carefully crafted actions intended to obtain maximum benefit from available resources, require careful thought and planning. These resources can be physical (e.g., space or equipment) and human; typically, human resources are the most important organizational resources, since individuals allocate money, materials, and equipment to accomplish specific objectives.

This chapter discusses basic administrative considerations, including the administrative environment and assumptions underlying the administrative process. The chapter also discusses specific factors related to administrative effectiveness. Following an overview of the decision-making process, discussion focuses on budgetary factors and the importance of personnel and staff training. And, finally, the chapter discusses the importance of conducting and consuming research as a basis for implementing administrative strategies. This brief chapter cannot cover the vast terrain of administration; however, the topics presented here are critical for managing

---

[1] Part of this chapter was adapted from Chapters 11 and 13 of <u>Public Access to Government Information</u>, 2nd edition (Norwood, NJ: Ablex Publishing Corp., 1988). Charles R. McClure of Syracuse University was primarily responsible for writing those chapters.

organizational records. A number of excellent administration textbooks offer more detailed information regarding administration (e.g., Stueart and Moran, 1987; Kast and Rosenzweig, 1985; and Hitt, Middlemist, and Mathis, 1986).

THE ADMINISTRATIVE ENVIRONMENT

Background

Before developing specific administrative strategies, records managers should assess the current records management practices and organizational understanding of the role and function of a records management program. Initially, they must:

o   Know the organizational goals and understand departmental activities within that context;

o   Identify the formal and information power bases within the organizational structure, and exploit each when necessary;

o   Be knowledgeable about total resources available to the organization so that they can compete successfully against other areas of the organization for adequate resources; and

o   Promote the importance and benefits of records management in order to receive political and moral support when required.

The reality of organizational political life is that records managers must justify their needs, clarify goals, and demonstrate accomplishments. Justification is necessary, in large part, because competition for scarce resources in an organization can be fierce.

The administrative environment does not exist by chance or happenstance. The above factors, which determine the nature of the environment, are allowed or encouraged to occur either by administrative design or neglect. If there is to be any modification in these and other factors, records managers must identify specific factors to be changed and develop administrative strategies to implement change.

Administrative Assumptions

The administrative philosophies of the chief executive officer, and those of other staff, affect the effectiveness of records management programs and services. Only rarely do records managers analyze the specific philosophies at work in the organization. But to develop strategies one must know where the other organizational members are "coming from." Further, records managers must identify their administrative assumptions as well. Thus, a brief summary of the basic administrative philosophies typically found in an organization will help to better understand "why decisions are made the way they are."

Since a number of textbooks and articles provide sophisticated descriptions of the various administrative philosophies, only a brief overview will be presented here (Koontz and O'Donnell, 1984). All the various administrative philosophies are based on assumptions -- which are difficult to prove or disprove. But one's assumptions toward work and people affect the actual behaviors and administrative strategies that are used.

A first basic set of administrative assumptions, known as classical managerial assumptions (Wren, 1987), are task oriented; the most important aspect of the work environment is getting the work done. There is strict adherence to centralization of authority, and staff participation in decision making is a privilege to be jealously guarded. Control, rather than flexibility and innovation, is stressed, while strict lines of authority are maintained.

A second set of assumptions, from the human relations school of thought (Argyris, 1973, pp. 257-269), sees workers valued as individuals, and the group processes of decision making and participation are at least as important as the task itself. Indeed, the assumptions are that the individual will respond to rewards other than money, that the organization can best be studied based on social interactions, and that people will work more effectively if they "like" each other and have respect for each other. Other assumptions are that open and honest communication within the organization is necessary, that the process of getting work done must be seen in a context of personal values, and that each individual has a right to provide upward communication and feedback to superiors.

Both of these schools of thought are based largely on principles that are applied, in general, to all employees in most organizations. Another school of administrative thought emphasizes the importance of environmental and situational factors rather than general principles (Luthans, 1976; Kast and Rosenzweig, 1985). Contingency management assumptions suggest that individuals are more likely to modify organizational behavior by manipulating environmental characteristics rather than by making direct threats and sweeping promises to individuals. Administrative strategies of an "if ... then ..." variety allow individuals to respond differently in different situations, yet still accomplish stated goals. Further, specific administrative strategies can resolve situations by taking into account the characteristics of the people involved, the environment itself, and decentralized information access (Samuels and McClure, 1982, pp. 23-24).

The three philosophies of classical, human relations, and contingency are defined more easily in theory than in practice. Many organizations operate under basic classical management assumptions, with a pseudo-interest in human relations assumptions. In this context, one finds either "paternal despotism" or "laissez faire" administrative environments. Despite the specific environmental situation, records managers must identify administrative assumptions and respond with contingency administrative strategies. Such strategies will be more effective if records managers are knowledgeable about the decision-making process.

DECISION MAKING

Decision making, which is an administrative process of critical importance for increasing organizational effectiveness, usually involves three related topics: the decision-making process, the decision maker, and the decision itself. Within each of these areas, decision making aims to influence value judgments held by other individuals. But, if one defines decision making as that process whereby information is converted into action, then decision making is largely concerned with the process of acquiring, analyzing, and reporting information to accomplish specific objectives. Because records managers have administrative responsibilities, they must convert effectively a broad range of information resources and research findings into a coherent plan of action.

Simply stated, effective decision making requires the setting of organizational goals and objectives. Furthermore, research is necessary to obtain and analyze appropriate information resources and to guide the evaluation process. Environmental input and feedback should assist records managers in assessing the effectiveness of all decisions made.

The comparison and evaluation of alternative decisions enable administrators to consider a broad range of possible solutions, encourage creativity, and introduce a planning perspective on the decision-making process. Of course, the decision must be implemented; that is, specific steps must be identified by the decision. Those steps or actions must be completed by the appropriate individuals at the appropriate time, and must meet previously agreed upon performance criteria. Based on the extent to which the decision results in the appropriate outcomes, as well as the consideration of additional or revised information from the environment, the decision outcomes should be evaluated against organizational goals and objectives; when necessary, goals should be revised. Underlying the entire decision-making process is the need to collect, analyze, and integrate information through regularly conducted research.

The decision-making process is sabotaged, and ineffective decisions are likely, without research taking place to identify, compare, evaluate, and select alternative decisions; to evaluate the success of the decision; or to determine the impact of the decision on the environment (Janis and Mann, 1977). Indeed, a typical (and usually ineffective) approach to decision making in some organizations is simply to define the situation in which a decision is necessary, and then implement the decision. This "two-step" process of decision making helps to explain why some records management programs neither flourish in today's complex information environment nor provide adequate access to an organization's records or information resources.

WORKING WITH UPPER MANAGEMENT

It is important that records managers maintain a cordial and productive working relationship with upper management. Upper management must be shown that a records management program saves space, improves records and information retrieval, reduces equipment and supply needs, assists in compliance with government regulations, and protects vital records. Records management should demonstrate program advantages through cost-effective and cost-benefit measures.

By enlisting the support of upper management, records managers reinforce the importance of the program to the accomplishment of the organization's mission, goals, and objectives. Records managers, as part of middle management, must maintain a cooperative relationship with each department of the organization and demonstrate that the cooperation benefits both the department and the records management program. In other words, the department *benefits* from that cooperation. The benefit may take the form of the records manager providing the storage space and retrieval services for departmental records.

When records managers find upper and middle managers who are unfamiliar with a records program, they must overcome this ignorance by discussing the value of the program to the organization and individual departments. At the same time, they must avoid the appearance of "empire building." A records management program is not a separate fiefdom; rather, it is an integral part of the daily operations of the organization.

ORGANIZATIONAL CHARTS

A organizational chart displays the structure of the organization and indicates who reports to whom within the organziation. There is not one, but many, organizational configurations that include the position of records manager. To be expected, smaller organizations have fewer employees and assign them a wider range of tasks. Larger organizations have more specialization or employees performing a smaller range of tasks.

Figure 10-1. Organizational Chart.

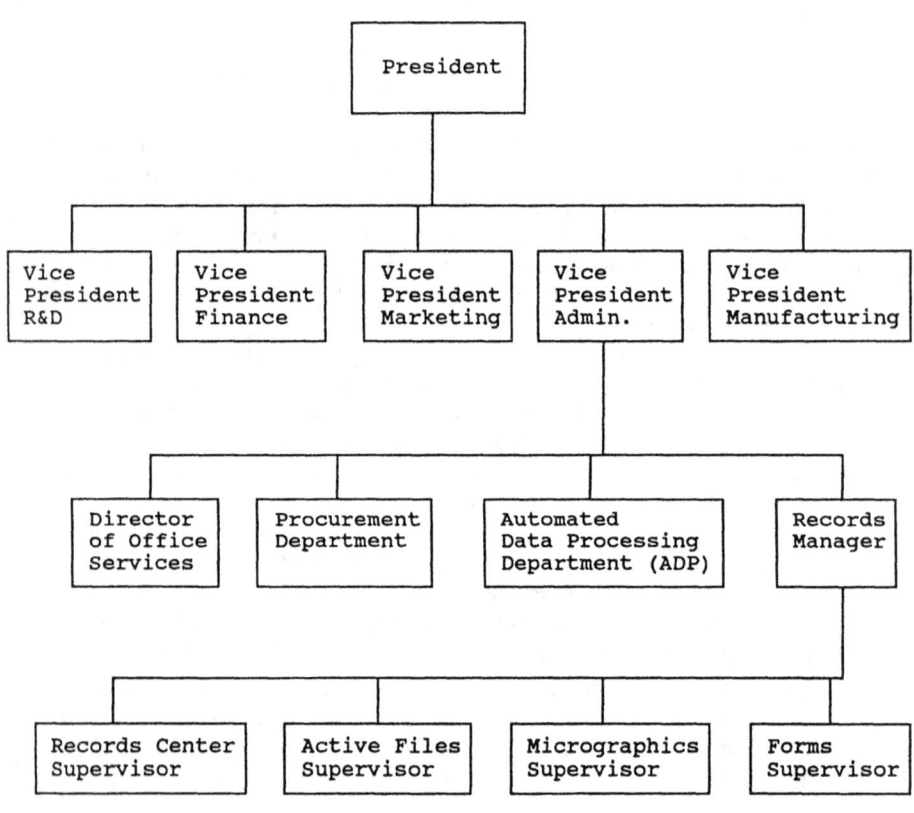

Figure 10-1 is an example of an organizational chart which places the records management program in its proper context. Textbooks, such as *Information Resources Management* (Ricks and Gow, 1988), offer other examples of organizational charts. In addition, many microcomputer software programs permit the drawing of organizational charts.

STAFFING

Staffing refers to the development of an organization through the recruitment, selection, development, and retention of individuals who will contribute to the accomplishment of the mission, goals, and objectives. Personnel departments may engage in transferring, discharging, and training personnel.

A job analysis examines the function, duties, and qualifications of a position. More specifically, the analysis focuses on the prerequisite formal education or training, type and length of experience, and personal characteristics. These characteristics might pertain to one's ability to work with or to motivate others, to engage in problem solving, and to work with minimal direction and guidance.

A *job description* is a written summary of the position that specifies the responsibilities and duties to be performed by the employee. Records managers should have a written job description and should as well develop one for each member of their staff. They can set performance objectives and ascertain, on a periodic basis, the extent to which the staff have accomplished objectives, such as "to place 15 record series on microfiche by the end of the week." The Association of Records Managers and Administrators (1991) has produced guidelines for the development of job descriptions. These guidelines enable organizations to standardize their job descriptions and to produce a degree of uniformity within and across organizations.

As McFarland (1979, p. 247) suggests, there need not be a precise matching of individuals with jobs and tasks. Yet, managers may make mistakes in the selection of staff and must realize that mismatching may present problems, such as incompetency, low morale, and job dissatisfaction. Occupational stress and burnout, if present in staff, impact on daily performance and on the ability of those individuals to work effectively with other members of the organization. The result might be an unwillingness of others in the organization to work with certain members of the records management team, forcing additional burdens on productive staff.

Managers must explore techniques for motivating and training staff. They must also consider every job vacancy as an opportunity to review the organization -- the range of positions within it, the expectations for each member of the *team*, the tasks and duties of those who will fill a vacant position, and the tasks and duties of those who serve in a related capacity (McFarland, 1979, p. 254).

Staff Training

Records managers should develop a supportive atmosphere, one in which staff obtain job satisfaction and motivation, that encourages staff to retain their positions. High turnover rates present an unstable situation that requires constant hiring and training of staff. It is important that staff realize their place and contribution within the organization -- see how they contribute to the larger environment.

Whatever training programs exist should be part of written policies and be standardized. Nonethless, training programs must be responsive to individuals and present them with an understanding of the records management program, specific tasks and responsibilities covered in the job description, career and advancement options, and standard procedures. New and other staff should be periodically reviewed, but the results of the review should not be used solely for salary, retention, and promotion decisions. The results should be incorporated into a training program.

Records managers, and their staff, should participate in the orientation of all staff new to the organization. All staff, including departmental records coordinators and department heads, should be familiar with the records management program, support its goals and objectives, and realize how that program benefits their own department or unit.

Personnel Development

Without adequately trained, knowledgeable, and forceful individuals serving as records managers, the value of records management will be negligible. Records management staff must be knowledgeable about specific areas of expertise, organizational goals, service philosophies for the user, and obtaining adequate resources from the organization in order to perform their duties.

As Garbarino (1990, p. 2) indicates,

> to a great extent, the overall effectiveness of the records management function will be determined by the extent to which ... [records managers] understand what is happening in this environment and prepare ... [their] colleagues to respond to it.

Staff development is a "key to remaining in touch with the realities and demands of ... [the] outside world" (Ibid.).

Five factors "force a records manager to consider the need for" personnel development (Ibid.). These are (Ibid.):

o   Technological change;
o   Changing customer or business needs;
o   New staff members;
o   New roles for existing staff members; and
o   Perceived deficiencies of existing staff.

Clearly, a changing world and work environment necessitate the need for staff to master new skills, competencies, and knowledge.

A program of personnel development can begin with a skills inventory, or the identification of specific areas in which personnel can become more effective during the performance of their duties (Mathis and Jackson, 1988). A skills inventory, however, should not be confused with a personnel evaluation process. Typically, personnel evaluation attempts to determine how well the employee has performed during the past year (or some given amount of time), and ranks that person in comparison to other organizational members. The results then can be translated into recommendations for salary increases or promotions (Kroll, 1983, p. 32). While both techniques can encourage skills development, a skills inventory should be a self-assessment process without direct pressure for evaluation.

A skills inventory, which comprises the first step in the process of personnel development, enables individuals to improve their knowledge, technical skills, attitudes, and overall effectiveness. In this sense, the emphasis is on the future, not the past, and on providing strategies for improvement to occur. In a number of instances, the problems with many records management programs and collections are attributable to the skills/knowledge deficiencies of the staff. On the one hand, many of them never received appropriate training before accepting the responsibilities of the position. On the other hand, those people who did receive some training may now find it inadequate or obsolete.

Yet, final responsibility for personnel development rests with both the individual and the organization. Regardless of whether the individual is classified as a manager or a clerk, his or her development in terms of improved skills and knowledge is essential. The unique nature of records management demands special skills -- and the application of rapidly changing technology to the field only adds to this demand. Ongoing training programs are essential if the quality of personnel is to be upgraded.

There must be formally developed training sessions for all personnel who begin work in a records department. Boss and Raikes (1982, pp. 147-170) reprint an excellent general outline for staff training. New staff members working with the organization's records should not be "dumped" there without considerable training. A program of staff training for all new employees, combined with a carefully planned program for continuing education, will greatly contribute to meeting management goals and objectives.

RECORDS MANAGEMENT MANUAL

A records management manual familiarizes staff with the organization and standardizes procedures, establishes or fixes responsibility, identifies the relationship between records management and other departments, updates procedures and communicates these changes, eliminates duplication of effort, and assists in employee training, evaluation, and improvement. The manual might take the form of a:

o   Policy manual documenting decisions, resolutions, and pronouncements;

o   Organizational manual delineating lines of responsibility;

o   Administrative procedures manual detailing standard methods of work, general procedures, and organization-wide records control; and

o   Operating procedures manual covering specific activities or departments.

As a first step, the organization forms a committee to determine the type of manual, the contents, and the number of copies to be generated. The committee sifts through manuals produced within the organization, interviews executives and staff, reviews company literature and policies (including minutes, memos, grievance records, and job descriptions), and examines checklists from supervisors (see "Records Management Policy," 1989). Committee members then organize the collected information into a manual that probably includes the following items:

o   Title, authorship, and date;
o   Signed authorizations;
o   Preface, including:
    purpose,
    definition of records management,
    solicitation of improvements, and
    instructions for updating;
o   Table of contents;
o   Organization charts;
o   Procedures;
o   Glossary;

Figure 10-2. Sample Playscript.

Records Manual

Number: A02-21
Page: 1
Date: 12/3/89

Subject: Obtaining a Photocopy of a Record from the Records Center.

Title		Task
Requester	1.	Contact Records Center (via mail or in person).
	2.	Complete Request Form (203-CC) or request completion of the form, noting that a photocopy is needed.
Records Center Manager	3.	Process the Request Form. o Check index for record's location. o If record is not listed, notify requester.
	4.	Give retrieval page (green page of Request Form) to Records Clerk.
Records Clerk	5.	Retrive record from carton.
	6.	Photocopy record.
	7.	Return original record to carton.
	8.	Forward photocopy to Records Center Manager.
Records Center Manager	9.	Send copy to requester.

o   Flowcharts;
o   Copies of all pertinent forms; and
o   Index.

The procedures might be presented in playscript form. As shown in Figure 10-2, each set of procedures is divided into two columns. The first column identifies the title of the person responsible for a task or decision, and the other column specifies the task to be done or the decision to be made.

The manual is probably placed in a binder, with a flexible numbering system. Such a manual is easy to update. The records manager retains the master copy but distributes copies throughout the organization. The manager might even distribute copies of sections while the committee prepares the manual. The purpose is to sensitize various departments and units with the records management program, the committee and its charge, and the importance of maintaining an active records management program.

BUDGETING AND RESOURCE ALLOCATION

Records managers need direct control over the budget for their area of responsibility. Without a regular budget and some direct control over that budget, records managers are effectively hamstrung and must rely on "handouts" from the administrative offices or other departments for support.

Records managers must realize that the allocation of resources is a systems process -- of which organizational records comprise one part. Records managers must make an effective argument for a broader view of budgeting than simply advocating the preservation of the organization's past. In its simplest form, budgeting is the process of outlining organizational activities and services in terms of dollar amounts, obtaining adequate financial support for the accomplishment of objectives, and allocating predetermined amounts of money to specific areas of organizational activities. In addition, a budget, a formal and written document that outlines these expenditures, has impacts in the following areas:

o   *Planning*: a budget expresses priorities for a specific planning cycle, usually a one-year period, and suggests which activities are to be funded and at what levels of support during the forthcoming year;

o   *Control*: a budget attempts to ensure that specific amounts of resources are expended for only certain activities and services by indicating which activities, or which departments/agencies, are to be allocated predetermined amounts of support, and by clarifying who is responsible for those expenditures;

Figure 10-3. Combination Program-Line Item Budget.

PROGRAM NAME: RECORDS DELIVERY SERVICE
PROGRAM OBJECTIVES:
1. To deliver a requested record to members of the organization within 1 hour of the original request.
2. To increase the speed with which the records management unit can provide accurate delivery of requested records.

ITEM NAME	JUSTIFICATION	COST
1. Clerical Staff	Clerical staff during hours of operation are required in order that someone is always available to deliver actual documents	$1000/mt
2. Copying	Copies of paper records will be provided unless there is a need for the original	245/mt
3. Film/Fiche Reader/ Printer	When there is a need for microfilmed records, "blow back" to paper copy will be provided	250/mt
4. FAX	Where immediate delivery is essential or distance is too great for expeditious delivery, the item(s) will be faxed	210/mt
5.		
6.		
7.		
8.	START-UP	
COMMENTS:	Clerical staff will be assigned additional responsibilities during the day. TOTAL COST	$1705/mt
DATES:	Program will begin September 1992, with monthly evaluation.	

o *Political relationships*: the budget expresses the relationships among the various departments/agencies funded by the institution, the degree to which department/agency heads can obtain support for their programs, and the perceived importance of those activities compared to other institutional activities; and

o *Basis for evaluation*: the budget also provides a basis by which the activities and services of records management can be evaluated in terms of *effectiveness* and *efficiency*.

Budgeting and resource allocation procedures at the department level is as important as budgeting procedures at the larger organizational level.

After itemizing basic expenditures, records managers can produce an annual budget summarizing the expenditures. Furthermore, they can examine those expenditures in terms of specific objectives.

A number of budgets have been suggested for organizational use. But, in general, the budgets tend to be either line item (each type of expenditure is given an individual line on the budget) or program-oriented (the expenditures are linked to specific program goals and objectives). Line-item budgets, which are easy and quick to produce, can specify individual expenditures clearly. However, they tend to inhibit creativity, encourage the department/agency to use the same categories (items) year after year, and support revisions based on a certain percentage of expenditures for all items rather than examining each item individually. A program budget, which is more difficult to produce, must include measurable program objectives. It fosters long-range planning, links expenditures directly to the accomplishment of objectives, and encourages evaluation of the program under consideration.

Figure 10-3 suggests a useful compromise between the two approaches. A program budget with line items is easier to complete than a straight program budget and simply incorporates the "items" or portion of items directly related to the program under consideration. In the example, the program "Records Delivery Service" is described in terms of clearly identified objectives.[2] The resources needed to accomplish the program objectives are specified with individual lines (items).

The monthly evaluation mentioned in the figure would focus on the computation of performance measures for both objectives. The measure for the first objectives is the percentage of records delivered versus those requested, while the measure for the other objective is the average time per

---

[2] Examples of forms could be constructed from the figures contained in Burk and Horton (1988).

delivery of records. The records manager might set the expected fill rate for the first objective at 85%, while an average of one hour or less would be considered successful for meeting the second objective. The manager, thus, has set the level of expectation against which actual performance can be evaluated.

Use of such a program budget has certain benefits:

o Costs directly attributable to the accomplishment of a specific objective are itemized;

o Performance measures are established for each objective and assist records managers in knowing the degree to which the program or activity is "successful;"

o Programs that are not cost-effective can be identified and either modified or eliminated; and

o The ability to justify costs and request appropriate resources in light of program objectives is significantly strengthened.

The use of budgeting information is essential for the computation of cost-effectiveness ratios. Such ratios express the cost (which could include personnel, time, materials, equipment, overhead, etc.) per unit measure of a product. For instance, the cost-effectiveness ratio of shelving microfiche records might be $1.50 per microfiche if professional staff do the filing, whereas the ratio might be 63 cents if clerical staff refile the microfiche. Cost-effectiveness ratios can be improved only by:

o Decreasing the cost associated with the production of the item, and at the same time maintaining the number of items produced; and

o Increasing the number of items produced from the process, and at the same time maintaining the level of costs associated with the process.

It is essential that records managers consider cost-effectiveness and cost-benefit ratios as a basis for decision making, planning, and the justification of resources and services (Ricks and Gow, 1988, pp. 37-38; Burk and Horton, 1988, Chapter 3).

SPACE MANAGEMENT

Space management is a process whereby the placement of physical facilities and services within a given area maximizes access to records and encourages records management staff to provide accurate, prompt, and effective services. Thus, the arrangement, organization, and relationship of physical facilities, as well as records services and sources, are primary areas for attention when considering space management.

An assessment of physical facilities and space cannot be made in isolation of the goals and objectives of the records program and the entire organization. Space utilization addresses the relationship between structure and function. Structure comprises the arrangement, the relationship of physical facilities and space to other factors in the area as well as to the organization, and the manner in which facilities are organized within the area. Function is simply the purpose for which something is intended, e.g., what is expected to be accomplished with this particular piece of equipment? Both factors must be considered together when assessing the overall strengths and weaknesses of the facility, since there is frequently a tradeoff relationship between them.

After completing an inventory of equipment and support facilities, the staff should make a diagram or floor plan of the records center, or whichever records office is under consideration. The floor plan simply illustrates the actual available floor space and the location of the physical facilities within the area. The floor plan should be drawn to scale -- usually one-quarter or one-eighth inch to a foot. By developing such an outline floor plan, copies can be made that, at a later time, can be used as a basis for designing new arrangements without constantly having to redraw the skeletal configuration.

Special attention should be given to assessing the relationship among the activities (service objectives) to be accomplished and their physical organization and arrangement. The records collection should not constitute an "obstacle course," and efficiencies in design must be recognized (Strain, 1979).

Given the growth in the number of records generated by an organization annually, staff must *plan* for an orderly growth and control over the records collection. In many instances, they might improve physical facilities and space utilization simply by rearranging the layout, functions, and location of resources and services within the area already established for managing the records collection.

CAREER CHOICE

Careers in records and information management focus on records and information managers, records administrators, senior records and information analysts, records and information analysts, and records and information supervisors. Of course, there are supportive positions.

Records managers plan and administer, coordinate departmental activities, ensure compliance, promote the concept of records management, supervise staff, plan and design space and technology use, analyze cost-effectiveness and cost-benefit measures, and prepare reports, manuals, and budgets. Supervisors supervise and train staff, submit reports and budgets, and design forms and workstations. Records analysts evaluate the usefulness and cost of records, and make recommendations for microfilming and photocopying.

Records managers can rise within an organization to the position of office resources or information resources manager. They might administer a large department with a substantial budget and number of staff under their direction.

Records management supervisors oversee records centers and activities, such as forms control and reprography. Known as records management assistants, systems analysts, reports analysts, forms analyst, active records supervisor, or records center supervisor, they need a working knowledge of their area's procedures, supplies, automation prospects, retention practices, equipment, and security regulations.

Because there is a shortage of qualified records managers, organizations might hire managers from other organizations. As an alternative, an organization might promote nonmanagerial staff to positions in records management. These staff members might receive training from outside consultants or training programs offered, for example, by ARMA.

A growing number of records managers might have their undergraduate degrees, or perhaps master's degrees, in business administration, economics, computer science, history, and/or library and information science. They might have supervisory experience, knowledge of systems analysis, and office experience.

Students enrolled in graduate programs of library and information science seeking positions in records management should take courses involving systems analysis, the application of technology, management, evaluation, research methods, preservation, and archives management.

Career advancement for these individuals will depend on factors such as technical knowledge, the ability to communicate (orally and in written form), to manage, and to engage in problem solving, and knowledge of technology. They must keep abreast of the latest technological advances and their implications for records management and retrieval. At the same time, they should participate in continuing education opportunities, and attend national and regional conferences. As managers, they should know their peers in other organizations and draw upon the insights and perspectives of these individuals as needed. Personal networking may also result in the awareness of carrer opportunities.

ESTABLISHING A RESEARCH BASIS FOR RECORDS MANAGEMENT

The topics discussed in this chapter all require accurate and timely information, if the organization expects to implement administrative strategies to increase the overall efficiency and effectiveness of records collections and services. Obtaining adequate and timely information requires that records managers be knowledgeable about both *conducting* and *consuming* research. The complexity of operating records programs requires greater knowledge about the research process, collecting and analyzing data, and awareness of how that process can impact and support decision making and planning. The importance of the research process can only increase as greater opportunities and challenges (and increased flexibility for funding records related services) becomes apparent.

Conducting and consuming research for the effective operation of records collections cannot be considered as a luxury. Many records managers may find it easy to rationalize their inability to exploit research for administrative decisions because of demands on staff time, solving day-to-day problems, holding the line against inflation, reduced budgets, rising costs, and limited knowledge about the research process. Realistically, the successful incorporation of the research process into a records management program calls for a restating of priorities and perhaps recognizing that, although all activities are important, some might be more so than others. Those activities of greater importance are likely candidates for investigation and research.

Conducting research to assist in the overall decision-making process is likely to take on increased importance because of the complexity of issues to be resolved and the limited resources available to resolve those issues. The type of research needed in most records management programs is *action research*. The primary difference between it and traditional research rests on the emphasis for improving the organizational effectiveness of a particular library/information center, as opposed to conducting research intended to have broad generalizability. Results from action research are intended to be *implemented* -- to effect change in the organization and, it is hoped, to improve organizational effectiveness. Swisher and McClure (1984) describe the process of action research, while Hernon (1991) discusses specific statistical procedures supporting action research.

The primary means to integrate research into organizational decision making and planning is to:

o   Have clearly written statements of the goals and objectives for the organization;

o   Link all research projects to a specific decision that is necessary or related to accomplishment of the organization's goals and objectives; and

o   Demonstrate how the results from the research can assist the organization in improving its overall effectiveness and efficiency.

Addressing these three points before any investigation is initiated is tantamount to asking "So what?" regarding the research to be conducted. If the answer to these questions is "It really doesn't matter and won't make an impact on the organization's effectiveness or efficiency," then other topics for research merit identification and implementation.

Intelligent answers to the above questions must come, indeed can only come, from records management personnel who have research knowledge, who can relate the research process to decision making and planning, and who understand the basic concepts of general systems as a means to describe and understand the operations of information services. Without such skills, the personnel will be forced to accept traditional assumptions currently operating in the organization and will be unable to conduct a competent needs assessment. They will be unable to respond to the changing environments affecting the organization and to demonstrate accountability and justify the existence of the collection if asked to do so. Further, the staff may continue to do well (efficiently) activities that need not be done (ineffectiveness). By understanding action research and statistical techniques, utilizing research to *support* decision making and planning, and encouraging professional staff's development of research competencies, records managers will be better able to plan and provide high quality and innovative programs.

In addition to having knowledge of the research process, information-handling technologies, and marketing strategies, records managers must be competent managers, ones able to plan, evaluate, administer a records program, supervise staff, and interact with others inside and outside the organization. They must be effective communicators and leaders, able to gain top management support as well as cooperation from everyone throughout the organization. Clearly, recruitment, selection, retention, and training are all essential factors for implementing a qualified and dynamic records management team that will face the challenges of today and tomorrow.

REFERENCES

Argyris, Chris. "Some Limits of Rational Man Organizational Theory," *Public Administration Review* 33 (1973): 257-269.

Association of Records Managers and Administrators. *Job Descriptions*. Prairie Village, KS: ARMA International, 1991. (ARMA International Guideline for Records and Information Management)

Boss, Richard W. and Deborah Raikes. *Developing Microform Reading Facilities*. Westport, CT: Microform Review, 1982.

Burk, Cornelius F., Jr. and Forest W. Horton, Jr. *InfoMap: A Complete Guide to Discovering Corporate Information Resources*. Englewood Cliffs, NJ: Prentice-Hall, 1988.

Garbarino, John. "Staff Training and Development," *The Records & Retrieval Report* 6 (October 1990): 1-10.

Hernon, Peter. *Statistics: A Component of the Research Process*. Norwood, NJ: Ablex, 1991.

Hitt, Michael A., R. Dennis Middlemist, and Robert L. Mathis. *Management: Concepts and Effective Practice*. St. Paul, MN: West Publishing Co., 1986.

Janis, Irving L. and L. Mann. *Decision Making*. New York: The Free Press, 1977.

Kast, Fremont E. and James E. Rosenzweig. *Organization and Management: A Systems and Contingency Approach*. 4th ed. New York: McGraw-Hill, 1985.

Koontz, Harold and Cyril O'Donnell. *Management: A Systems and Contingency Analysis of Managerial Functions*. New York: McGraw-Hill, 1984.

Kroll, Rebecca H. "Beyond Evaluation: Performance Appraisal as a Planning and Motivational Tool in Libraries," *Journal of Academic Librarianship* 9 (March 1983): 27-32.

Luthans, Fred. *Introduction to Management: A Contingency Approach*. New York: McGraw-Hill, 1976.

Mathis, Robert L. and John H. Jackson. *Personnel-Human Resource Management*. St. Paul, MN: West Publishing Co., 1988.

McFarland, Dalton E. *Management Foundations and Practices*. New York: MacMillan, 1979.

"Records Management Policy," *The Records & Retrieval Report* 5 (May 1989): 1-16.

Ricks, Betty R. and Kay F. Gow. *Information Resource Management*. Cincinnati, OH: South-Western Pub. Co., 1988.

Samuels, Alan R. and Charles R. McClure. "Toward a Theory of Library Administration." In *Strategies for Library Administration*, edited by Charles R. McClure and Alan R. Samuels. Littleton, CO: Libraries Unlimited, 1982, pp. 421-431.

Strain, Paula M. "Efficiency and Library Space," *Special Libraries* 70 (December 1979): 542-548.

Stueart, Robert D. and Barbara B. Moran. *Library Management*. 3d ed.

Littleton, CO: Libraries Unlimited, 1987.
Swisher, Robert and Charles R. McClure. *Research for Decision Making: Methods for Librarians*. Chicago, IL: American Library Association, 1984.
Wren, Daniel A. *The Evolution of Management Thought*. New York: Wiley, 1987.

DISCUSSION POINTS

1. Evaluate a decision made by a records manager. Present background information and analyze the basis on which the decision was made. Compare the decision to alternative choices. Was the best decision made?

2. Is every records manager an administrator?

3. Are leadership and management the same thing? Discuss.

4. What leadership qualities should records managers possess?

5. Develop and justify a budget for a records management program. Furthermore, prepare the budget on a spreadsheet and explore how "what if" scenarios impact budgetary expenditures.

6. How should the performance of staff be monitored? Should performance evaluation be linked to salary and promotion decisions? Discuss.

7. Study different organizational charts and the role of records management within various settings. What are the similarities and differences? Discuss.

8. Examine job announcements for positions as records managers. What educational background, experiences, qualifications, and personal traits do employers seek?

9. Develop or review a records management manual.

Chapter Eleven

Evaluation and Planning

Simply stated, evaluation, a component of the planning process, involves the identification and collection of data about specific services or activities, the establishment of criteria by which the success of these services and activities can be assessed, and the determination of both the quality of the service or activity and the degree to which the service or activity accomplishes stated goals and objectives. As such, evaluation is a decision-making tool that is intended, primarily, to assist managers in allocating necessary resources to those activities and services that *best* facilitate the accomplishment of the organization's mission, goals, and objectives.

In one sense, evaluation is an information gathering, analysis, and reporting process. Managers identify specific activities, questions, or areas as appropriate for evaluation, and then they -- or someone delegated the responsibility -- develop research procedures (designs and methodologies) to guide the evaluation. In addition, they collect data that specifically assess a particular service, program, or activity, and analyze the data in such a way that they can describe and compare the quality and performance of the service, program, or activity against appropriate criteria. Next, they report and implement the results of the investigation in order to effect change or improvement.

Although change, simply for the sake of change, is of little value for any organization, all organizations constantly respond to changing internal and external conditions. Policies emanating from the federal and state governments, technological developments, institutional mandates, changing demographics of the organization's constituencies, and new or different competitors providing similar services are only some of the external environmental factors that impact organizations.

Internal conditions include legal and regulatory requirements, budgetary increases or decreases, the addition of new personnel, evolving or revised organizational or institutional missions, change in clientele served, and new methods of organizing and accessing resources and services. Thus, an organization may have to change its services and activities *just to maintain* its current level of effectiveness! Determining what to change, and how to change it, is an important component of evaluation.

USE OF EVALUATION

Decision makers might engage in evaluation to gain information and data useful in deciding whether or not to continue or discontinue a program, service, or activity; in improving practices or procedures; in adding or dropping program strategies and techniques; in instituting similar programs elsewhere; or in allocating resources among competing programs. Evaluation incorporates planning, systems analysis, research, and change, and ongoing evaluation is integral to a dynamic, effective, and efficient organization. Evaluation involves five concepts that lend themselves to measurement:

o   *Extensiveness*, or the amount of a service provided in relation to the population served. This criterion is generally a measure of quantity rather than quality;

o   *Effectiveness*, or the extent to which a service or activity accomplishes stated objectives. This criterion might also examine the extent to which a service satisfies the demands that users place on it;

o   *Efficiency*, or the appropriateness of resource allocations. This criterion might be judged in the context of stated objectives;

o   *Cost-effectiveness*, or the accomplishment of objectives expressed in terms of costs; and

o   *Cost-benefit*, or the justification for the expense of providing a service or program in terms of the benefits derived from it.

Much evaluation in records management is extensiveness oriented. An extensiveness measure might focus on the number of records acquired, processed, and used. When decision makers view such numbers within the context of organizational goals and objectives, these measures become a type of effectiveness indicator. Assuming reliable and valid data collection, such measures suggest "how much." However, this is not the same as reporting "how well." In other words, looking at merely the number of records acquired, processed, and used portrays quantity not quality of a service, program, or activity.

To conduct a cost-effectiveness or cost-benefit study, managers determine all costs -- direct, indirect, immediate, and long term -- related to a specific activity or service. The difference between a cost-effectiveness and cost-benefit study is that the former compares costs to the actual impact of a service or activity, and the latter requires the assignment of a monetary value to that service, program, or activity (see Rossi and Freeman, 1989; Burk and Horton, 1988, Chapter 3, pp. 75-114; Balough, 1991).

BASIC EVALUATION APPROACHES

Formative evaluation is an ongoing assessment that provides information to monitor and improve an in-progress activity or service. *Summative* evaluation determines the level of program success or failure. The purpose of formative evaluation is to *improve*, while that of summative evaluation is to *prove*.

One purpose for engaging in evaluation is to monitor the degree to which the organization or program meets stated goals and objectives, and to readjust a program to accomplish specific objectives better. As such, the approach is effectiveness- oriented and done on a formative basis. An example of such evaluation is the regular monitoring of the degree to which clientele obtain a specific record (that they already have in mind). If their "success rate" suddenly drops, the formative nature of the evaluation process is a warning that records managers need to take corrective action.

Another purpose of evaluation is to provide a "once only" assessment of how well the organization or individual programs meet stated goals and objectives. In this instance, the evaluation, although effectiveness-oriented, is concerned with whether to continue or discontinue the program, service, or activity.

A third purpose of evaluation is to monitor the manner in which organizational resources are allocated. This approach is efficiency-oriented because it assesses how the organization uses standard resource categories (personnel, equipment, books and other information resources, supplies, and other forms of budgeted items). Another type of efficiency criterion includes time. For instance, the number of records processed per day is an efficiency assessment, and if such an assessment is conducted on an ongoing basis, it can identify and monitor delays in processing.

Summative evaluation of resource allocation takes less effort than formative evaluation of resource allocation, which in turn takes less effort that summative evaluation of organizational/program effectiveness. Formative evaluation of organizational/program effectiveness may require the greatest effort. This is because:

o Evaluation of effectiveness criteria requires the existence of clearly stated goals and objectives; and

o Formative evaluation involves *ongoing* monitoring of an activity and requires the establishment of regular data collection and analysis procedures. In contrast, summative evaluation is a "one time" activity.

Thus, the greater the use of effectiveness-oriented evaluation that relies on formative assessment procedures, the greater is the evaluation effort in terms of planning, staff time, commitment, and resource support. The greatest payoffs, in terms of meeting the information needs of the records program's clientele, competing successfully against other information providers, and offering improved access to information resources and services, come from the use of evaluation that is formative and effectiveness-oriented.

PLANNING

Evaluation supports a number of organizational and administrative activities. Many of these activities (e.g., decision making, needs assessment, development of goals and objectives, and communication) are essential ingredients for planning. Effective planning cannot be accomplished without an evaluation component, and evaluation has little practical utility unless staff members initiate specific strategies to integrate study findings into the planning process.

Planning is the process of (1) conducting a needs assessment of the organization and the environment, (2) developing written goals and objectives, (3) implementing services and activities to accomplish those objectives, and (4) evaluating the overall quality and success of those services and activities vis-à-vis stated objectives (McClure, Owen, Zweizig, Lynch, and Van House, 1987). The conduct of evaluation research requires the setting of organizational priorities and an assessment of the quality of services, programs, and activities provided.

Integrating the evaluation process within organizational planning is essential because planning tends to focus attention on the library or records center as a whole, whereas evaluation focuses on specific aspects of an activity, program, or service without considering the impact of that activity, program, or service on the entire organization. In addition to relating the "parts" of records management activities to overall organizational goals, planning assists in the setting of priorities for what should be accomplished through the program. Because libraries and records centers cannot do *everything*, they must determine which activities, programs, and services are most important and *should be* done.

The main components of planning comprise a hierarchy ranging from the articulation of the mission of the organization to the:

o   Setting of goals and objectives;

o   Implementation of services, programs, and activities;

Figure 11-1. Hierarchy of Planning Components.

Mission:

The Brightstar Company makes widgets and engages in related R&D activities to ensure that the company's products remain state of the art and competitive in international markets.

The Records Management Department monitors and manages the life cycle of the company's information resources on widgets. The Department manages company records and provides appropriate personnel with access to these records. The more sensitive records remain accessible only to corporate leadership and the company's research scientists.

Goal:

Company research scientists are able to obtain records and services that support their R&D activities.

Objectives:

1. To assess the records and service needs of research scientists by August 199X.

    Activity: Survey the information needs of these scientists.

    Measure: Production of a final report.

2. To increase scientists' use of company information resources by 25% by June 199X.

    Activity: Current awareness/publicity campaign.

    Measure: Scientist program participation per capita.

Goal:

Company managers have access to a wide range of high quality services.

Objective:

To increase the number of requests managers make per capita by 35% by June 30, 199X.

    Activity: Discussion groups focusing on the records and information requests of managers.

    Measure: Program participation of managers per capita.

o   A review of these activities, programs, and services against organizational goals and objectives; and

o   Making adjustments or changes as necessary.

The mission is a philosophical statement that broadly sets forth areas perceived to be important to the organization. Such statements are value assessments of what the organization *should* be doing (see McClure et al., 1987) (see Figure 11-1). Goals, on the other hand, are long-range statements of activity areas (usually three to five years) and suggest activities that will receive priority for organizational resources. Goals might focus on collections, services, and administration.

Typically, a goal has numerous objectives. Objectives typically begin with an action verb and must be measurable, challenging, time-limited, and clearly understood. They suggest what is to be done and not *how* to do it (Ibid.). Each objective has programs, which in turn may specify *performance measures* for assessing the effectiveness of the program and the degree to which an objective is accomplished.

In times of austerity, the setting of goals and objectives and formalized planning take on increased importance. Indeed, there is an increased need to establish "realistic" goals and objectives, i.e., those that accurately represent the needs and intentions of the organization and have a likelihood for success (Johnson, 1984). Furthermore, as Pings (1980, p. 61) suggests, "the mark of a healthy organization does *not* rest on goal statements or on studies to set goal statements, but it does rest on the fervor with which it tests goals." This constant testing, or reassessment, comprises the evaluation component of planning.

ACTION RESEARCH

Understanding the relationship between planning and evaluation is essential for improving the effectiveness of the records management operation. The research process, as typified by action research, links planning to evaluation. Action research is a process of collecting and analyzing data specifically for the purpose of making changes and improvements in organizational services and activities (Swisher and McClure, 1984, pp. 22-29).

Action research supports the planning process by supplying empirical evidence regarding the success with which goals and objectives are accomplished, resources allocated, and the quality of individual services and activities assessed. In short, action research is targeted at problem solving, improved decision making, and increased organizational effectiveness. In contrast, basic and applied research has a broader intent -- the generation and testing of a theory or model, leading perhaps to revision of that theory or model (see Hernon, 1991).

Records managers and their staffs simply are too busy, have too many responsibilities, and have too few resources to waste on evaluation projects that are not likely to have immediate and significant payoffs. Indeed, if the evaluation process does not have a high probability of having a direct impact on decision making and planning, a library or records center should allocate resources to other areas or activities rather than supporting action research and a superficial and nonproductive evaluation study. Thus, it is likely that organizational efforts will be designed in the context of action research.

PERFORMANCE MEASURES

Performance measures represent a broad managerial concept that encompasses both *input* (indicators of those resources essential to records services) and *output* (indicators of the services resulting from records activities) measures. Performance measures can assess the extent, effectiveness, and efficiency of various organizational operations, services, and programs. Perhaps with the exception of those measures that only indicate extensiveness or the amount of service provided, the purpose of performance measures is to direct the attention of records managers to the question, "How well is the organization doing what it claims to be doing?" (McClure, 1986), and to the identification of the services that the organization wants to provide and improve. Performance measures can assist records managers in determining the degree to which the organization accomplishes specific goals and objectives, in setting priorities for resource allocation, in justifying services, and in demonstrating organizational effectiveness to external agencies (Van House, Weil, and McClure, 1990, p. 9).

The primary utility of a performance measure is for "internal self-diagnosis of ... services and activities" (McClure, Zweizig, Van House, and Lynch, 1986, p. 51). Managers must select and use measures having value to their organization and the information needs of their clientele. They should not consider a particular score derived from calculating a measure as "inherently 'good' or 'bad'" (Ibid.). Rather, managers must place a score in the context of their expectations and their organization's goals and objectives.

When they compare the performance of one organization to that of another, they may be distorting the mission, goals, and objectives of each organization. They must also recognize the strengths and weaknesses of the sampling frame (sample selection and sample size), self-reporting questionnaires, referral records, and other methods of data collection. Furthermore, they might question the extent to which evaluators collected reliable and valid data.

Performance measures encourage records managers to re-examine their priorities and the extent of their commitment to the provision of services that meet the information needs of clientele. Without such priorities and commitments, clearly stated and examined on an ongoing basis, many organizations will not be future- (or change-) oriented: They will not improve the quality of their information services. Without available data, records managers will make decisions based on intuition or else they will avoid making decisions. Consequently, they may fail to recognize service areas that require immediate attention and improvement.

When records managers select possible performance measures for local use, they should consider the appropriateness, validity, reproducibility, comparability, and practicality of the measures (see Orr, 1973). Appropriateness refers to whether the measures accomplish what records managers want, and validity questions whether the measures mean what the managers think they do. Reproducibility refers to whether someone else would get the same answer from the same data, while comparability questions whether others using the same procedures and definitions would discover similar findings. Practicality questions whether the organization can afford the time, money, and effort to gather data for these measures.

Certain factors must be remembered when using performance measures:

o   Each measure only emphasizes one facet of records management. Measures are best used in conjunction with each other;

o   Conditions can be manipulated to improve the performance on a particular measure without always improving the quality of the service or operation, e.g., increase the *referral rate* simply by moving records to inactive storage too early;

o   There are no "right" or "wrong" scores on a performance measure; the scores are tied to specific goals and objectives, and provide "benchmarks" to assess the effectiveness of activities;

o   A primary use of a performance measure is to identify areas where change is desired, to determine if change has occurred, and to identify areas where additional research is required;

o   Performance measures should suggest not only what is happening in records management operations, but also the quality of what is occurring, "without going into the details of how those outputs were produced." Performance measures "do not in themselves diagnose the causes of inadequate performance" (Van House et al., 1990, p. 8);

o   Output measures reflect services delivered or uses made of the records collection. The archival function of the collection is not fully reflected. In some instances, this is a major consideration (Ibid.);

o   Measures reflect user success with the records program, not simply organizational performance. The final outcome is a function of the records center, the user, and the record center's success in anticipating user needs and assisting in the user's search (Ibid.); and

o   Measures reflect the interaction of users and organizational resources, constrained by the environment in which they operate. The meaning of a specific score on any measure depends on a broad range of factors including the organization's goals, the current circumstances of the organization and its environment, the users, the manner in which the measure was constructed, and how the data were collected (Ibid.).

Examples of Measures

Output Measures for Public Libraries (Van House, Lynch, McClure, Zweizig, and Rodger, 1987) identifies a number of performance measures and discusses their computation and data collection procedures. Some of the measures that records managers might find useful include:

o   *Document delivery* (percentage of requested materials available/received per a particular time frame). This measure examines the number of hours or days to get materials from storage or other locations from the shelves;

o   *Referral completion rate* (proportion of referral transactions successfully completed that same day, in the opinion of the staff); and

o   *Program participation per capita* (program participation per person in population served, or a target group).

Each measure, in fact, portrays extensiveness or the number served. However, measures, such as *document delivery*, might be modified to take into account different types of records and locations. The emerging picture has more value to managers in identifying strengths and weaknesses in collections, services, and facilities.

The measures also offer viewpoints from the perspective of the staff. They do not represent users, their information needs, information gathering behavior, and satisfaction. Such insights go beyond performance measures and indicate that evaluation is multifaceted. It can focus on whatever records managers decide are important at a particular time. Again, it merits mention that records managers and the organization decide what is important to know. This might be a performance measure or some other method of assessment.

DOING A RECORDS MANAGEMENT STUDY

Balough (1990) shows that records managers set up and conduct records management studies within the context of an organization's goals and objectives. Using three case studies, she outlines the steps involved in planning and conducting a study. Planning includes the use of probability sampling (e.g., random or cluster sampling) to investigate study objectives, such as "to determine the size of the records collection and its growth pattern" and "to determine who uses the records and what they use them for" (Ibid., pp. 4-5). For a more complete discussion of sampling, including determination of sample size, see Hernon (1991). This work also highlights *descriptive statistics* (Chapter 5), a set of procedures for organizing and describing observations, and *inferential statistics* (Chapters 7-9), a set of procedures for drawing inferences and generalizations from a sample.

Balough (1990) briefly discusses the use of selected descriptive and inferential statistics to guide data interpretation. Three short appendices present data collection techniques appropriate to the three case studies, mention when and how to use the techniques, and identify the advantages and disadvantages associated with the use of each technique.

Her paper explains the value of research and statistics to an organization "contemplating a large investment, especially when the operations of the organization will also change" (Ibid., p. 2). "Studies are also appropriate when:

o   Gathering data to defend a cutback or elimination of services;

o   Acquiring a new organizational unit that is to be merged with another;

o   Relocation or reorganization is planned;

o   Performance is poor;

o   All or part of a budget needs to be defended; and

o   A response is needed to a specific problem, such as a change in regulatory record keeping requirements, a disaster, or a lawsuit." (Ibid.)

She views research and statistics as proactive tools leading to or justifying change. Research and statistics may become subjective tools which support positions that records managers want or intend to take, or have already taken. Such uses would undoubtedly encourage upper management to question research results and the decisions that records managers make or plan to make. It is important that the organization have confidence in the objectivity of research findings and that its members do not disagree over the quality of a study. In sum, although Balough (Ibid.) offers some useful information and insights, records managers should be careful about the introduction of any study whose honesty and neutrality are called into question. The negative repercussions might outweigh the positive rewards of having conducted a study which contains sampling and uses statistics.

DECISION SUPPORT SYSTEMS

A decision support system (DSS) is "a category of information systems used in organizations to assist managers in semi-structured decision processes" as opposed to making more routine and programmed decisions (Akoka, 1981, p. 131). A DSS is designed to conform to the individual style and needs of a manager so as to assist him or her in problem solving (Bommer and Chorba, 1982, p. 13). With a DSS, managers have predetermined the topical areas of central interest to them, and they query the system within the narrowly prescribed areas.

Microcomputer-based DSS systems serve as a reminder that records management departments should not merely maintain "a file cabinet of data and information" (Fingerman, 1989, p. 199) in hard-disk memory. Records managers should collect data for a reason (or purpose) and put the datasets to use.

Primary reasons for developing an information base useful for organizational decision making are to (McClure, 1984, p. 7):

o   *Reduce ambiguity by providing an empirical basis for decision making*: There is a need to reduce uncertainty by validating assumptions without replacing creativity and by searching for opportunities;

o   *Provide intelligence about the environment*: Ignorance of the environment perpetuates ignorance of opportunities, isolates records management, reduces knowledge of competitors, and confuses the "proper" role of the records management department;

o   *Assess historical, current, and future states*: Various scenarios must be considered to deal with the future effectiveness of record keeping; past and present performance can assist in developing those scenarios; and o   *Evaluate process and monitor progress*: The accomplishment of objectives cannot be determined, remedial action taken, resource allocations changed to meet different contingencies, or planning for the development of new goals and objectives cannot occur without evaluation.

The creation of a decision support system may increase centralized control over whatever information is collected and used, the costs associated with information collection and analysis, the percentage of staff time spent in administrative activities, and the need for managers to become more sophisticated users and consumers of statistical analyses.

According to McClure, Hagerty-Roach, Ruth, and England (1989, p. 192), a management information system and a decision support system "should support a number of different types of decision making [activities], including:

o   Operational decisions (day-to-day decision making);

o   Strategic planning decisions (determining appropriate objectives and accomplishing those objectives);

o   "What if" questions (If we increase expenditures on a particular service, what would the impact be on another service?);

o   Exceptions (Use of inactive accounting records has increased drastically during the last month -- why?); and

o   Resource control (ensuring that resources are expended on appropriate activities or items)."

These authors also indicate that the system supplies decision makers with data elements that can be combined and presented "in a standardized and individualized format" (Ibid.).

Large organizations may operate their DSS on mainframe computers. In such instances, the DSS handles large and discrete datasets. The records managers can move among different datasets and make projections. Smaller organizations create decision support systems that operate on microcomputers. Such systems are more limited than those functioning on mainframe computers.

The current literature of library science and records management focuses on the microcomputer environment and identifies spreadsheet and database management software that records managers can use to create decision support systems. Lotus 1-2-3, dBase, Inmagic, Paradox, Info Mapper, and Reflex, among other software packages, have been used to develop and maintain DSS systems. Any package used must be capable of number crunching or the numerical manipulation of large datasets.

Some examples of the types of data that might form part of a records management operation in a library might serve as illustration. According to Clark (1989, p. 184), a decision support system might "include data on financial transactions, [human resources:] personnel and staffing, library resources, and library use." Financial transactions include expenditures, encumbrances, and budgets. Personnel and staffing data explain "who works where, when, how much, and doing what ..." (Ibid.). Resources include the number and types of interlibrary loan transactions, circulation, titles acquired and withdrawn from the collection, facilities, equipment, cataloging work flow analysis, and so forth. And, finally, library use encompasses both users and nonusers, and reports on their information-gathering behavior. Clearly, a decision support system quantifies and summarizes variables and library or information center activities. It does not deal with *qualitative* matters. Such a system, therefore, is not all-encompassing; rather, it provides a regular and reliable means of providing records managers with *some relevant* data useful in making decisions.

Practical DSS?

Most often records managers want summary statistics that they can use in making decisions and engaging in planning. They might receive frequency counts and percentages presented in the form of tables and graphs. As more records managers use word-processing and graphics software that simulates desktop publishing, the uses of descriptive statistics in annual and other reports will increase.

Readers wanting graphic displays of the types of data and statistics that decision support systems can provide should consult Clark (1988). He produces figures showing frequency distributions, bar charts, crosstabs, the calculation of measures of central tendency, and determination of Z-scores using Reflex.

For instance, records managers could produce bar charts that depict the amount of expenditures for preservation supplies, over time. They might also engage in "what if" scenarios and make forecasts using regression analysis. Clearly, a decision support system could include a variety of data elements, and records managers could use different methods of data analysis. Again, it is important to repeat that managers must decide what they want to know and be certain that they collect the proper data elements and use the appropriate measurement scale. Whatever data they collect must demonstrate reliability and validity, and capture the "essence" or certain characteristic that they need to know for making decisions.

Effective use of decision support systems requires some knowledge of the research process, reliability and validity indicators, and statistics. Readers needing some knowledge of these areas might consult Hernon (1991) or Hernon and McClure (1990).

OBSTACLES TO EVALUATION

Organizational and individual obstacles to evaluation may exist in any organization. Perhaps the most deadly and insipid obstacle is the belief that "everything is fine in my organization or department." In the vast majority of instances, managers simply do not *know* how well activities, programs, and services meet the information needs of clientele, if specific services and programs are effective and efficient, or if resources could be *better* spent on supporting different activities, programs, and services.

One set of obstacles related to the conduct of evaluation is that the managers/evaluators could apply evaluation inappropriately or merely serve organizational or administrative self-interests (Suchman, 1972, p. 81). For example, evaluation might be used to:

o   Justify a weak or bad program by deliberately selecting for evaluation only those aspects that "look good" on the surface. Appearance replaces reality;

o   Cover up program failure or errors by avoiding objective appraisal. Vindication replaces verification;

o   "Torpedo" or destroy a program regardless of its effectiveness. Politics replaces research;

o   Treat evaluation as a "gesture" of objectivity or professionalism. Ritual replaces research; and

o   Delay needed action by pretending to seek the "facts." Research replaces decision making.

Staff members could subvert the evaluation process by deciding to "fool" someone or a governing body. Evaluation under such circumstances is a waste of time, personnel, and other resources. Furthermore, it damages the credibility of the organization and the morale of the organizational staff.

In some instances, there is a real fear of evaluating record-keeping services and activities. Such fears can result from recognition that evaluation will, in fact, show that the records management program is ineffective or inefficient; that existing resources are poorly allocated to activities that do not fulfill clientele information needs; or that records managers may be identified as incompetent, inadequately trained, or lacking specific knowledge and skills necessary to perform their responsibilities effectively.

The attitude that evaluation is not really necessary, that records managers *really* know what is happening in their organization, and that records managers have a good "feel" for knowing when a service, program, or activity is effective or ineffective is an obstacle to the completion of a successful evaluation study. Faith in "common-sense" approaches to organizational effectiveness is simplistic and unrealistic in these times of complex organizations, innovative technologies, and limited available resources.

Another area of obstacles to successful evaluation comes from inadequate training of records managers to conduct evaluation research. In most schools of library and information science, for instance, many students simply do not take courses on research methods, planning and evaluation, and systems analysis, for various reasons. Once in the field, these people then find it difficult to conduct evaluations because they are unfamiliar with data collection and analysis techniques, evaluation research designs, and methods for the implementation of evaluation results.

Other obstacles to successful evaluation include the perceived lack of resources to support the evaluation process, and, upon completion of the study, an unwillingness on the part of decision makers to implement study recommendations. Implementation requires a knowledge of planning techniques and an ability to develop practical strategies and recommendations.

Records managers who want to establish a meaningful program of evaluation can do it. All that is necessary is: (1) a commitment to evaluation, (2) learning of basic planning and evaluation skills and competencies, and (3) recognition that evaluation must be accomplished if the organization is to meet its mission, goals, and objectives in an effective and efficient manner.

ACCOUNTABILITY

Information and data comprise tools useful for acquiring and retaining power. Information may enable an organization to advance its image and role as dynamic and meeting its mission, goals, and objectives. Even in dynamic organizations, decision makers might want to monitor carefully any evaluation study that was contemplated and determine the extent to which findings conform to that image and their expectations. Because of the inherent problems associated with attempting to *control* research and study findings, image protectors and inflators probably would prefer not to engage in evaluation. Rather, they would merely rely on perceptions and subjective impressions. Evaluators would probably be reluctant to conduct studies in a repressive or restrictive environment. Evaluation is most conducive in an open organization truly interested in planning and self-improvement.

Evaluation involves compromises and a process of negotiation. Evaluation is more interested in attacking practical problems than in developing new knowledge. However, the emergence of new knowledge may be a by-product. Clearly, there are many reasons for not conducting evaluation studies and for not engaging in planning. However, effective and efficient management requires both planning and evaluation.

The expectation that more organizations will justify their budgets and operating expenses and rely on "hard evidence," not mere testimonials, underscores the importance of planning and evaluation. The desire to hold organizations accountable indicates that external pressure to engage in planning and evaluation may be an important impetus for gathering information and data that address specific goals and objectives. Records managers can use such information and data to improve, and to justify, decision making.

THE CHALLENGE FOR THE PRESENT AND FUTURE

The challenge for records managers is to become more familiar with planning and evaluation, research methods, past, present, and future technologies, management and decision making, systems analysis, and modeling. They also require interpersonal skills and the ability to interact effectively with a host of individuals, ranging from the public to the bureaucrat and the politician. Indeed, managers must constantly learn and challenge themselves to be visionary. It may be that few individuals can absorb all these attributes and be dynamic leaders. Most people might prefer to focus on one or two areas and fall into their niche. Proper planning and management of evaluation and decision support systems discourage a narrow perspective. It is important that records managers have sufficient educational opportunities to assist them in becoming more well rounded and better able to cope with present and future challenges.

REFERENCES

Akoka, J. "A Framework for Decision Support Systems Evaluation," *Information and Management* 4 (1981): 133-141.

Balough, Ann. "Designing and Conducting a Records Management Study," *The Records & Retrieval Report* 6 (November 1990): 1-16.

_____. "Cost Benefit Analysis and Presentation," *The Records & Retrieval*

Report 7 (January 1991): 1-16.

Bommer, Michael R. W. and Ronald W. Chorba. *Decision Making for Library Management*. White Plains, NY: Knowledge Industry Publications, Inc., 1982.

Burk, Cornelius F., Jr. and Forest W. Horton, Jr. *InfoMap*. Englewood Cliffs, NJ: Prentice-Hall, 1988.

Clark, Philip M. "Statistical Description and Analysis with Reflex, the Database Manager." In *Microcomputer Software for Performing Statistical Analysis*, edited by Peter Hernon and John V. Richardson. Norwood, NJ: Ablex, 1988, pp. 127-146.

_____. "Developing a Decision Support System: The Software and Hardware Tools," *Library Administration & Management* 3 (Fall 1989): 184-191.

Fingerman, Joel. "Painting the Picture -- Personal Computers and Graphical Presentation of Statistics," *Library Administration & Management* 3 (Fall 1989): 199-204.

Hernon, Peter. *Statistics: A Component of the Research Process*. Norwood, NJ: Ablex, 1991.

_____ and Charles R. McClure. *Evaluation and Library Decision Making*. Norwood, NJ: Ablex, 1990.

Johnson, Edward R. "A Realistic Objectives Management Program." In *Austerity Management in Academic Libraries*, edited by John F. Harvey and Peter Spyers-Duran. Metuchen, NJ: Scarecrow Press, 1984, pp. 161-175.

McClure, Charles R. "Management Information for Library Decision Making." In *Advances in Librarianship*, volume 13, edited by Wesley Simonton. New York: Academic Press, 1984, pp. 1-47.

_____. "A View from the Trenches: Costing and Performance Measures for Academic Library Public Services," *College & Research Libraries* 47 (July 1986): 323-336.

_____, Liz Hagerty-Roach, Lindsay Ruth, and Pat England. "Design of a Public Library Management Information System: A Status Report," *Library Administration & Management* 3 (Fall 1989): 192-198.

_____, Amy Owen, Douglas L. Zweizig, Mary Jo Lynch, and Nancy A. Van House. *A Planning and Role Setting for Public Libraries: A Manual of Options and Procedures*. Chicago, IL: American Library Association, 1987.

_____, Douglas L. Zweizig, Nancy A. Van House, and Mary Jo Lynch. "Output Measures: Myths, Realities and Prospects," *Public Libraries* 25 (Summer 1986): 49-52.

Orr, R. H. "Measuring the Goodness of Library Services: A General Framework for Considering Quantitative Measures," *Journal of Documentation* 29 (September 1973): 315-332.

Pings, Vern M. "Use or Value of Goals and Objectives Statements," *Journal of Library Administration* 1 (Fall 1980): 55-62.
Rossi, Peter H. and Howard E. Freeman. *Evaluation: A Systematic Approach.* Newbury Park, CA: Sage, 1989.
Suchman, Edward A. "Action for What? A Critique of Evaluation Research," in *Evaluating Action Programs*, edited by Carol H. Weiss. Boston, MA: Allyn and Bacon, 1972, pp. 52-84.
Swisher, Robert and Charles R. McClure. *Research for Decision Making: Methods for Librarians.* Chicago, IL: American Library Association., 1984.
Van House, Nancy A., Beth Weil, and Charles R. McClure. *Measuring Academic Library Performance: A Practical Approach.* Prepared for the Association of College and Research Libraries, Committee on Performance Measures, Ad Hoc. Chicago, IL: American Library Association, 1990.
_____, Mary Jo Lynch, Charles R. McClure, Douglas L. Zweizig, and Eleanor Jo Rodger. *Output Measures for Public Libraries: A Manual of Standardized Procedures.* Chicago, IL: American Library Association, 1987.

READINGS

Baker, Sharon and F. W. Lancaster. *The Measurement and Evaluation of Library Services.* 2d ed. Arlington, VA: Information Resources Press, 1991.
Burke, Cornelius F., Jr. and Forest W. Horton, Jr. *InfoMap: A Complete Guide to Discovering Corporate Information Resources.* Englewood Cliffs, NJ: Prentice Hall, 1988.
Hernon, Peter and Charles R. McClure. *Evaluation and Library Decision Making.* Norwood, NJ: Ablex, 1990.
Place, Irene and David J. Hyslop. *Records Management: Controlling Business Information.* Reston, VA: Reston Pub. Co., 1982.
Ricks, B. R. and K. F. Gow. *Information Resource Management.* Cincinnati, OH: South-Western Pub., 1987.
Robbins, Jane and Douglas Zweizig. *Are We There Yet? Evaluating Library Collections, Reference Services, Programs, and Personnel.* Madison, WI: University of Wisconsin, School of Library and Information Studies, 1988.
Rossi, Peter H. and Howard E. Freeman. *Evaluation: A Systematic Approach.* Newbury Park, CA: Sage, 1989.
Wallace, Patricia E., Dexter R. Schubert, J. A. Lee, and U. S. Thomas. *Records Management.* New York: Wiley, 1987.

DISCUSSION POINTS

1. Locate an evaluation study in the published literature on records management and critique it as a research investigation and analysis having utility for decision making.

2. Develop a prototype DSS for records management. What fields would you include, and what software would you use? Discuss.

3. Review the goals and objectives of a records management unit of some organization. Test a performance measure following the procedures outlined in Van House et al. (1987). How useful is that measure? Does the measure require modification? Discuss.

4. How similar and dissimilar are evaluation and systems analysis?

Chapter Twelve

Information Resources Management

Information resources management, which is commonly known as IRM, is an integrated, coordinated approach to managing the *life cycle* of information produced within an organization or agency. By extension, IRM includes obtaining, retaining, and providing access to those resources needed by the staff to meet the mission, goals, and objectives of the organization or agency. IRM officers offer guidance in (and direction to) the management of those resources produced and needed by the organization or agency. IRM is clearly related to records management, but might be regarded as a broader concept.

The purpose of this chapter is to provide an overview of information resources management, as well as to suggest its relationship to records management. Readers seeking additional information on IRM might consult sources, such as those listed in Figure 12-1, as well as *Public Administration Review*, and indexes, such as *Social Sciences Citation Index, Library Literature, Business Periodicals Index, ABI/Inform, Trade & Industry Index,* and *Information Science Abstracts*.

INFORMATION LIFE CYCLE

Figure 12-2 depicts the information life cycle from the collection or creation of information, be it in automated or nonautomated form, to the retirement of an information resource. Not all information created, collected, and produced becomes available to everyone within and outside of the organization or agency. Governments, industrial firms, and corporations, for example, reserve some internally produced information (e.g., proprietary information) for the exclusive use of a few. The United States government, as an example, classifies and limits access to certain scientific, technical, military, business, and other types of information. It also restricts the distribution and export of some information.[1]

Organizations and agencies often treat *distribution* as a passive approach -- individuals must know that an information resource is available and they can request a copy. In contrast, *dissemination* is a more proactive concept, one in which the organization or agency markets its resources, or shares copies of them with a clearinghouse (e.g., the National Technical

---

[1] See Hernon (1989a,b), Relyea (1989), and Finding Common Ground (1991).

Figure 12-1. Selected Readings on Information Resources Management.

Caudle, S. L. "Federal Information Resources Management after the Paperwork Reduction Act," *Public Administration Review* 48 (1988): 790-799.

_____ and D. A. Marchand. *Managing Information Resources: New Directions in State Government*. Syracuse, NY: Syracuse University, School of Information Studies, 1989.

Guimaraes, T. "Information Resources Management: Improving the Focus," *Information Resources Management Journal* 1 (1988): 10- 21.

Horton, F.W.,G Jr. *Information Resources Management*. Englewood Cliffs, NJ: Prentice-Hall, 1985.

The IRM Organization: Concepts and Considerations. Prepared by Federal IRM Planning Support Center. Falls Church, VA: Office of Software Development and Information Technology, 1989.

Levitan, K. B. and J. Dinneen. "Integrative Aspects of Federal IRM," *Information Management Review* 1 (1986): 61-67.

Lytle, R. H. "Information Resource Management: A Five-Year Perspective," *Information Management Review* 3 (1988): 9-16.

Marchand, D. A. and J. C. Kresslein. "Information Resources Management and the Public Administrator." In *Handbook of Information Resource Management*, edited by J. Rabin and E. M. Jackowski. New York: Dekker, 1988, pp. 395-455.

Ricks, B. R. and K. F. Gow. *Information Resource Management*. Cincinnati, OH: South-Western Pub., 1987.

Robek, M. F., G. F. Brown, and W. O. Maedke. *Information and Records Management*. Encino, CA: Glencoe, 1987.

Figure 12-2. The Information Life Cycle

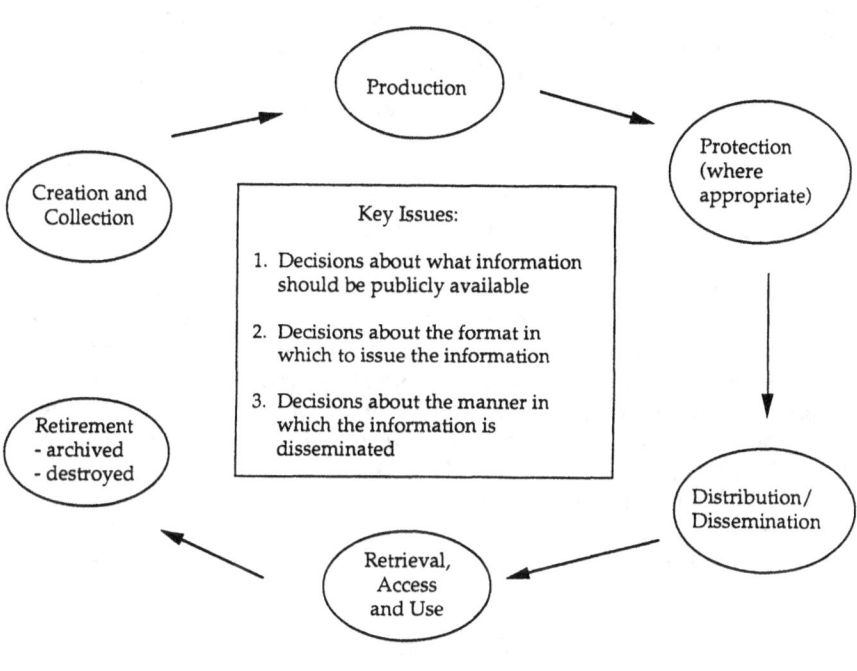

Information Service or the Educational Resources Information Center), or the private or nonprofit sector.

Organizations and agencies often fail to consider retrieval, access, and use as part of the life cycle. They assume that their resources have little value, use, or interest to others. Thompson (1991), an Assistant Comptroller General of the U.S. General Accounting Office, disagrees with such assumptions. He calls for those agencies and organizations directly serving the public to define the level of service [quality] they expect to provide. He asserts that "service quality cannot be defined internally but must be defined as meeting the public's expectations," thereby ensuring that the public gets its "money's worth from the federal government" (Ibid., unpaged). The challenge, he notes, "is to meet the rising demands for public services in an environment of continual revenue shortages" (Ibid., p. 3). To achieve higher service quality and meet rising expectations, agencies and organizations must understand and respond to the information needs of those served.

Few agencies and organizations, however, have determined the information needs of their clientele, anticipated future ones, and shaped part of the information life cycle to accommodate the needs and preferences of their clientele. Instead, the constraints and preferences of the organization or agency determine which resources are produced and made publicly available, and in what format.

To librarians and some other professional groups, retrieval, access, and use comprise the most critical part of the life cycle. To others (and contrary to the views of Thompson), these might be viewed as secondary issues, perhaps within a cost-benefit or cost-effectiveness framework. Government information policies tend to underscore this dichotomy. United States national policies, guidelines, and laws often concentrate on creation, production, and protection. However, librarians and other information professionals trying to impact policy formulation typically focus on retrieval, access, and use. As a result, they may fail to influence other components of the information life cycle (see *Federal Information in the Electronic Age*, 1990). However, it appears that the U.S. Office of Management and Budget (OMB) is beginning to side with the professional groups and expect agencies to become more involved with information dissemination. As discussed later in the chapter, OMB's view of dissemination, however, has not yet been articulated.

INFORMATION RESOURCES MANAGEMENT

What Is It?

Information resources management views information as a significant resource that, like other resources, must be used and managed effectively and efficiently, if the organization or agency is to accomplish its mission, goals, and objectives. IRM, therefore, is "not an end in and of itself" (Sprehe, 1987, p. 39).

IRM, as a philosophy of information management, concerns itself with managing the life cycle of information produced by the organization or agency, as well as the collection and use of information useful to the organization or agency in meeting its mission, goals, and objectives. IRM also considers the management of related resources, "including personnel, equipment, funds, and technologies of data processing, telecommunications, office systems and information management" (General Services Administration, 1985, p. 3). IRM, therefore, is more than the management of information-handling technologies, databases, and electronic information. It requires knowledge of those served by the organization or agency, and the information needs, information-gathering behavior, and information use patterns of these individuals. Information-handling technologies must accommodate the needs, preferences, and information-gathering behavior of these individuals, not vice-versa.

The two key components of information resources management are *information resources* and *management.* Information resources encompass print and nonprint resources that require *management* throughout their life cycle; these include records themselves. IRM, in its broadest sense, is the management of agency or organizational information and records. Management includes the application of principles relating to strategic planning and management, evaluation, information policy, systems analysis and design, records management, information networking, and knowledge engineering. As already noted, technologies have created additional opportunities to manage information. As a result, it is now more obvious to many people that information resources deserve to be (and can be) managed and that they command the attention of senior management.

Succinctly stated, information resources management is a response to a growing demand for organizations to practice stategic planning. As such, it "seeks to harness information for the benefit of the organization as a whole by exploiting, developing, and optimizing information resources" (Burk and Horton, 1988, p. 5). IRM includes technologies, where appropriate, and the following components:

o Information systems;
o Information resources;
o Information policy;
o Information users; and
o Information services.

Information management includes planning, evaluation, and systems analysis to ensure that any system is more than the mere sum of its parts. As such, information management is part of each of the five components as well as a thread linking each component to the mission of the organization or agency.

With advances in the development and use of expert systems, artificial intelligence, and decision support systems, information resources management is becoming more sophisticated and technologically based. The integration of information technologies with the management of information processes suggests a number of applications for decision making and more effective management of organizational operations, services, and programs (Marchand, 1985). Nonetheless, an organization or agency may not have access to all of its information in automated form. This other information may be important and require proper management as well.

Principles of IRM

Information resources management is based on five principles:

o   Information is a vital asset of the organization (Synnott, 1987) and is on par with other resources, e.g., personnel or capital (Burk and Horton, 1988);

o   Information is a public good and must be treated accordingly;

o   Information, at the same time, is an economic resource, with value and a cost of production. Information is not a free good;

o   Information has a clearly identifiable life cycle; and

o   Information should be managed in a coordinated and systematic manner based on established and widely accepted management principles and practices.

In the case of information resources management as practiced by the U.S. national government, accountability and management of information resources do not occur in a centralized environment.

Information resources management practiced by the public sector necessitates the consideration of issues such as confidentiality, privacy, and preservation of records documenting policy making and decision making. These issues must address the public's right to know. A proper balance between withholding and releasing information in an electronic and information age is difficult to achieve and maintain. Too often, the scales have tipped towards withholding information. With the end of the Cold War and the collapse of communism in the Soviet Union and eastern Europe, the U.S. government is beginning to relax certain restrictive policies and to disclose more information. Yet, it still withholds information dating back to 1917.

Coverage of IRM in Federal Policy Instruments

The Commission on Federal Paperwork (1977b, p. 56), formed to investigate information policy issues, concluded:

> The absence of a body of doctrine covering the effective and efficient management of information resources has fostered overlap

and duplication in both the administrative controls over, and organizational structures which manage, information gathering, processing, and dissemination.

Furthermore, IRM, the report maintained, could help to solve the growing paperwork problems by managing government information in the most cost-effective manner.

The Paperwork Reduction Act (PRA) of 1980 (P.L. 96-511) incorporated the recommendations of the Commission, recognized information as a valuable and manageable resource, and centralized the information policy function into the new Office of Information and Regulatory Affairs (OIRA) within OMB. Section 3505 of the Act required the Director of the new office to:

> develop and implement Federal information policies, principles, standards, and guidelines and ... provide direction and oversee the review and approval of information collection requests, the reduction of the paperwork burden, Federal statistical activities, *records management activities*, privacy of records, interagency sharing of information, and acquisition and use of automatic data processing, telecommunications, and other technology for managing information resources. (italics added)

Moreover, the Director would develop and implement "uniform and consistent information resources management policies and [oversee] the development of information management principles, standards, and guidelines and ... [promote] their use." The Director was also assigned planning, evaluation, and research responsibilities related to information resources management.

In December 1985, OMB published Circular No. A-130, "The Management of Federal Information Resources" (Office of Management and Budget, 1985). That circular, among its many provisions, prescribed a general policy framework for the management of federal information resources and thereby discharged one of OMB's functions under the 1980 Act. The Reagan administration used the circular to press the privatization of government information services, programs, and resources. The Bush administration has expressed some reservations about the interpretation of the circular (e.g., the imbalance between government information as an economic resource and a public good) and called for its replacement.

On April 29, 1992, OMB released, for public comment, a draft of the replacement circular (see 57 *Federal Register* 18296). At some unspecified date (perhaps toward the end of 1992), OMB will produce the actual circular. Until then, the orginally produced circular, with a few modifications in 1987 and 1989 (see 57 *Federal Register* 18296) remains in effect and directs agency practices regarding the availability and dissemination of government information.

The draft circular covers information dissemination and defines information resoruces management (IRM) and records management. Both share four common activities: planning, organizing, directing, and training. IRM also encompasses budgeting and managerial control over government information, while records management involves controlling, promoting, and other administrative activites. IRM, furthermore, includes strategic planning, goal setting, and the accomplishment of measurable objectives.

The 1985 circular defines IRM as "the planning, budget, organizing, directing, training, and control associated with government information. The term encompasses both information itself and the related resources, such as personnel, equipment, funds, and technology" (see point 6i). According to Sprehe (1987, p. 34),

> The first sentence in the definition is a paraphrase of the definition found in S. 2433. The second sentence embodies OMB"s view ... that 'information resources management' is a term susceptible to two meanings, and that in fact both meanings are valid and necessary to the concept of information resources management. The twofold meaning of information resources management is critical, because it is also the organizational principle for the Circular's policy section: policies are divided into those dealing with the management of information and those dealing with the management of information systems and technology.

He continues that (Ibid.):

> The Circular's emphasis on the application of contemporary information technology to information resources management responds not only to the perceived potential of new technology for efficiencies in agency program management and delivery but also to the growing realization that many voluminous federal information collections are excellent candidates for automation.

The success of federal IRM is limited to the management and procurement of information technology. IRM has been less successful in designing information products, services, and systems that meet the information needs and preferences of users, and in implementing federal information policies.

The 1986 legislation reauthorizing the Paperwork Reduction Act (P.L. 99-591) defined IRM "in response to concern about how well the concept was understood and implemented" (Congress. Senate Committee on Governmental Affairs, 1990, p. 41). However, there remained "a lack of commitment and full understanding of the term and the potential benefits which can be derived from its wider use in government" (Ibid., p. 28).

With the expiration of the reauthorized Paperwork Reduction Act on September 30, 1989, some members of Congress and others considered it an excellent opportunity to examine the Act in greater detail and OMB's powers under it, and to improve the management of federal information resources. They noted that OMB exceeded its paperwork reduction mandate, interfered with substantive agency decision making on policies and programs, provided little direction required for the management of federal information resources, and did not concern itself with records management.

Congress began reconsideration of the Act but continued to let OMB fund OIRA from its general appropriations until reauthorization legislation could be implemented. The attempt to enact new legislation was slow, difficult, and eventually unsuccessful. *Federal Information in the Electronic Age* (1990) summarizes some of the issues preventing enactment of new legislation. Suffice to say, policy differences emerged within Congress and between Congress and the White House.

Three bills were at the center of discussion and debate within the executive and legislative branches of government. The House of Representatives considered the "Information Policy Act of 1989" (H.R. 2381) and the "Paperwork Reduction and Federal Information Resources Management Act of 1989" (HR. 3695). These bills addressed some issues relating to IRM but failed to consider that many federal IRM personnel do not understand the concept of IRM, do not know how to implement these concepts within their agency, are unaware of the larger federal information policy system, and define IRM solely in terms of technology management and procurement.

The Senate bill (S. 1742), the "Federal Information Resources Management Act," offered a much more expansive view of IRM: "Federal information resources management as a comprehensive and integrated process for improving the efficiency and effectiveness of government information activities" (Congress. Senate. Committee on Governmental Affairs, 1990, pp. 40-41). According to the bill, IRM is (Ibid.):

> a complex term which encompasses the process of defining information needs to accomplish agency mission[s]; of managing information resources to efficiently, economically and equitably meet defined information needs; and integrating the skills of individuals in various information functions. Additionally, the process extends through all stages of information collection, use and disposition and includes the management activities of planning,

budgeting, organizing, firecting [sic, directing], controlling and evaluating the use of information.

Title I, "Information Resources Management of Federal Departments and Agencies," seeks to:

o Ensure the greatest possible public benefit from information collected, maintained, used, disseminated, and retained by the federal government;

o Minimize the federal paperwork burden;

o Emphasize federal information resources management as a comprehensive and integrated process for improving the efficiency and effectiveness of government information activities;

o Improve the quality and use of federal information to strengthen decision making, accountability, and efficiency in government and society;

o Ensure automatic data processing, telecommunications, and other information technologies are acquired and used to achieve all purposes of federal information policy under chapter 35 of title 44, *United States Code*;

o Coordinate, integrate, and to the extent practicable and appropriate, make uniform federal information policies and practices;

o Improve the accountability of the Office of Management and Budget and all federal agencies to Congress and the public for the effective implementation of this chapter; and

o Ensure that the collection maintenance, use, dissemination, and retention of information by the federal government is consistent with applicable laws.

The bill required the appointment of career Chief Information Resources Managers, who are (Ibid., p. 42):

> well qualified through experience or training to carry out all the programs and activities authorized by this law. Each agency is required to establish an agency-wide IRM program; to provide formal training on IRM concepts and educate program officials about IRM as a managerial discipline. Agency responsibilities for

identifying information needs for developing information systems, for maintaining inventories of information resources, for issuing IRM plans, and for establishing a system for dissemination of information, regardless of format are spelled out.

The Senate bill encouraged the conduct of policy research on IRM and the information needs of agency staff and the constituency of an agency. The bill might be regarded as an attempt to reverse a trend in which the federal government places too much emphasis on the acquisition and production of information and accords significantly less attention to the management, organization, dissemination, and use of information. Reversal of the trend requires the enactment of mechanisms to deal with people "drowning in data," the task of making data usable, and the treatment of data centers as "data cemeteries" ("Early Data: Losing Our Memory," 1989).

The bill also addressed a concern of some officials within the General Accounting Office. Socolar (1990, p. 2), a senior official of that agency, noted that "federal agencies are facing a crisis in managing their information resources." According to him, the government spends about $20 billion each year on information technology. Yet, the General Accounting Office "could not identify a single large systems development project that met each of three important criteria -- satisfying user needs, coming in on time, and reasonably meeting original cost estimates" (Ibid.).

In summary, a significant contribution of the Senate bill was its recognition of the importance of knowing the information needs, information preferences, and information-gathering behavior of agency staff and constituent groups. The conduct of policy research and evaluation studies is important if the government is to manage information resources properly -- effectively and efficiently.

Due to policy differences between the two branches of government, these bills failed to become law. In 1991, two bills (S. 1044 and S. 1139), both of which lack the strong IRM framework of the previously mentioned legislation, were introduced into the Senate. One bill (S. 1044) covers information dissemination in broad terms, while the other bill (S. 1139) focuses on reducing the paperwork burden on citizens, business, and industry. The fate of both bills is uncertain; they might be altered, they might perish like the previous legislation, or the information dissemination provisions (weak as they are) might be extracted and treated as separate legislation. Suffice to say, if neither bill materializes as law, A-130's replacement, may comprise the only general information policy framework having government-wide applications and implications.

AN INVENTORY/LOCATOR SYSTEM

An inventory/locator system enables organizations or a government to monitor and manage the information life cycle. The system might also alert individuals external to organizations or a government about the information resources produced and held internally. A benefit of an inventory/locator system within government is that it could track information resources produced by various agencies or branches of government. Such a system might contain information resources that are publicly available and whose use is not restricted by the Privacy Act (5 U.S.C. 552a), the Freedom of Information Act (5 U.S.C. 552), and other statutes.

A number of agencies with the U.S. national government operate individual information inventory and locator systems. Authors, such as McClure, Bishop, Doty, and Bergeron (1990, 1991), maintain that these systems provide piecemeal access to information resources produced and retained by government agencies. Cabell (1987, p. 65) regards the locator system within OMB as "impotent" and "not cost effective," while Bass and Plocher (1991, p. 14) state that the same system "is a Federal information locator system in name only."

McClure et al. (1991) argue for a new government-wide system to compensate for the decentralized approach to federal information resources management and the inability of government to coordinate the various systems and the finding aids they produce. A government-wide system, they maintain, should contain complete citations, with abstracts, to the entire array of publicly available information resources produced by each agency, regardless of format. Moreover, the system could serve as both an inventory mechanism and a locator system. As such, it has utility for information resources management and the dissemination of agency information resources to the public, or the clientele served by that agency.

Background

The Commission on Federal Paperwork (1977a, p. 3) observed that "the Federal Government does not know what information it collects, with what frequency, from whom, and for what uses." To remedy this, the Commission advocated the creation of a federal information locator system, which would be "the equivalent of the library card file for information collected and stored by the federal government" (Cabell, 1987, p. 67). More specifically, the system was supposed to contain a dictionary of government information resources identifying agency data holdings, public reporting requirements, etc.; a dictionary of data elements or a compendium of standard terms and definitions in information and reporting systems; and a national information referral system linking the public to the locator system.

Information Resources Management 209

In brief, the Commission favored a management system that would (Bass and Plocher, 1991, p. 15):

o   Assist agencies in planning, coordinating, and evaluating their information requirements;

o   Maximize the use of data and information already available;

o   Assist agencies in fulfilling their responsibilities under the Freedom of Information Act and the Privacy Act;

o   Help detect, identify, and root out generic, similar, and identical data elements duplication;

o   Serve as a research and analytical instrument; and

o   Serve as an authoritative, centralized reference and finding aid.

Through the Paperwork Reduction Act of 1980, Congress mandated the development of a government-wide FILS to "assist agencies and the public in locating existing government information derived from information collection requests" (Ibid., p. 18). The printed or microfiche version of the resulting Federal Information Locator System is available, in part, from NTIS and the Government Printing Office's depository library program. In addition, the public can gain access to the system through OMB's Office of Information and Regulatory Affairs.

As defined in 44 *United States Code* 3507-3511, the intent of FILS was to:

o   Be an authoritative register of all information collection requests;

o   Assist agencies and the public in locating government information derived from the information collection requests; and

o   Eliminate duplication in information collection activities.

The system, in fact, contains only paperwork cleared by OMB. According to Bass and Plocher (1991, p. 19),

> It does not include other agency information, such as internal documents, inter-agency reporting information, public dissemination products, and archived information. Moreover, because the system is not fully searchable and because the data

elements are not catalogued, it cannot begin to locate potentially duplicative information collection. Finally, the system cannot be accessed directly by other agencies or the public.

(For a discussion of OMB and its measurement of the paperwork burden, see Rubinstein, 1990.)

In summary, FILS has not been that successful. First, the amount of duplication and overlap in existing government information collection activities is minimal. Second, compliance with FILS may actually result in additional information collection activities because agencies must determine if a similar information request is already on file. If a request is on file, an agency would have to make its request sufficiently different. Third, FILS entries are inadequately indexed and abstracted. Fourth, FILS does not quantify the reduction in paperwork as specified in the Paperwork Reduction Act (Cabell, 1987). And, finally, FILS is more a listing of agency information collection requests than a locator system or a means of gaining access to government information resources.

Development of a Government-Wide Information Inventory/Locator System

Correcting the inadequacies of FILS is not enough, so claim McClure et al. (1991). The concept of FILS is firmly entrenched and limited in its application. They recommend its replacement with a government-wide inventory and locator system, which is not a mere listing of agency information collection requests. Bass and Plocher (1991, p. 20), on the other hand, disagree and maintain that FILS should not automatically be rejected or replaced. As they explain, the original version of the system could still guide planning for a locator system. Moreover (Ibid., p. 20),

> the problems of FILS were in its implementation, not its concept or vision. The history of FILS is replete with consistent themes of what FILS could and should be, and that agencies would like FILS to serve as a tool to help them better manage information resources.... [McClure et al.] should not reject aspects of FILS simply because of past problems of implementation.... [They] should also not ignore the strikingly similar findings and recommendations regarding FILS made over more than a decade [ago] and instead try to reinvent the wheel.

Despite the differences between Bass and Plocher, and McClure et al., a government-wide inventory/locator system requires (McClure et al., 1990, 1991):

- Government recognition of its responsibility for development of the system;

- Having OMB set policy guidelines but not operate the system;

- Recognizing, understanding, and addressing the information needs of agency clientele;

- Design and operation of the system based on input from various stakeholders;

- Having the agencies themselves function as the locus of responsibility and control;

- Providing agencies with incentives and rewards for participating in the government-wide system;

- Integration of the system into agency IRM functions;

- Obtaining congressional support for system development and maintenance;

- Keeping the system simple and develop it incrementally; and

- Generating multiple products in different formats from the system.

According to Bass and Plocher (1991, p. 22), "what is needed now is a clear reaffirmation of FILS' purposes and a definition of its mission in such concrete terms as to pragmatically guide the design and operation of the system."

The system must meet the information resource management needs of agencies as well as those of the executive and legislative branches of government concerning "public information collection requests and requirements, regulatory requirements, inter- and intra-agency reporting requirements, dissemination products and services, archived materials, and other information holdings" (Ibid.). It is important that IRM officials monitor the array of information resources produced and maintained by an agency. At the same time, the system must serve the needs of various groups, for instance, state and local governments, businesses, public interest groups, and libraries. As Bass and Plocher (Ibid., p. 23) caution,

> There is certainly a danger ... [however, in the system] trying to be all things to all people -- ending up too diffuse and unworkable.

That is precisely why a vision and plan need to be developed. Nonetheless, that vision can and should be very broad.

Potential Approaches

McClure et al. (1991) identify approaches for a governmentwide system. They mention, for instance, the *Information Resources Directory* (Environmental Protection Agency, 1989); *The Federal Information Sources and Systems* (General Accounting Office, 1984); *InfoFind*, an online register of information sources produced by New Jersey (see Stone, 1988); and *InfoMapper*, a software program based on dBase IV useful in identifying information resources.[2]

The government might produce a machine-readable database that is a comprehensive inventory of information holdings produced and maintained by each agency. Each agency could submit a list of available finding tools, together with abstracts of the tools, to a central source, which would compile all submissions into one database and serve as a gateway to the information resources of the federal government. The gateway enables the public to identify and access needed government information forms and resources.

McClure et al. (1991) and Bass and Plocher (1991) detail their visions of how the government might develop the system. McClure et al. emphasize information resources dissemination, but do consider dissemination as an integral part of information resources management. Bass and Plocher (1991), however, disagree with this distinction and the emphasis placed on dissemination.

McClure et al. (1991) note that the development of a government-wide system could be one of the most significant government information policy initiatives of the decade, and could improve public access to government information resources. They also remind us that the successful design of such a system requires five ingredients: leadership, resources, commitment, planning, and involvement from a wide range of stakeholders. At the national level, involvement of the Office of Management and Budget, General Services Administration, and the National Archives and Records Administration is essential to the realization of an effective government-wide information inventory/locator system. At the state and local levels, agencies performing similar roles must be an active participant in planning and policy formulation. Policy execution should be left to the individual agencies.

---

[2] InfoMapper is available from Information Management Press, P.O. Box 19166, Washington, D.C. 20036.

RECORDS MANAGEMENT: A PART OF IRM

Within the United States government, records management dates back to 1889 and the General Records Disposal Act, which improved "the efficiency of records disposition" (Caudle and Marchand, 1989, p. 17). Congress was attentive to considerations of federal records management when it adopted the Budget and Accounting Act of 1921 (amended most recently in 1982, P.L. 97-258, 96 Stat. 877). This 1921 statute created the Bureau of the Budget (later renamed OMB) and authorized internal agency controls over the quantity of federal records produced. A body of records management principles and practices emerged in the 1940s (Ibid., p. 18), in part attributable to the Federal Reports Act of 1942 (56 Stat. 1078). IRM, on the other hand, is a more recent concept, one developed in the 1970s.

As Caudle and Marchand (Ibid., p. 16) note, a program of information resources management

> should include information management policies, information resources plans, information cost accounting, information auditing and evaluation, and systems such as those to locate information, handle data and database administration, and *ensure there is records management* (italics added).

The chief information resources manager has records management responsibilities, such as those covered in Figure 12-3. More importantly, that person views records management within a broader context -- application of organizational planning and management to the life cycle of information produced internally, and the development of resource collections to meet the information needs of the staff. The manager (Ibid., p. 17)

> must understand information resource functional activities such as paperwork management, records management programs, data processing, telecommunications, and office automation, and have knowledge of information handling technologies and trends in product and service development as well.

Moreover, that person must also interact with other officers throughout the organization and gain a thorough knowledge of the life cycle for information produced internally (Diebold, 1985). Clearly, the mere equation of information resources management with information technology management limits the vision and utility of IRM as a management strategy for dealing with the information life cycle.

Figure 12-3. Records Management as Part of IRM.*

Records management includes:

o   Correspondence management: The implementation of agency standards for the creation, tracking, and control of correspondence.

o   Mail management: The implementation of standards and procedures for the receipt, delivery, collection, and dispatch of mail.

o   Micrographics management: The management of the technology and procedures for document and information microfilming, associated microform storage, and retrieval systems, and optical disk storage and retrieval systems.

o   Printing and publications management: The overall management and control of the policies, procedures, and activities involved in printing and publishing an agency's documents. It can include everything from desktop publishing to in-house printing operations, and printing/publication services from outside sources.

o   Directives management: The management of the creation, classification, issuance, and maintenance of written management policy and operating procedures.

o   Forms management: The management of the creation, revision, reproduction, storage, and distribution of forms, including the elimination of nonessential and duplicative forms.

o   Reports management: The control of the agency's requests for information from the public, other government agencies and internal sources, ensuring that report formats, content, timing, and distribution fulfill the intended purpose.

o   Privacy Act management: The establishment of safeguards to protect agency-held information concerning individuals from unauthorized access, in accordance with the Privacy Act of 1974.

o   Copy management: The development of agency policy and standards for copying services and the acquisition, use, and inventorying of copying equipment.

o   Files management: The maintenance of files in an appropriate manner and facility, including electronic and manual files.

o   Records disposition management: The development of agency records control schedules, the transfer of records to the National Archives and Records Administration, and appropriate disposal of records.

o   Vital records program management: The management of an agency's emergency operating records and rights and interest records.

o   Audiovisual and cartographic records management: The management of the agency's film, video- and audiotape, photographic, and cartographic records.

o   Electronic records management: The management of records stored in a form that can be processed only by computer. It includes magnetic tape, optical and digital disks, and diskettes.

The IRM Organization (1989), pp. 15-16.

BARRIERS TO OVERCOME

Caudle and Marchand (1989, p. 22) note "difficulties in IRM adoption:"

> As with the development of any new management function, IRM is not without its problems. Some impediments might include difficulties in visualizing information as a corporate resource, problems in measuring the costs and value of information resources, lack of involvement in strategic planning, resistance in bringing all information resources together under one management structure or new roles for various information professionals, limitations in the amount of resources that can be devoted to IRM, problems in finding the skilled personnel to staff IRM efforts, difficulty in getting control, coordination, and commitment from people who come from all parts of the organization, and representing different perspectives, lack of a "natural" constituency for IRM, the length of time change takes, and just plain inertia.

Furthermore, when IRM managers adopt an approach calling for the centralization of power and decision making, their strategies may not be effective. It is difficult to apply "top-down" approaches to the management of *all* information produced internally and to overcome bureaucratic resistance and organizational politics.

Agencies and organizations may (*The IRM Organization*, 1989, p. 3):

> lack an accurate picture of their total information resources and the relationship of those resources to agency missions. In this regard, the following questions have continued to surface with alarming frequency: How much money are we spending on information-related activities? Are all of our systems legally mandated? How can we control the information resources budget? What is the quality of our information? Are all of our information needs being met? And most importantly, are our information-related activities supporting the agency's [and organization's] mission?

A barrier, therefore, is that these questions have not been answered or perhaps even raised. The agency or organization may not fully value IRM, have continuity in the staffing and budget of the IRM unit, and have introduced the "incentives to motivate program managers to implement sound information management practices" (Ibid., p. 40). Staff training will become more of an issue and concern as agencies and organizations develop their IRM practices. Training is crucial because the staff serve as planners, change agents, and managers who look to the agency's or organization's past, present, and future.

DOING IRM AS A RECORDS MANAGER

Every unit within an organization produces, collects, and retains numerous records and information resources. Information resources management serves as a reminder that records managers should take an expansive view of their role, responsibilities, and opportunities. They should determine who needs and uses which information resources, the types of information resources generated and retained within each department, and the relative importance of different information resources.

Records managers should assess the information needs, information preferences, and information-gathering behavior of members of the organization. They might promote the development of an internal locator system that monitors the information resources produced within the organization and that calls these resources to the attention of others within the organization.

Records managers and their staff should conduct interviews within each department of the organization. The interviews should identify the individuals responsible for managing departmental records, review the life cycle of the records and other information resources, the facilities for the storage and retrieval of records, the existence of a records management manual, the types of information and data needed for compliance with governmental regulations, and records security. The purpose is to determine the fate and utility of existing records as well as the degree of receptivity to the program initiated by the records manager.

The records manager should promote the services of his or her department and the advantages of forging a partnership for managing the records and other information resources. Equally as important, the records manager should see that department successes become known throughout the organization. The purpose is to show each department that cooperation is in their interests and that the records manager is not interested in empire building.

It is important that records managers anticipate, not react, to the needs and preferences of individual departments. At the same time, they should attempt to standardize operations and practices across units within the organization. The goal is the creation of locator and decision support systems available to everyone within the organization. In some instances, however, certain information and records might be protected and eligible for use on a selective basis. This is all the more reason for the creation of standardized policies and practices, and management of the information resources of the organization.

Records managers need a broad vision of their role and responsibilities.

This vision recognizes the broader information environment and the short-term and long-range needs of the organization and its members. They should engage in referral and understand the practices of other organizations. The purpose is to improve their own internal operations.

Example

Burk and Horton (1988) provide various data collection instruments for ascertaining the use of information resources within a large organization. Using such instruments, records managers can survey individual staff members, managers and nonmanagers, or specific departments about their information needs, information-gathering behavior, and satisfaction with source utilization.

Figure 12-4 depicts the internal communities of a public library and illustrates the types of information facilities that they might use. A records manager might develop such a figure and show the frequency and nature of use made by each community. The purpose is to map the organization's information facilities showing who uses and does not use them, what escapes use or receives *minimal* use, the reasons for limited and nonuse, what is used, and where facilities are located. Records managers might compute cost-effectiveness or cost-benefit ratios, indicating the cost of use and value derived from the use of these facilities. From the insights gathered, records managers can engage in strategic planning while setting, revising, and cancelling programs and services. Service quality (effectiveness, efficiency, and user satisfaction), not service quantity, becomes the central focus of records management activities. As such, the review of organization policies, practices, and decision making depends more on performance measures (outputs, outcomes, and impacts) than on input measures (see Van House, Weil, and McClure, 1990).

INFORMATION POLICY

IRM deals with policies, decision making, planning, and so forth. As such, it requires a knowledge of information policy and the legal, political, and economic contexts in which decisions are made and plans implemented. The next chapter discusses the concept of information policy as a means to maximize the benefits and value of information to specific user groups. Building upon the discussion of the Paperwork Reduction Act, its possible reauthorization, and A-130, this chapter highlights other government information policies pertaining to records management.

218 Records Management and the Library

Figure 12-4. Use of Information Facilities in a Public Library.

INFORMATION FACILITIES

PERSONNEL	Photocopy Machine	Copy Center	OPAC	Online System	OCLC	DP Services	Micro Lab
Trustees							
Library Director							
Public Services Director							
Reference Librarians							
Reference Staff							
Technical Services Director							
Cataloging Head							
Cataloging Prof. Staff							
Cataloging Paraprof. Staff							
Coll. Dev. Head							
ILL Head							
ETC.							

REFERENCES

Bass, Gary and David Plocher. "Finding Government Information: The Federal Information Locator System (FILS)," *Government Information Quarterly* 8 (1991): 13-34.

Burk, C. F., Jr., and F. W. Horton, Jr. *InfoMap: A Complete Guide to Discovering Corporate Information Resources.* Englewood Cliffs, NJ: Prentice-Hall, 1988.

Cabell, Christine. "Viewpoint: The Federal Information Locator System: A Personal Perspective," *Information Management Review* 3 (1987): 65-73.

Caudle, Sharon L. and Donald A. Marchand. *Managing Information Resources: New Directions in State Government.* Syracuse, NY: Syracuse University, School of Information Studies, 1989.

Commission on Federal Paperwork. *The Federal Information Locator System.* Washington, DC: GPO, 1977a.

_____. *Final Summary Report.* Washington, DC: GPO, 1977b.

Congress. Senate. Committee on Governmental Affairs. *Federal Information Resources Management Act.* Report 101-487. Washington, DC: GPO, 1990.

Diebold, J. *Managing Information: The Challenge and the Opportunity.* New York: Amacom, 1985.

"Early Data, Losing Our Memory," *Science*, 244 (June 6, 1989): 1250

Environmental Protection Agency. *Information Resources Directory.* Springfield, VA: NTIS, 1989 (PB90-132192).

Federal Information in the Electronic Age: Policy Issues for the 1990s. Washington, DC: The Bureau of National Affairs, Inc., 1990.

Finding Common Ground: U.S. Export Controls in a Changed Global Environment. Washington, DC: National Academy Press, 1991.

General Accounting Office. *The Federal Information Sources and Systems.* Washington, DC: The Comptroller, 1984.

General Services Administration. Office of Software Development and Information Technology. *Strategic Information Resources Management Planning Handbook.* Washington, DC: GPO, 1985.

Hernon, Peter. "Protected Government Information: A Maze of Statutes, Directive, and Safety Nets." In *United States Government Information Policies*, edited by Charles R. McClure, Peter Hernon, and Harold C. Relyea. Norwood, NJ: Ablex Pub. Corp., 1989a, pp. 245-268.

_____. "Protection of U.S. STI under the Reagan Administration." In *United States Scientific and Technical Information Policies*, edited by Charles R. McClure and Peter Hernon. Norwood, NJ: Ablex Pub. Corp., 1989b, pp. 87-108.

The IRM Organization: Concepts and Considerations. Prepared by Federal IRM Planning Support Center. Falls Church, VA: Office of Software Development and Information Technology, 1989.

Marchand, Donald. "Information Management: Strategies and Tools in Transition," *Information Management Review* 1 (1985): 27-34.

McClure, Charles R., Ann Bishop, Philip Doty, and Pierrette Bergeron. *Federal Information Inventory/Locator System: From Burden to Benefit*. Syracuse, NY: Syracuse University, School of Information Studies, 1990.

_____, Ann Bishop, Philip Doty, and Pierrette Bergeron. "OMB and the Development of a Government-Wide Information Inventory/ Locator System," *Government Information Quarterly* 8 (1991): 33- 57.

Office of Management and Budget. Circular No. A-130, "The Management of Federal Information Resources," *Federal Register* 50 (December 24, 1985): 52730-52751.

Relyea, Harold C. "Access to Government Information: Rights and Restrictions." In *United States Government Information Policies*, edited by Charles R. McClure, Peter Hernon, and Harold C. Relyea. Norwood, NJ: Ablex Pub. Corp., 1989, pp. 141- 160.

Rubinstein, Gwen. "The Quantification of Information: The Paperwork Budget and the Birth of the Burden Hour," *Government Information Quarterly* 7 (1990): 73-81.

Socolar, Milton J. (Special Assistant to the Comptroller General, General Accounting Office) (February 21, 1990). "Federal Information Resoruces Management Act (S. 1742)," testimony before the Senate Committee on Governmental Affairs.

Sprehe, J. Timothy. "Developing Federal Information Resources Management Policy: Issues and Impact for Information Managers," *Information Management Review*, 2 (Winter 1987): 33-41.

Stone, Nidia. "InfoFind: A Practical Tool for Managing Information," *Information Management Review* 3 (1988): 39-46.

Synnott, W. R. *The Information Weapon*. New York: Wiley, 1987.

Thompson, Lawrence H. "Service to the Public: How Effective and Responsive Is the Government?" Statement of the Assistant Comptroller General, Human Resources Division, U.S. General Accounting Office, before the House Committee on Ways and Means, May 8, 1991 (**GAO/T-HRD-91-26**).

Van House, Nancy A., Beth Weil, and Charles R. McClure. *Measuring Academic Library Performance: A Practical Approach*. Chicago, IL: American Library Association, 1990.

DISCUSSION POINTS

1. Has the Paperwork Reduction Act been reauthorized, and has a

replacement to Circular A-130 been implemented? Regardless of the answer, discuss the implications for IRM and records management within the federal government.

2. Interview an IRM officer within an agency or organization, and identify other *barriers to overcome*.

3. Analyze the concept of the information life cycle and its application to records management. Do/should records managers have control over all phases of the life cycle?

4. "For many in both the public and private sectors, 'managing information' is not an easy concept to embrace. It has always been easier to manage the filing systems, the computers, and other related information resources because these resources have physical substance" (*The IRM Organization*, 1989, p. 1). Discuss.

5. How can IRM (and by extension, records management) personnel obtain top management support for their programs and services? Discuss.

6. Has a government-wide locator system materialized? Is one included as part of any legislation currently before Congress? Discuss.

Chapter Thirteen

Information Policy

Information policy, a field encompassing both information science and public policy, treats information as both a commodity adhering to the economic theory of property rights and a resource to be collected, protected, shared, manipulated, and managed. Although the literature often refers to information policy in the singular, there is no single all-encompassing policy. Rather, information *policies* tend to address specific issues and, at time, to be fragmented, overlapping, outdated, and contradictory.

Information policy is a set of interrelated principles, laws, guidelines, rules, regulations, and procedures guiding the oversight and management of the information *life cycle* (see Figure 12-2). Information policy embraces access to, and use of, information. Collectively, policies form a framework that "profoundly affect[s] the manner in which an individual in a society, indeed a society itself, makes political, economic, [technological,] and social choices" (Mason, 1983, p. 93).

Information policy embraces developments at all levels of government, as well as international concerns. Moreover, information policy occurs outside of government; it takes place within and among organizations, associations, and other groups. Government policies provide a framework within which organizations and agencies function. These policies often determine what types of publications will be issued, the availability of government funds, and how funds will be allocated and spent. Obviously, records managers must understand the policy arena and the necessity of influencing the policy-making process.

Another reason why records managers should be knowledgeable about information policy is that they are part of a larger organization, for example, a city government or a corporation. The internal policies set by that organization impact on them and set the constraints under which they operate. Moreover, external policies also have an impact on their ability to meet stated goals and objectives.

In brief, information policies determine which information is publicly available and guide organizations in their information resources management practices. The policies ensure agencies adherence to principles formulated by elected officials. In the case of nongovernment organizations, information policies frame what information is reported to government and ensure that organizations accomplish their mission, goals, and objectives. Information policies also cast records management as part of a planning and

Information Policy 223

evaluation process relating records creation, use, and retention to decision making and accountability.

The purpose of this chapter is to provide an overview of information policy emanating from the federal government. The chapter identifies key policy areas and stakeholders, shows how policy is formulated, and discusses issues central to an understanding of information policy in the 1990s. Moreover, the chapter demonstrates that there is no single corpus of statutory or administrative law to coordinate information policies of federal agencies and to eliminate ambiguities in government information policies. Some policies pertain to an agency and specific activities; others apply to a branch of government, have government-wide application, or have international ramifications. At any rate, government policies affect society and its ability to function on an orderly basis.

INFORMATION POLICY AT THE CORPORATE/INSTITUTIONAL LEVEL

Information policies set by government bodies have a profound impact on nongovernment organizations and institutions. Federal, state, and local governments dictate the type of information and data that these groups must provide as part of governmental regulatory and data collection activities. Although the literature on information policy focuses on government policy, there is still nongovernment information policy. Organizations and institutions set their own policies which staff must honor. Records managers, therefore, must be knowledgeable about the policies emanating from their own organization as well as those government and nongovernment bodies to which the immediate organization reports or must supply information or data.

THE LITERATURE

Figure 13-1, together with the reading list contained at the end of this chapter, identifies selected source material on information policy. A number of recent writings focus on privacy, telecommunications policy, information resources management, scientific and technical information policy, and electronic recordkeeping. The congressional Office of Technological Assessment has produced a number of introductory texts on topics, such as intellectual property rights, the management of government records, and electronic recordkeeping.

Figure 13-1. Selected Source Material on Information Policy.

INDEXES
    Information Science Abstracts (1966-)
    Library Literature (1921-)
    Resources in Education (ERIC) (1966-)
    PAIS Bulletin (1915-)
    Social Science Index (1974-)
    Monthly Catalog of United States Government Publications (1895-)

PERIODICALS
    Government Information Quarterly (1984-)
    Government Publications Review (1973-)
    Information Hotline (1969-)
    Journal of Policy Analysis and Management (1981-)
    Science (1880-)

NEWSPAPERS
    The Chronicle of Higher Education (1966-)
    Government Computer News (1981-)

NEWSLETTERS
    Access Reports/Freedom of Information (1975-)
    Privacy Times (1981-)
    Privacy Journal (1974-)

POLICY ISSUES

Overview

Since publication of the Porat study (1977), little progress has been made in developing detailed typologies of policy issues, using sophisticated methods to organize and relate issues or to produce better methods of clarifying issues and their interrelationships. Many policy issues are part of both a larger and smaller issue, and resolution of one issue often depends on resolution of another.

Hernon and McClure (1987), who analyzed a wide range of policy issues, underscore that:

o   The published policy literature is repetitive in the broad themes that it addresses;

o   Surprisingly little duplication exists among specific policy issues; each issue tends to emphasize specific and unique aspects of the broader themes;

o   The literature devotes little attention to issues related to the information needs and gathering behaviors of the public;

o   The issues become more technological than user-driven with the passing of time; and

o   Policy issues can be isolated in terms of their impact on other policy issues.

Policy issues impacting on the effectiveness with which the federal government provides information might be grouped under a typology, the central components of which include:

o   *Federal organization for information policies*: the structure of the government regarding the provision of federal information;

o   *Relationship between the federal government and other stakeholders in the information sector*: responsibilities and roles of agencies and organizations engaged in the production, distribution, and dissemination of government information;

o   *Information technology*: applications of information technology and their effect on the government's provision of federal information;

o   *The economics of government information*: costs and benefits of government provision of federal information;

o   *Public access to (and availability of) government information*: the rights of the public and the responsibilities of the government to make federal information accessible and available;

o   *Freedom of information and privacy protection*: the rights of the public to gain access to government agency records, while at the same time protecting information that should not be released; and

o   *Secrecy and protection*: the rights of the government to withhold information for the common protection of the public and national security.

These categories are not mutually exclusive, but they offer a means for organizing various policy issues and realizing that some issues have a broader impact than do others.

The categories suggest policy issues related, for example, to: information disclosure, international communications facilities and capacities, privacy protection, freedom of information statutes, the economics of information, information networking, the setting of standards, computer regulation, transborder data flow, intellectual property rights, the role of government and government participation in the marketplace, scientific and technical information (STI), information resources management, national security, national competitiveness, and the public's right-to-know and gain access to government information.

National and International Information Policies (1991) discusses information policies of the United States, Canada, Europe, the Asian Pacific Rim, and developing countries. The chapter on the United States, alone, identifies more than 75 basic information policy issues grouped under the above-mentioned categories. These issues, for example, indicate that significant debate and research remain concerning implementation of the National Research and Education Network (NREN) as a high-speed computing network; see also McClure, Bishop, Doty, and Rosenbaum (1991); and P. L. 102-194, the "High-Performance Computing Act of 1991," which President Bush signed into law on December 9, 1991.

An even larger typology of policy issues might address topics related to energy, housing, health care, the environment, transportation, etc. No wonder that from the 95th through the 100th Congress, 1977 through 1988, more than 300 public laws dealing with information policy were enacted (Chartrand, 1989, p. 1). Added to this, many authorization and appropriations bills contained provisions that directed agency information policy activities. Furthermore, numerous administrative rules and regulations were proposed and implemented during this time period. Consequently, information policies have enormous societal and other consequences.

According to the Bureau of National Affairs, "the speed of technological change has easily eclipsed the development of policy" ("Electronic Access to Federal Information Prompts Debate," 1989, p. c-1):

> As a result, some extremely basic questions remain only partially answered. They include:
>
> What information should the government distribute electronically?
>
> When should the government distribute the electronic

information, and when should it rely on the private sector?

Should the government make more of its computerized information available through computer-to-computer telephone links via modems?

How much should the government charge for electronic information, and what provision should be made for those unable to pay for electronic information?

Technology has a profound effect on the collection and availability of government information. Some agencies offer current information to those making queries using telecommunications software.

POLICY FRAMEWORK

At the federal level of government information policy may be made a variety of ways and prescribed in a number of different forms. The prescribed way for Congress to establish information policy is largely through the constitutionally specified legislative process. A member of Congress formally introduces a proposal in the form of a bill or a joint resolution. Usually the measure is endorsed by the member, but legislation can be offered "on request" on behalf of the President. Ideally, the proposal is referred to the appropriate committee of jurisdiction, given a hearing, where public comment is received, marked up in accordance with committee wishes, reported to the floor, and voted upon by the chamber membership. After the other House of Congress completes similar action on the measure or on one nearly like it, a conference committee may resolve differences in the two adopted versions. After both Houses have agreed on the compromise bill, that bill is presented to the President for signature. When signed into law, the measure attains the status of a statute and, usually, is inserted into the *United States Code*. If the President vetoes the bill, Congress has an opportunity to override and, if successful, the measure becomes a statute.

There are, however, other techniques and procedures available to Congress for setting policy. Within its own domain, each Chamber of Congress adopts rules and standards which constitute policy. Committees of the House and Senate set rules for themselves which constitute information policy.

Congress also appropriates funds for the departments and agencies. This fiscal authority can be directly and indirectly used to set policy. A generous appropriation for an information program may be accompanied by a verbal understanding or committee report language concerning the operation and/or expansion of the program in question. Similarly, funds may be denied or withheld for a program. Moreover, a permanent prohibition may be instituted through the appropriations process.

Finally, policy may be set through informal but, nonetheless, documented agreements. A powerful committee chairman may ask an agency head to conduct some information operation in a particular way; the verbal agreement, extracted at a hearing, is captured in the transcript of the proceeding. In the same regard, an exchange of letters may be used to set policy. Sometimes, of course, a record documenting an informal setting policy may be difficult, if not impossible, to locate. At other times, no such record exists.

The federal courts also make information policy. When a judicial decision is rendered on a dispute, that decision may uphold the status quo or modify an existing policy. Moreover, in writing an opinion on a decision, a judge or judges may offer views or prescribe a procedure which have policy implications.

Courts and individual judges also enjoy a considerable amount of authority for setting information policy for their domains. Federal court rules, practices, and procedures, not inconsistent with legislative enactments, have the force and effect of statutes, but any such rule which is inconsistent with a statute is inoperative. The Supreme Court promulgates rules for itself and the separate lower federal courts. These are for the general guidance of the courts. However, since the individual Courts of Appeals in their circuits and Federal District Courts throughout the country encounter special local conditions and circumstances, they are empowered to make their own special rules, not inconsistent with the rules of general application set down for them by the Supreme Court. Furthermore, within all of these rules, presiding trial judges have some latitude to control information -- e.g., issue a protective order, seal documents, or perhaps close a portion of a proceeding. Such actions may be viewed as policy making; their significance will vary depending on their public effect.

Judicial opinions, once filed, are publicly available at least in typescript form at the court house of the authoring judge(s). Some judges, however, may be slow to file their prepared views. Commercial publishing firms obtain these opinions and produce various compilations.

Within the executive branch, information policy may be prescribed through a wide variety of forms emanating from the Oval Office, an agency fulfilling a government-wide responsibility, or an agency serving only its own personnel. In the first category, the President may set policy through the issuance of a directive, such as an executive order or a national security directive, a letter, a memorandum, or simply an announcement. In almost all cases, such policy making cannot conflict with statutory expressions and is of an administrative nature and internal to the government. Occasionally, however, the President may exercise some constitutional authority -- e.g., Commander in Chief powers -- resulting in policy expression in conflict with congressionally legislated policy. Conflicts between a congressional and a presidential policy expression are sometimes settled by the courts, but are oftentimes left to political settlement.

Government-wide policy on a matter may be set by a particular agency. For many years, the Office of Management and Budget (OMB) has issued circulars, announcements, and guidelines on a variety of fiscal and administrative matters. Some interpretive materials of OMB and other agencies have been controversial, not only because Congress did not legislatively mandate them, but also because of the questionable views they have offered. Indeed, it is expected that any guidance will not conflict with existing statutes and will otherwise be a faithful explanation of legislative intent. As the legal arm of the executive branch, the Department of Justice may also express policy through formal legal opinions of the Attorney General or the Office of Legal Counsel/Office of Legal Policy.

Finally, each individual agency produces forms of policy. Again, the expectation is that these agency expressions of policy will not conflict with statutes, presidential directive, and so forth. Agencies issue regulations implementing and interpreting statutes and presidential policy instruments, internal administrative orders and directives governing their organization and operation, and staff manuals, all of which contain expressions of policy. Most agency regulations can be found in the *Code of Federal Regulations*. New regulations and some other agency orders and directives may be published when first issued in the *Federal Register*. Nonetheless, some material is unpublished and fugitive.

A new and important player in federal regulatory activities is Vice President Quayle's Council on Competitiveness, which is a direct successor to the Reagan Administration's Task Force on Regulatory Relief. Contrary to its name, the Council oversees OMB's regulatory review functions, reviews any regulation of an executive branch agency it dislikes, and pressures that agency to change its regulatory practices or enforcement procedures (see Triano and Bass, 1992). Furthermore, the Council operates outside the open government rules that apply to federal regulatory agencies. Because it carries out its regulatory interference behind a veil of secrecy, the Council's activities cannot be traced through sources, such as the *Code of Federal Regulations* and the *Federal Register*.

ROLE OF SELECTED AGENCIES

Three important agencies include: the National Institute of Standards and Technology (NIST), the National Archives and Records Administration, and the General Services Administration (GSA). NIST has been charged with developing standards, guidelines, and technical methods that the government needs (see Radack, 1990). The merging of computer and telecommunications technologies and the increasing complexity of systems will make standards for the interconnectivity of systems, portability of computer software, and the protection of computer information important as NIST initiatives for the future.

Among its many activities, the National Archives and Records Administration advises agencies in the preservation and storage of records, and it houses some records no longer retained by the agencies themselves. Electronic records present unique problems, ones which the National Archives has not fully resolved. For example, agencies may not leave a trail of electronic records documenting the evolution of a policy.

The Federal Records Act of 1968 (44 USC 29) assigned to the GSA a management role in records management, while the Federal Property and Administration Services Act of 1949 (63 Stat. 377) initially involved the GSA in the management and procurement of automated data processing equipment; the Procurement of ADP Resources by the Federal Government (Brooks) Act of 1965 (40 USC 759), which governs federal acquisition and management of such equipment, expanded this role.

The GSA sets policy for the efficient management of agency records. It maintains an Information Resources Management Service, which coordinates and directs a "governmentwide program for the management, procurement, and utilization of automated data processing and telecommunications equipment and services" (*The United States Government Manual 1990/91*, 1990, p. 605). The Service also plans and directs "programs for improving federal records and information management practices" (Ibid.).

Chapter 29, Title 44, of the *United States Code* covers "Records Management by the Archivist of the United States and by the Administrator of General Services." The chapter covers:

o   Definitions;
o   Objectives of records management;
o   Custody and control of property;
o   General responsibilities of Administrator;
o   Establishment of standards for selective retention of records;
o   Security measures;
o   Inspection of agency records;
o   Records centers and centralized microfilming services;
o   Regulations; and
o   Retention of records.

According to Section 2901 of that chapter,

the term 'records management' means the planning, controlling, directing, organizing, training, promoting, and other managerial activities involved with respect to records creation, records maintenance and use, and records disposition in order to achieve adequate and proper documentation of the policies and transactions of the Federal Government and effective and economical management of agency operations.

Section 2902 presents the goals and objectives of records management:

It is the purpose of this chapter, and chapters 21, 31, and 33 of this title, to require the establishment of standards and procedures to assure efficient and effective records management. Such records management standards and procedures shall seek to implement the following goals:

(1) Accurate and complete documentation of the policies and transactions of the Federal Government;

(2) Control of the quantity and quality of records produced by the Federal Government;

(3) Establishment and maintenance of mechanisms of control with respect to records creation in order to prevent the creation of unnecessary records and with respect to the effective and economical operations of an agency;

(4) Simplification of the activities, systems, and processes of records creation and of records maintenance and use;

(5) Judicious preservation and disposal of records;

(6) Direction of continuing attention on records from their initial creation to their final disposition, with particular emphasis on the prevention of unnecessary Federal paperwork; and

(7) Establishment and maintenance of such other systems or techniques as the Administrator or the Archivist considers necessary to carry out the purposes of this chapter, and chapters 21, 31, and 33 of this title.

Chapter 31 of Title 44, which covers "Records Management by Federal

Agencies," includes the following sections:

o   Records management by agency heads; general duties;
o   Establishment of program of management;
o   Transfer of records to records centers;
o   Certification and determinations on transferred records;
o   Safeguards;
o   Unlawful removal, destruction of records; and
o   Authority of Comptroller General.

Section 3101 of the chapter explains that:

> The head of each Federal agency shall make and preserve records containing adequate and proper documentation of the organization, functions, policies, decisions, procedures, and essential transaction of the agency and designed to furnish the information necessary to protect the legal and financial rights of the Government and of persons directly affected by the agency's activities.

Chapter 33 of Title 44 discusses the "Disposal of Records." The first section (3301) defines records as:

> all books, papers, maps, photographs, machine readable materials, or other documentary materials, regardless of physical form or characteristics, made or received by an agency of the United States Government under Federal law or in connection with the transaction of public business and preserved or appropriate for preservation by that agency or its legitimate successor as evidence of the organization, functions, policies, decisions, procedures, operations, or other activities of the Government or because of the information value of data in them. Library and museum material made or acquired and preserved solely for reference or exhibition purposes, extra copies of documents preserved only for convenience of reference, and stocks of publications and of processed documents are not included.

Other parts of the *United States Code* address records management practices and principles. Readers might peruse the general index to this source of statutory law. They might also examine the *Federal Register* and *Code of Federal Regulations* for the rules implementing these provisions.

GOVERNMENT INFORMATION SAFETY NETS

Overview

In the mid-1980s, OMB, the congressional Joint Committee on Printing (JCP), and various writers associated the concept of a safety net with government information policy. For example, OMB's Circular A-130 referred to the depository library program administered by the Government Printing Office as "a kind of information safety net" (Office of Management and Budget, 1985, Appendix IV, section 12).

A safety net refers to a kind of insurance, a device to cushion the impact of a fall by a person walking a high wire or performing on a trapeze. In a political context, the concept of a safety net protecting the public probably dates from the New Deal and the desire of the Roosevelt administration and Congress to guarantee a minimum standard of living, to reform financial practices, and to protect the public through old-age pensions, unemployment insurance, etc. The Johnson administration, with its vision of a Great Society, expanded the role that government played in managing the economy and improving the overall condition of (and opportunities for) the American people.

National discussion of a safety net has focused on both economic issues and social welfare. The policy literature suggests that there are various safety nets for separate segments of society that could "fall" -- e.g., for child welfare, education, low-income and poverty, pensions and old-age assistance, and health care.

The concept of a safety net underscores a fundamental question: "What is the *basic* responsibility of government and society to assist the 'truly needy', those experiencing difficulty in caring for themselves?" A safety net maintains power balances among the branches of government, helps people, and ensures that governmental policies and practices are equitable. Fiscal retrenchment, record federal deficits, and a political philosophy advocating less federal intrusion into state and local activities have had an undeniable impact on society's willingness to support certain safety nets. It seems that both government and society are now questioning their ability to support a number of safety nets at the same level of commitment provided in the past.

Examples

The FOI Act and GPO's depository library program are the most frequently mentioned government information safety nets protecting the public's right to know ("Electronic Access to Federal Information Prompts Debate," 1989, p. C-8). OMB, the JCP, and various authors have referred to the depository library program as an information safety net guaranteeing that the public has a minimal level of access to government publications/ information. The adjective *minimal* is the key qualifier. The policy literature, in fact, does not regard safety nets as comprehensive channels for the provision of government information to the public.

If the depository library program comprises one safety net serving in minimal capacity, what are the complementary ones that, together, ensure the public has access to all publications and information products labeled as public information or as falling within the gray area?

TOWARD NATIONAL INFORMATION POLICY

Origin of the Term

In July 1976, the U.S. Domestic Council submitted a report, *National Information Policy*, to President Ford. The principal recommendation was that "the United States set as a goal the development of a coordinated National Information Policy ... that is comprehensive, sufficiently sensitive to new technology, and responsive to the implications of the Information Age" (Domestic Council, 1976, pp. vi, 183-184). The report advocated a unified approach to information policy coordinated in the Office of the President. That approach never materialized.

The Concept

Discussions of information policy have encouraged the development of a "requisite arterial system" for "the free and equitable flow of all nonproprietary, nonconfidential information to each individual, regardless of location, level of comprehension, economic status, or other circumstances" (Kaser, Blake, Chelton, Josey, Malinconcio, Sullivan, and Swartz, 1978, p. 545). Such discussions focus on national information policy, but for either government or nongovernment information. Rarely has such policy been viewed as a marriage of all information resources, be they government or nongovernment.

Many writers, including Bearman (1986) and Rosenberg (1982), have considered the terms national, federal, United States, congressional, and executive branch information policy as synonymous. Of course, U.S. government policies have national and international ramifications. The Paperwork Reduction Act created a climate whereby the three branches of government profess a common goal -- reduction of the federal paperwork burden and the effective and efficient management of government information resources. Various policies, therefore, may have government-wide implications (or create the impression that they do).

Brinberg (1989) recognizes a hierarchy in information policy and has a vision of a national information policy articulated by the President and his advisors. His vision, however, is largely technologically oriented; there should be both a national communications network and standard protocols. National policy, he maintains, is shaped largely by administration and congressional leadership.

Foundation of National Information Policy

The Glenerin Declaration (1987) is a tri-national statement emanating from the U.S. National Commission on Libraries and Information Science, the British Library, and the Canadian Institute for Research on Policy. The Declaration, in effect, might be a preamble for national, or international, information policy that recognizes the impact of information on national economies and societies. The policy might also articulate an agenda of issues, initiatives, and strategies for achieving the marriage of all information resources.

Briefly, national information policy conveys a sense of national purpose and represents guiding principles leading to the integration of all publicly available government information in the United States, regardless of the level of government producing that information. Moreover, that integration combines government and nongovernment information, extends bibliographic control over that information, and produces mechanisms (i.e., safety nets) for gaining effective and efficient access to that information. In contrast, federal information policy has the force of law and variously binds the federal government to prescribed courses of action.

One purpose of national information policy is to improve coordination among safety nets and to bring pertinent government information resources produced in the United States to the resolution of various information needs. Of course, national information policy might have another component: the identification of significant foreign source material that, for example, will lead to a U.S.-based patent, scientific breakthrough, or economic advantage. National information policy should encourage differentiation between quantity and quality of information and discourage the generation of information that merely adds to *information overload*.

REFERENCES

Bearman, Toni Carbo. "National Information Policy: An Insider's View," *Library Trends* 35 (Summer 1986): 105-118.

Brinberg, Herbert R. "Realities and Opportunities in the Global Information Economy," *Government Information Quarterly* 6 (1989): 59-65.

Chartrand, Robert L. "Information Policy and Technology Issues: Public Laws of the 95th through 100th Congresses." Washington, DC: Library of Congress, Congressional Research Service, 1989.

Domestic Council. Committee on the Right to Privacy. *National Information Policy*. Washington, D.C.: National Commission on Libraries and Information Science, 1976.

"Electronic Access to Federal Information Prompts Debate," *Daily Report for Executives* [the Bureau of National Affairs, Inc.] 154 (August 11, 1989): C-1 - C-17.

"Glenerin Declaration: Statement of Policy," *Federal Register*, 52 (December 10, 1987): 46980-46981.

Hernon, Peter and Charles R. McClure. *Federal Information Policies in the 1980s*. Norwood, NJ: Ablex Pub. Corp., 1987.

Kaser, David, Fay Blake, Mary K. Chelton, E. J. Josey, S. M. Malinconcio, Peggy Sullivan, and Roderick Swartz. "Toward a Conceptual Foundation for a National Information Policy," *Wilson Library Bulletin* 52 (March 1978): 545.

Mason, Marilyn Gell. *The Federal Role in Library and Information Services*. White Plains, NY: Knowledge Industry Publications, Inc., 1983.

McClure, Charles R., Ann P. Bishop, Philip Doty, and Howard Rosenbaum. *The National Research and Education Network (NREN)*. Norwood, NJ: Ablex, 1991.

National and International Information Policies. Edited by Wendy Schipper and Ann Marie Cunningham. Philadelphia, PA: The National Federation of Abstracting and Information Services, 1991.

Office of Management and Budget. Circular A-130: "The Management of Federal Information Resources," *Federal Register* 50 (December 12, 1985): 52730-52751.

Porat, Marc. *The Information Economy*, vol. 1. Washington, DC: GPO, 1977.

Radack, Shirley M. "More Effective Federal Computer Systems: The Role of NIST and Standards," *Government Information Quarterly* 7 (1990): 37-49.

Rosenberg, Victor. "National Information Policies." In *Annual Review of Information Science and Technology*. White Plains, NY: Knowledge Industry Publications, Inc., 1982, pp. 3-32.

Triano, Christine and Gary D. Bass. "The New Game in Town: Regulation, Secrecy, and the Quayle Council on Competitiveness," *Government Information Quarterly* 9 (1992), forthcoming.

The United States Government Manual 1990/91. Washington, D.C.: GPO, 1990.

READINGS

American Science and Science Policy Issues: Chairman's Report to the Committee on Science and Technology. Washington, DC: Congress,

House, 99th Cong., 2nd sess., 1986 [Committee Print].
Association of Research Libraries. *Technology & U.S. Government Information Policies: Catalysts for New Partnerships.* Washington, DC, 1987.
Bennett, James R. *Control of Information in the United States: An Annotated Bibliography.* Westport, CT: Meckler Corp., 1987.
Caudle, Sharon. *Federal Information Resources Management: Bridging Vision and Action.* Washington, DC: National Academy of Public Administration, 1987.
Committee on the Records of Government. *Report.* Sponsored by the American Council of Learned Societies, the Social Science Research Council, and the Council on Library Resources. Washington, DC: The Committee, 1985.
Congress. House. Committee on Government Operations. *Electronic Collection and Dissemination of Information by Federal Agencies: A Policy Overview.* Washington, DC: GPO, 1986.
Congress. Office of Technology Assessment. *Informing the Nation.* Washington, DC: GPO, 1988.
Federal Government Information Technology: Management, Security, and Congressional Oversight. Washington, DC: Office of Technology Assessment, 1986.
Flaherty, David H. *Protecting Privacy in Surveillance Societies.* Chapel Hill, NC: The University of North Carolina Press, 1989.
Hernon, Peter and Charles R. McClure. *Federal Information Policies in the 1980s.* Norwood, NJ: Ablex, 1987.
_____ . *Public Access to Government Information*, 2d ed. Norwood, NJ: Ablex, 1988. Chapter 2: "Federal Information Policies."
Information Technology R&D: Critical Trends and Issues. Washington, DC: Office of Technology Assessment, 1985.
Lawrence, John S. and Bernard Timberg. *Fair Use and Free Inquiry.* Norwood, NJ: Ablex, 1989.
McClure, Charles R., Peter Hernon, and Harold C. Relyea. *United States Government Information Policies.* Norwood, NJ: Ablex, 1989.
_____ and Peter Hernon. *United States Scientific and Technical Information Policies.* Norwood, NJ: Ablex, 1989.
Newberg, Paula, ed. *New Directions in Telecommunications Policy*, 2 vols. Durham, NC: University of North Carolina Press, 1988.
Riley, Tom, ed. *Access to Government Records: International Perspectives and Trends.* Bromley, Kent (England): Chartwell-Bratt Ltd., 1986.
Shapley, Deborah and Roy Rustum. *Lost at the Frontier: U.S. Science and Technology Policy Adrift.* Philadelphia, PA: ISI Press, 1985.

DISCUSSION POINTS

1. Select an actual organization, information center, or library, such as the ones presented in Chapters 14-16. What information policies impact their records management practices?

2. Examine the life cycle of government information and its implications for that organization, information center, or library.

3. Assess the role of the National Archives or the General Services Administration regarding records management.

4. Why should all records managers be familiar with government information policy? Discuss.

5. Select a portion of a law on records management from the *United States Code*. Trace congressional intent through congressional hearings and reports and any judicial interpretations. Has that law been contested? Has the law evolved over the past decade, and does it need further refinement?

6. Is Congress currently considering any legislation relating to records management?

Chapter Fourteen

An Overview of the Weston Records Management Project

by Kate Jones-Randall

BACKGROUND

History

The Weston Public Library was built in 1899 to serve a rural population of 2,000 people, primarily adults. It was constructed at a cost of $40,000, housing a collection of 12,423 volumes in closed stacks, and staffed by one librarian. It is now governed by six Library Trustees elected by the voters for three-year terms. They determine library policy, appoint personnel, request adequate funds through town appropriation, and supervise the expenditure of funds. The library is administered by a Library Director supervising three professional (MLS) department heads.

In 1922, the Rosamond Freeman Room was remodeled from space on the lower level and dedicated to Children's Services with a gift of $5,000 from Louisa Case. In the 1940s and 1950s, the Weston Public Library enjoyed the reputation of being one of the best small public libraries in Massachusetts, and was selected, along with the Boston Public Library, to be visited by librarians from other countries.

The second internal modification to the building came in 1960 and was considered of a temporary nature in view of the frequent recommendations for an expanded or wholly new building. The remaining part of the lower level was adapted for staff work and meeting space and two rest rooms. The proliferation of records keeping paralleled the population growth, which has reached 11,800 and is expected to top off at 15,000 people.

Between the 1940s and 1980s the services and materials increased as the population became more demanding and sophisticated, gradually usurping most patron seating while the stack area was filled to double density. The library currently provides in constricted form all contemporary public library services, except online database searching, and much programming that cannot be accommodated except in off-site locations.

Library Building Program

The Library Building Committee, the Trustees, and the Director devised a Building Program which would complement the services already provided: automated circulation through the Minuteman Library Network, with annual circulation numbering 140,000 from 62,000 items (excluding microforms) which include print and audiovisual materials, programming for children and adults, and availability of services 61 hours per week, 7 days per week.

In fact, the need to automate the extensive specifications for each location in the new building (functional area designations) making up a significant portion of the Building Program spurred the Records Management Project. Realizing that the majority of records currently separated by two floors contained critical material necessary for the completion of the Building Program, the Library Director instigated the Project. Other reasons, in addition to the goals of the Project, included the pressing need to create an automated base of library administrative materials, and the then-current availability of the consultant.

While previous library building initiatives did not succeed, the town of Weston in May 1991 voted to allocate $4.4 million to build a new library building. In addition to the increased space for people to meet and work, and for books, tapes, videos, and other materials, technological developments will "catch up" to the existing equipment and services. In addition to Apple and Macintosh computers used in Children's Services, three IBM-compatible microcomputers allow access to computer indexes to the local newspapers, the oral and local history collections, the records management system, the library building program specifications, and numerous internal databases, such as new fiction or books on tape listings. Holdings are downloaded by subject, author, etc., from the Minuteman Network automated system to create other specific database/lists.

LIBRARY RECORDS OPERATIONS

Records Management

Administration of records at the Weston Public Library is carried out individually at present by the personnel who create and/or handle the various records which pertain to their duties. This, of course, results in some duplication, but is mostly divided by job description.

For example, the day-to-day administrative records, including personnel, are maintained by the Secretary to the Director; the financial records, especially purchasing and budgeting, by the Bookkeeper; the executive records, including special information or subject files, by the Director; and individual departmental records by the various department heads of

Circulation/Adult Services, Children's Services, and Technical Services.

Library Organization

Twenty-six staff members are presently employed by the Library, including the Pages and Maintenance worker; there are 14 full-time equivalents in total. All of the staff that work with the public have bachelor's degrees or the equivalent. No organizational chart exists at this time although it is easy enough to extrapolate. The Director is at the top of the chart, with each of three department heads supervising two or more nonprofessional staff members or student pages. The Secretary and the Bookkeeper are also answerable to the Director, as is the Maintenance worker, although he most often deals directly with the Secretary.

THE RECORDS MANAGEMENT PROJECT 1988-1989

Scope of the Project

This particular project was restricted to the administrative, financial, and executive records; models of records operations were created which, in theory, could then be passed on to the library department heads as well as to other town departments, such as Recreation or Water Resources Management. While the library departments could readily adopt the system, the town departments did not do so. A centralized minicomputer system in use in the Town Hall made this infeasible.

Goals of the Project

The goals of the Records Management Project listed below elaborate the role of records management within staff duties: particularly, retention and disposition schedules formed a primary objective for the three areas which were under examination.

The Records Management Project began in September 1988, and the first phase ran through March of the next year. The library automation consultant (who had developed the microcomputer indexes to the local newspapers and the oral and local history collections) conducted the project. The second phase began in September 1989, and ended in December of that year; it was undertaken by a library science graduate student who was also a part-time employee of the Weston Public Library. The original goals of this Project were very specific; they were to:

o   Analyze the filing system for all records pertaining to the Weston Public Library to determine what corrections or innovations must be made in order to increase the efficiency of the system and make it cost-effective;

- Inventory existing records and determine the type and volume of records currently contained in multiple physical locations. Measure the number of cubic feet necessary for inactive and active storage to be incorporated into the Library Building Program;

- Analyze records according to their content, and classify them by usage, with procedures developed to be used both in active and inactive storage;

- Determine the value of existing records, and recommend retention periods for all records. Assist in establishing a vital records protection program;

- Design and test a database structure for a total records management program. In particular, provide access through subject classification techniques to materials known to exist but not found without extensive searching, if at all; and

- Provide training and instruction for staff in records handling and storing procedures. Include within the training period the initial implementation of the records management database, with subsequent data entry to be performed by staff and evaluation of the database to be conducted jointly by staff and records analyst.

Phase Two goals included the following:

- Work with the Executive files and implement the inventory:
  - Match inventory sheet with actual files;
  - Sort files based on recommendations by active, inactive, professional, file, or discards; and
  - Place the files in new file cabinets with new subject headings.

- Learn how the database works and ensure the executive files are kept up to date; and

- Keep the program going after the semester to ensure updates and usefulness.

Table 14-1. Records Questionnaire.

o **Active Records**

- o Are records conveniently located for users? Yes, mostly, except for the director's files.
- o Are files well maintained? Are materials unfiled? No; no authority tables are used, no deaccessioning is done, and there is no determination of actual use. Yes; the Executive materials are often "in use," on both desk tops (third and first floors) or in piles on chairs or other pieces of furniture.
- o Is equipment appropriate? Yes, it is acceptable, but needs to be "weeded." Everything is full, with things on top of each cabinet as well!
- o Has procedure for moving out inactive materials been standardized? No, and we really need this.
- o Have retention schedules been developed? No; only the information file has a retention schedule, but it is not followed. Perhaps a stamp with blocks of spaces of dates to fill in would work?
- o Who controls new equipment purchases? The Director has final say over staff recommendations.
- o Is filing system uniform? No, it is idiosyncratic at best, with no standard headings, and similar subject files which should be consolidated.
- o How much duplication of records exists? Sometimes up to three copies per invoice, advertisement, or other internal document is made.
- o Is there a vital records preservation program? The payroll records are also kept on microfilm at the Town Hall, but otherwise there is a need to identify vital records and then develop a preservation program for them.
- o What programs involve microforming, computing, or other technology? Serials management, monthly reports to Trustees, standing orders, payroll, financial statements do. The Town Hall stores past payroll information on microfilm and current data in its minicomputer.

o **Inactive Records**

- o Do central or departmental storage areas exist? Yes; the Field School is a designated area but it is not safe for anything but books to be stored there. One area on the third floor, in the bathroom, is used for inactive storage, but everything else is interfiled with active materials in the main staff work room.
- o Are storage areas adequate in size and protected from moisture, excessive temperatures, dirt, rodents, etc.? No, there is simply not enough room. No; there is no major deterioration yet, but the ceiling in the upstairs bathroom has had water damage. The library is closed for several days during the summer each year due to extremely high temperatures. No mice, though!

Table 14-1. (Continued)

- o Are legally required records protected? Probably; the payroll and personnel records are also kept to some extent at the Town Hall. We need to know what the legal requirements are.
- o Who services and maintains records and storage areas? The people who create and use them, sort of.
- o How are inactive records accessed? The boxes are numbered and have information pasted on the outside according to their arrangement by year.
- o What records are maintained of records movement? Sometimes a note is left in the previous active file, but mostly the Director's memory is the source!
- o Have retention schedules been established for inactive records? No; no one has any real idea of the value of the inactive records, and they should probably be weeded.
- o Who checks retention and destroys outdated records? The people who create and use them check for timeliness, but the Director has the final say in their destruction. Only rarely is anything thrown away.

PROJECT PROGRESS

Systems Analysis

The Records Management Project analyzed the filing system for the records pertaining to the administrative, financial, and executive departments of the Weston Public Library. An oral survey of the appropriate staff members determined the actual status of active and inactive records.

The insufficient space allocated to staff work areas contributed to filing confusion; it was also quite inefficient to have the executive files located in two separate working areas, one on the third floor and the other on the first floor of the building. Obviously, construction of a new library facility will ameliorate this condition. The questions asked of the staff can be seen in Table 14-1.

Subject Headings Reclassification

A systematic subject classification more clearly defined the contents of each records operation, and reduced confusion and redundancy within each broad area of records operations. Initially, a Library of Congress-style of headings predominated, such as "Vendors and Equipment -- Photocopiers." This was continued, albeit in a simplified format, with the broad heading (Vendors and Equipment) used only once, and the specific headings (Photocopiers) identifying each individual folder. The following examples show the development of the professional subject, or vertical file, headings:

Management and Administration
Performance Evaluation - MBO Guidelines

Management and Administration
Personnel Administration in Small Public Libraries

Personnel
Certification of Sub-Professionals

Personnel
Collective Bargaining

Personnel
Job Responsibilities
Professional and Sub-Professional

The Library of Congress, or inverted, style of subject headings was considered important because printed information was the major focus. While the database software can search an entire record for any word or phrase in any position, the physical files must group items together by like concept, and be simple to grasp by regular users.

Inventory

The inventory was the first, and most difficult, task completed. A map was created, assigning cabinet and drawer numbers to each piece of equipment, and a Records Inventory Form was used. At that time, a substantial number of records were more than three years old, and required space in an inactive storage area. The inactive records were stored in a bathroom in the upstairs Director's office on the third floor, an arrangement which was less than satisfactory.[1]

The inventory was, of necessity, continued in Phase Two of the Project, as five months had elapsed in between each phase, and the executive files had not been attended to during that period. Many of the original file locations were invalid, and new materials had been accumulated. Since the

---

[1] The new library facility will incorporate storge space for important records, while the disposal schedule will be implemented to remove unnecessary or duplicate materials, of which there were many.

executive files also included a great deal of subject information requiring the establishment of a "professional vertical file," its development was especially important.

Figure 14-1 reproduces the Records Inventory Form, which is designed to carry each records series, or files, through from initial discovery to final analysis for retention and disposition. The form incorporates "see also" references with a complete description of the type and amount of items inventoried, as well as determining vital records status.

Vital Records

No efforts were ever made to separate what might be considered vital records from other records, nor were there any attempts to dispose of records more than three years old or otherwise outdated and no longer useful. In particular, a vital records protection program is of some consequence, as the library has already been devastated once by a fire, and until library services are relocated in the new building, this is still a considerable concern. The recommendation to locate vital records in a separate building, such as the Town Hall, has not yet been incorporated except in already microfilmed payroll records.

Automation of Records Management

Databases for personnel records, a records management control system including records and equipment inventory and inactive/ archival records, as well as the professional subject files, were devised using INMAGIC textbase software.[2] The results have been mixed.

A relational database management software program is more suitable to work in conjunction with spreadsheet data from Lotus 1-2-3 in order to be fully effective for the personnel files, although INMAGIC is used regularly to produce a list of current staff members including addresses, telephone numbers, and job designation. This listing is updated regularly by the Secretary to the Director, and printed as needed.

---

[2] INMAGIC is the registered trademark of Inmagic, Inc., 2067 Massachusetts Avenue, Cambridge, MA 02140-1338 (617-661-8124). It is available through a registered INMAGIC dealer, such as Randall Research Associates, 35 South Avenue, South Dartmouth, MA 02748 (508-997-7939), or directly from Inmagic Inc.

Weston Records Management Project

Figure 14-1. Records Inventory Form.

LOCATION

Department Name	Office

Contact Person	Cabinet or Drawer Number

IDENTIFICATION

Working Records Series Title

Contents/Description

Use/Retrieval Terms

DESCRIPTION: Circle all that apply

Arrangement
- subject
- alpha
- numeric
- geo
- org
- chrono

Storage
- cabinet/shelf
- desk drawer
- boxed
- other

Format
- < letter
- letter
- legal
- \> legal
- mag media
- photos
- dp printout
- bound vols
- maps, charts
- microfilm
- online
- AV media

Volume
total cu. ft.:

Inclusive Dates
from: to: present

Activity
- multi/daily
- daily
- weekly
- monthly
- other

User reference (years after creation)
- < 1
- 1
- 2
- 3
- 4
- 5
- 6
- other
- while current

Figure 14-1. *(Continued)*

DESCRIPTION continued

<u>User Retention</u>

in office   in inactive storage

STATUS: Circle all that apply

<u>Legal Status</u>   <u>Restrictions</u>   <u>File Integrity</u>

■ official   ■ vital   ■ file breaks/
                                                   missing items
■ supporting files   ■ confidential   ■ related
                                                   files elsewhere
■ reference materials   ■ archival

                        ■ subject to audit

<u>Public Disclosure</u>   <u>Information Duplicated Elsewhere</u>   ■

■ required

■ prohibited   <u>Information Summarized Elsewhere</u>   ■

ANALYSIS

Official Records Series Title

Retention Period

in office   in inactive storage   authority

Microfilm Recommendations

Automation Recommendations

Date   Surveyor

■ add   ■ change   ■ delete

Remarks

The *Records Management Control System* consists of three similar databases designed to inventory and control records at the Weston Public Library. Each database has been developed to be searched in a comparable fashion, and each has several features in common. Were INMAGIC software to incorporate a relational function, these databases could easily be linked, although each is designed to operate independently and individually at this time.

A *Searching Guide* to all the databases has been developed to explain the contents and preferred searching strategies for each field of each database, with appropriate examples. The use of SearchMAGIC,[3] however, makes it easy for staff members unfamiliar with any of the Records Management Control System databases to search and retrieve particular records without previous training. SearchMAGIC is INMAGIC's front-end search "engine" which allows browsing of field contents, cutting and pasting search words or phrases, and printing of results from an easy-to-use menu interface.

The *RecInv* (Records Inventory) database structure mirrors the Records Inventory Form (see Figure 14-1). The fields correspond directly, while the choices under "Arrangement," "Format," etc., such as "subject" or "letter" become the controlled vocabulary to be entered into the appropriate field. RecInv contains the inventory taken in print of all the records (files or other stored information) held by the library in the first and third floor administrative offices, located in different types of storage (file cabinets, shelves, and boxes), and is comprised of four categories of materials. To make searching quick and easy, the *Recno* field is divided into numbers which begin with either E, A, F, or P, corresponding to the *E*xecutive, *A*dministrative, *F*inancial, and *P*rofessional materials. A sample record appears in Figure 14-2.

The *Reconsys* (Records Control Inactive/Archival) database is an inventory of all the records (files or other stored information) held by the Library in archival or inactive storage in either the first or third floor administrative offices, and located in different types of storage containers (file cabinets and boxes). While it contains some of the same fields as the *RecInv* database, it also includes the disposition method and date, as well as the ability to loan out and reclaim records. It is comprised of the four categories of materials used in the RecInv database, with the *Recno* field divided into numbers beginning with either *E*, *A*, *F*, or *P*, corresponding to the *E*xecutive, *A*dministrative, *F*inancial, and *P*rofessional materials. A sample record appears in Figure 14-3.

---

[3] SearchMAGIC is also a registered trademark of Inmagic, Inc.

Figure 14-2. Records Inventory Database Sample Record.

```
                        RECORDS INVENTORY
Page: 1                                             Date: 02/28/89
------------------------------------------------------------------
LOCATION
--------
   Record #: E001                    Dept: Exec
   Contact Person: Alice Douglas     Location #: UP

IDENTIFICATION
--------------
   Official Records Series Title: Building Programs

   Contents: architects' proposals; detailed specifications by
      function; furniture and equipment; correspondence and other
      documents; consultants; journal articles; other library
      building programs; Brandeis Study; Field School Proposal

DESCRIPTION
-----------
   Arrangement:        Format:          Storage:         Vol. cu. ft.:
      subject             <letter          cabinet/shelf    4.5
                          letter
                          legal
                          >legal
                          photos
                          maps, charts

      Inclusive dates:                  Activity:
         1959                              daily
         present

      User reference:                   User retention:
         other                             in office

STATUS
------
   Legal Status:       Restrictions:            Public Disclosure:
      official            some confidential
      supporting files    some archival
      reference materials

   File Integrity: related files elsewhere with Building Committee

ANALYSIS
--------
   Retention Period:
      In office: P              Inactive storage:   ARC

   Recommendations: separate journal articles, other library
      programs and prepare bibliography; discard obsolete  items;
      sort and discard duplicate items before archiving.

   Jan/89, KJR
                              ******
```

The *EquipInv* (Equipment Inventory) database is an inventory of tools and equipment held by the Library in various locations, and is comprised of three categories of materials. It includes items like electric staplers, photocopiers, microcomputers, and contracts and warranty information on all major pieces of equipment. The *Recno* field is divided into numbers which begin with either *T*, *W*, or *C*, for the tools, typewriters, and computer equipment. A sample record appears in Figure 14-4.

Most successful of all, the Director's professional subject files have been fully indexed for maximum accessibility. The main subject headings appear in inverted style, and are supplemented with descriptive language which is also searchable so that specific information can be pinpointed easily. New lateral file cabinets were acquired to house both types of Executive files, and Phase 2 inventory and placement completed the relocation of subject and less active file folders to their appropriate addresses.

Figure 14-3. Records Control System Sample Record.

```
                        RECORDS CONTROL SYSTEM
Page: 1                                                  Date: 02/28/89
------------------------------------------------------------------------
LOCATION:
   Record #: E001                        Dept.: Executive
   Location #: UP 1v14 1-4

IDENTIFICATION:
   Official Records Series Title: Building Programs

DESCRIPTION
   Format:              # of boxes:  4      Other copies?:
     <letter                                  w/Building Committee
     letter
     >letter
     photos
     maps

DISPOSITION:
   Destruction Code:   ARC               Destruction date: N/A

   Checkout Date: Jan 4, 1989; AD        Claim Date: Jan 31, 1994

                                ******
```

Figure 14-4. EquipInv Sample Record.

```
                       EQUIPMENT INVENTORY
Page: 1                                        Date: 02/28/89
-------------------------------------------------------------
Equipment: printer, laser                   Record #: C005

Location: UP, AD

Manufacturer: Okidata

Model #: Laserline 6, EN 2300A              Serial #: B 012240

Vendor: PC Connection, 6 Mill St., Marlow, NH 03456;
        1-800-243-8088

Date Purchased:          Cost:             Warranty Expires:
   Nov 12, 1987           $ 1,398.00          Nov 12, 1988

Service Contracts by Company, Date, and Cost:
   Xerox Service Center, 194 Forbes Rd., Braintree MA 02184;
   (617) 848-5750

Maintenance record by Date and Description:
   Mar 22, 1988; shipped for paper jam repair to
                 Xerox Service Ctr.
   Nov 1988; excess toner; cleaned drum and vacuumed interior
   Dec 1988; replaced toner cartridge at 5104 count
   Jan 1989; inventory

                            ******
```

RESULTS AND OUTLOOK

The Weston Public Library staff proved responsive to the introduction of records handling and storage procedures, albeit reluctantly embracing the actual disposition [read destruction] of outdated records. They have been willing to work with and generate automated data, in some cases replacing printed forms with improved automated formats, although reducing the number of copies generated per document is still problematical.

The costs of the Records Management Project included the consultant's fees, which totaled $6,975.00 for the seven-month period at roughly 15 hours per week (see Figure 14-5), and the cost of a new lateral file cabinet at $754.00. The library science graduate student was already on the payroll, and the internship (work study) costs resulted in $572.00 for the five hours' work per week for 12 weeks. The INMAGIC and SearchMAGIC software and computer hardware, including a printer, had been previously purchased for earlier automation projects, and this project required no further equipment outlays.

Figure 14-5. Timeline for Weston Records Management Project, September 1988-March 1989.

```
                                              1988              1989
PROJECT                                       SEP OCT NOV DEC   JAN FEB MAR APR MAY JUN
************************************************************************************

Records Management, Weston
[To be supplemented 5 hrs/wk by internship Sep-Dec]

Systems Analysis                                                 ■  ■
-----------------------------------------------------------------------------------------
Records selection and Inventory                                  ■  ■  ■
-----------------------------------------------------------------------------------------
Database design and testing                                             ■  ■
-----------------------------------------------------------------------------------------
Records retention/disposition scheduling                                ■  ■
-----------------------------------------------------------------------------------------
Database implementation and evaluation                                     ■  ■  ■
```

The Weston Records Management Project is expected to carry on for 15 hours/week for 26 weeks; the internship period, therefore, will be occupied only with the systems analysis and records selection and inventory portions of the entire project. The goals of this project are as follows:

1) Analyze the filing system for all records pertaining to the Weston Public Library to determine what corrections or innovations must be made in order to increase the efficiency of the system and make it cost-effective.

2) Inventory existing records and determine the type and volume of records currently contained in multiple physical locations. Measure the number of cubic feet necessary for inactive and active storage to be incorporated into the Library building program.

3) Analyze records according to their content, and classify them by usage, with procedures developed to be used both in active and inactive storage.

4) Determine the value of existing records, and recommend retention periods for all records. Assist in establishing a vital records protection program.

5) Design and test a database structure for a total records management program. In particular, provide access through subject classification techniques to materials known to exist but not found without extensive searching, if at all.

6) Provide training and instruction for staff in records handling and storing procedures. Include within the training period the initial implementation of the records management database, with subsequent data entry to be performed by staff and evaluation of the database to be conducted jointly by staff and records analyst.

In general, the Records Management Project has been termed a success, although, like any project of this nature, its continuation is the real benchmark upon which success must be measured. The administrative files have consistently been continued by the Secretary to the Director, and new categories are introduced as necessary, often after consultation with the original consultant. The executive files are erratically continued, particularly when the Secretary to the Director can enter the data and update previous records. The professional subject files grow "like topsy," with the database usually well behind the actual contents of the file cabinet. Financial data have been automated yet not truly incorporated into the Records Management Control System, as the Bookkeeper is a part-time employee and lacks training in INMAGIC. The financial records in the database, therefore, are inactive only.

Were a Records Manager (either the Administrative Secretary or the Bookkeeper) to handle the rest of the data entry, inventorying, data linking, and maintain the retention and disposition of inactive records, the project would become an unqualified success. As it stands, it is an excellent foundation upon which to build in the new library building.

Chapter Fifteen

MARC AMC and the Government Records Project at the Massachusetts Archives

by Nancy Richard and Kathryn Hammond Baker

The purview of librarians, particularly in special and institutional libraries, is expanding to include records created by the parent institution; those establishing records management programs may seek to automate management information. Librarians who are familiar with the MARC format can benefit from the use of the MARC AMC format in their records management programs. Unlike commercially available software, which has traditionally focused on records center operations, programs utilizing the MARC AMC format offer a framework for describing the characteristics of original records. The format and required authorities, borrowed directly from library practice, enhance the efficiency and effectiveness of management and archival activities, and are a step toward the integration of management and bibliographic information. The Massachusetts Archives recently participated in a two-year grant project, the Government Records Project, to test the use of MARC AMC format for the appraisal and description of government records.

DEVELOPMENT OF MARC AMC

MARC format was designed to facilitate the automation and exchange of cataloging records. Although the Library of Congress (LC) issued the MARC format for Manuscripts in 1973, it was not useful as an archival descriptive tool until its data elements were revised by the National Information Systems Task Force (NISTF), a task force of archivists appointed by the Society of American Archivists (SAA). The result of the collaboration between LC and SAA was the MARC AMC format, approved in 1983 by the Committee on Representation in Machine-Readable Form of Bibliographic Information (MARBI), a joint committee of three divisions within the American Library Association (see Weber, 1990). The original MARC for manuscripts, an extension of the MARC format for books, was based on a fundamental misunderstanding of both the nature of archival records and how they are managed.

The initial MARC for Manuscripts was designed to treat archival materials as just another format, like books or maps. Unlike books, meant by the author to be read and understood as a single entity, archival materials are the product of a group or individual as a result of an activity. "They are the means to an end, not the end in themselves" (Roe, 1990, p. 147). A single function may continue over many years, and the responsibility for fulfilling it may change hands more than once. Where book cataloging usually concerns describing a single item, static in nature, archival records are unique and dynamic. The records created to document a function may consist of one or many forms of material filed separately or interfiled into one series. Understanding archival materials, in order to render an adequate description, requires understanding the context in which they are created.

Moreover, unlike book cataloging, actions taken upon records by records managers and archivists are important to an understanding of the record series. Cataloging does not change the nature of an entity, alter its level of comprehensiveness or arrangement; however, sampling, weeding, and reorganization of records are tasks not atypical of the records management and archival professions. It was essential that the archival principles of provenance and life-cycle management be the basis for the revised MARC format. The *Report of the Working Group on Standards for Archival Description* (1989, p. 450) provides this insight into archival description:

> Archivists (and their close allies, records managers) have accepted the challenge of providing control of and access to records and the information they contain throughout their life cycle, from creation through disposition. In the process they capture, manipulate, and provide information about the records in many forms to serve many functions.

TESTING THE FORMAT

Although the revised MARC AMC format incorporated the archivist's point of view and method of description, it was not until archivists and records managers tested the format in national bibliographic databases that the practical applicability of MARC AMC format could be evaluated.

The Seven States Project (SSP)

In 1984, the Research Libraries Group (RLG) adopted the MARC AMC format for use in the Research Libraries Information Network (RLIN) research database. Initially, members of RLIN using the MARC AMC format consisted primarily of college and university libraries and archives. This changed, in 1986, when RLG was awarded a grant from the National Historical Publications and Records Commission (NHPRC) to include the first MARC AMC descriptions of state and local government records in a national utility. Seven states (Alabama, California, Minnesota, New York, Pennsylvania, Utah, and Wisconsin) were asked to participate. The goals of this grant were to create a base of approximately 25,000 descriptions of state record series, to improve access to descriptions of the records of other archival institutions, to provide a tool to assist government archivists to manage their holdings throughout their life cycle, to improve the appraisal of public records, and to create an authority list of agency functions.

To further refine the MARC AMC format for description of government records, the Seven States Project introduced several innovations. First, to clearly ground the series by its provenance, they developed the agency history record, an expanded authority record consisting of multiple 545 or history fields used to describe the history of the creating agency, its functions, and its varying name changes. This is a separate record linked to the descriptions of each series created by an agency (the 773 field provides a machine link in RLIN). The second idea, the development of an agency function vocabulary, was developed to index the function statement provided in the 520 or summary field of the series description. This access point (657) was added to allow searches across creating agencies for series developed to document similar functions (i.e., a search for the documentation for teaching mentally handicapped, or for reviewing grant proposals).

The Seven States Project also proposed innovations to enhance the usefulness of the system for records management activities. The first facilitated the documentation of public records throughout their life cycle. These nonstandard uses of MARC AMC format permitted appraisal archivists to enter information about archival and nonarchival series still in creating offices, or types of series created by a specific functional area of government or by many units of government regardless of unit function. The second, the addition of two local data fields, the LDA to contain an appraisal note, and LDB to document disposition decisions, was designed to test the utility of RLIN for comparative, or "shared" appraisal.[1] Difficulty in sharing appraisal data led participants to conclude, in part, that a vocabulary of forms of material was necessary in order for effective cooperation.

---

[1] LDA and LDB are MARC-AMC Local Data fields A and B.

The Government Records Project (GRP)

The momentum generated by the Seven States Project was renewed by RLG in a second NHPRC grant. The Government Records Project (GRP) in which the Massachusetts Archives participated along with Georgia, Kentucky, Nevada, Oregon, and Virginia, the archives of the District of Columbia, the City of New York, and the National Archives and Records Administration, continued the work begun by the Seven States Project and enlarged the body of government records in RLIN.

The goals of the second grant were to contribute approximately 30,600 additional series descriptions, agency history records, and records schedules to RLIN, to develop an authority list for forms of material, to continue testing shared appraisal for state and local records, to continue testing and developing standard terms to represent government functions and activities, to develop guidelines for standardized descriptive practice among state archival agencies, and to collaborate with the National Archives and Records Administration (NARA) in testing shared appraisal and access to intergovernmental records. Working groups in standardized vocabulary, appraisal, and description were established to complete these goals.

The vocabulary working group was responsible for developing authority lists for form of materials as well as functions and activities. These lists have been incorporated into the Art and Architecture Thesaurus and are now online in RLIN. A manual of descriptive guidelines consisting of discussion papers, written by the descriptive working group, has been compiled. "The Guide to Government Records in RLIN," designed to explain to researchers the use of government records in the database, was produced by the group as a whole. This publication includes sample records and search strategies, and diagrams a complete MARC AMC series description (see Figure 15-1). Results of a test of reference use of RLIN in participating institutions will be published in a statistical report.

The appraisal working group's basic goal was to develop standards for sharing appraisal data. The SSP had established experimental formats for recording appraisal information and scheduled records in RLIN; it fell to the GRP's appraisal working group to refine and improve these preliminary guidelines. Two specific tasks assigned to the group were to continue testing models for shared appraisal, and to collaborate with the National Archives in testing a shared approach to the management of intergovernmental records.

Many of the early concerns of the working group focused on the results of the SSP. The first project had concluded that the appraisal data entered was "inconsistent and often unsatisfactory in terms of quality, as well as quantity" (National Archives and Records Administration, 1990, p. 87).

Massachusetts Archives 259

Figure 15-1. Government Records in the RLIN Database.

— 5 —

What are the components of a records series description?*

The agency that created these records, and the title of the records series.	{ Massachusetts. Bureau of Municipal Facilities. State program grant files, 1979- [ongoing] <100 cubic ft.>	} The inclusive dates of the series — here, starting in 1979 and continuing as an active series — and the volume of material being described; various units of measure are used.
The structure and sequence of the records in this series.	{ Organization: Arranged by grant program, thereunder by project number.	
Why this series was created; the activities it documents; the kind of information it contains.	{ Summary: To further the mandate of the Department of Environmental Protection, the Bureau of Municipal Facilities was established in 1989 under the department's deputy Commissioner for municipal assistance to administer grants to municipalities for water supply and water pollution projects, previously administered by the Division of Water Pollution Control and the Division of Water Supply. This series was created by those divisions and is maintained by the bureau to administer grants in the form of outright allocations of funds, reimbursement of costs incurred by municipalities, or low-cost loans. Grant files contain applications, correspondence, revisions to grants, engineering reports, approved and executed specifications, contracts, change orders, approved and as-built plans, and closure documents. Files include information about project planning, facility location and features of proposed site, facility design, construction process, equipment and materials used, costs, and funding sources. In some cases, specifications and plans may be stored separately.	
	Appraisal statement: Files have administrative value until closure. Fiscal information is not audited in this office. Since the approved application is an agreement, records have a legal value that expires at 6 years after closure with the statute of limitations of actions on contracts. The record copy of this series is held by the municipal engineering department, local water district and/or the facility itself, which holds certain of the the materials, such as executed specifications and as-built plans, permanently.	} The value of these records for various purposes — administrative, legal, historical, etc; the period for which those values are presumed to exist.
How long these records are retained, and where.	{ Retention and disposition: Retain in office until closure then retain at state records center for 7 years then destroy.	
	Location: Dept. of Environmental Protection. 1 Winter St. Boston, MA 02108.	} Where the records are located.

---

* This particular example, while a real entry in the RLIN database, is shown here as an amalgam of two different presentations of the data that an RLIN user might choose to view at any moment. The Organization and Summary paragraphs are highlighted in one of RLIN's selectable display formats, while the Appraisal and Retention paragraphs are highlighted in another. They have been combined here simply to illustrate the contents of records series descriptions.

The working group also entered series descriptions and appraisal notes in two subject categories: corrections, a branch of criminal justice, and environment, specifically records relating to the Clean Water Act of 1977 (P. L. 95-217, 91 Stat. 1566). When, at the conclusion of the SSP, participants attempted to test the usefulness of the appraisal information in the database, they discovered that there were not enough records to produce statistically significant test results; the GRP participants selected these two very narrow areas in which to enter records in order to provide enough depth for a test.

Statistically significant test results might point to ways in which effective standards could be developed for sharing appraisal information. Unfortunately, the GRP's steering committee determined that not enough records had been entered to test; instead, it was decided that a survey of participating institutions' appraisal practices, method, and documentation would be conducted. The resulting Appraisal Profile would permit participants to examine the realities of appraisal in government archives, and establish a firm foundation on which to develop standards and definitions. The survey has been completed, and the results are now being analyzed.

Intergovernmental Records Project (IRP)

The Intergovernmental Records Project, a collaboration between NARA and the state archives of Virginia and Wisconsin, ran concurrently with the GRP. It set for itself a number of different tasks, a small portion of which related to sharing appraisal information about intergovernmental records. The IRP asked:

> Since intergovernmental records are held at different levels of government, would knowing how records were scheduled at one level be useful in scheduling records at another? Does shared appraisal information assist the appraiser by providing a broader context for the appraisal decision? Could RLIN serve as a source for information about related records scheduled by other states or the federal government? (Nelson, 1990, p. 3)

To answer these questions, the IRP and some GRP participants entered information about records created by the Environmental Protection Agency (EPA) and state environmental agencies that administer the Federal Water Pollution Control Act of 1972 (P. L. 92-500, 86 Stat. 816). These RLIN entries served as a pool of test data that was then studied by the IRP. This study was the only test conducted on the effectiveness of shared appraisal, since the GRP chose not to do a test.

The IRP arrived at a number of conclusions and recommendations.

Overall, despite problems with the quantity and quality of information in records, the report concluded that online access to interrelated records enables appraisers to better understand the context in which records were created as well as their usefulness, and aids in improving the quality of appraisal decisions.

IMPLEMENTATION

Definitions and Guidelines

When the Massachusetts Archives agreed to participate in the GRP, we felt that use of the MARC AMC format and comparative appraisal would have a positive impact on our records management program. The archives' appraisal methodology and documentation, although fairly consistent, had never been standardized; use of the MARC AMC format would require more standardized practice. Comparative appraisal, where archivists compare appraisal decisions made for parallel series created in multiple states, had been practiced in the past by exchange of information through the mail and over the phone with only modest success. We accepted the MARC AMC format and innovations to it developed by the SSP as tools we would use to achieve the goals set by RLG, and were ready to make the necessary programmatic changes (see Figures 15-2 through 15-4).[2]

The Appraisal Worksheet

Our first step was to develop a data-gathering tool for field work. The information needed to appraise and schedule series properly is not substantially different from that required to write agency histories, MARC format series descriptions, and LDA and LDB entries. Thus, we developed an Appraisal Worksheet (see Figure 15-5), which prompts the analyst to collect contextual and descriptive information, in addition to the data relating to records values needed for analysis.

---

[2] Definitions and guidelines were submitted by the GRP for consideration by RLG in August 1989 and September 1990. While not yet approved, these are the most recent proposals. Additional guidelines for agency history and series description records are available in the Compendium of Practice, which the RLG will soon issue.

Figure 15-2. Definitions of Record Types.

This figure identifies the types of online records created by members of the RLG-Government Records Project. A record type is a group of data elements created and used as a logical unit to document actions taken and to describe, explain, or make information available. Two categories of record types are represented here: authority records and bibliographic records. Within each category, a range of record types are defined.

All records created by Project members should fall into one of the identified categories. If alternate records types appear to be necessary to meet an institution's needs, a proposed definition and format should be submitted for review by the Descriptive Practices Working Group.

AUTHORITY RECORDS

Definition: A description of information necessary to understand the context, background, or conditions which may affect the physical conditions or intellectual content of the described items. Authority records do not describe specific, existing records, but attributes of and information related to the context and creation of these records.

Types of Authority Records:

<u>History records</u> are records providing information on the organization, history, and functions of an organizational body which is useful in explaining or ensuring an understanding of an organization.

o   <u>Government agency history</u>. This provides background information on the organization, functions, and major accomplishments of a government agency. It provides important contextual information for understanding the records the agency subsequently creates.

o   <u>Government agency subdivision history</u>. Like the agency history record, this record provides background information on a subdivision in order to further understand the organization and functions specifically related to this subdivision, and only generally referred to in the agency history record.

o   <u>Government program unit history</u>. This type of history record is yet another smaller version of the agency history record, again providing background information on the organization and function of a specific program unit.

<u>Record type records</u> describe common, general types of records produced. The record type records currently being created include:

o   <u>Schedule summary record</u>. This describes a whole schedule, explaining the process and purposes by which a group of records have been analyzed to identify their retention and disposition, and the purposes for scheduling their retention and disposition as a group. Like the agency history record, it provides background information for the user to help that person understand other scheduling records. The schedule can represent either general scheduled items, generic scheduled items, or real scheduled items. Examples of this might be a schedule for school districts, a personnel records schedule, or a schedule for one whole agency as as a Department of Energy schedule. The type of schedule described will depend on the scheduling practices of the particular institution.

Figure 15-2. (Continued)

o   General schedule series record. This describes a specific kind of record common to several or all government organizations based on the record's form and/or function. These record items describe kinds of records that may be found in either specific functional areas of government or kinds of records found in many units of government, regardless of unit function. Examples of form would be payroll, budget, or personnel records. These are not the same as bibliographic records, because they describe something that might exist. General scheduled item records also include items that are scheduled around a particular functional area, such as a county board of elections or a city manager. There is no volume, dates, or specific agency of creation in any of these records.

BIBLIOGRAPHIC RECORDS

Definition: A description of the physical characteristics and intellectual contents of a body of records. These records describe specific records of some kind in existence.

Types of Bibliographic Records

An archival record is a description usually at the series level, to provide information for research purposes as well as archival control purposes. Archival bibliographic records currently being created include:

o   Series records. A description of a group of records created to serve a particular function or activity, have a particular form, or some similar relationship.

o   Subseries records. A description of a logical subdivision of a series.

o   Item records. A description of a single archival document or other form of material.

A scheduled record. A description of current and noncurrent government records to provide information for management and control. Those records currently being created include:

o   Schedule series records. The scheduled item record provides appraisal and disposition information and general bibliographic information about actual records. This item contains the same types of information normally found in archival bibliographic records. Different organizations may schedule in different ways, so this record will encompass records above or below the series level, but it will adhere to basic standards for archival bibliographic records.

Figure 15-3. Guidelines for Records Schedules and Scheduled Records.

Records schedules are an administrative mechanism by which archival repositories and other responsible agencies manage the life cycle of many kinds of official records. Simply stated that life cycle consists of the creation of records, by an agency or office, and their use there for some period of time; the possible transfer of those records to another storage location, such as a Records Center, for less frequent access; and the ultimate disposition of the records - either destruction or permanent archival retention. Schedules may refer to actual record series, e.g., prisoner case files, or to types or categories of records, e.g., payroll records for all agencies within a particular state government.

Schedules are established based on an appraisal of the specific records or types of records; that is, a determination of the informational, evidentiary, and historical value (among other aspects) of the material. A schedule indicates, typically, the length of time records stay in the office or origin before transfer to the Records Center, how long they are kept at the Center, and what happens to them at the end of that period. An example might be employment records retained in the Personnel Office for three years after the termination of employment; they are then transferred to the Records Center and retained for 25 years; records are then destroyed, except for a 1 percent sample extracted each year for permanent retention in the County Archives.

There are two levels of schedule records: (1) a schedule summary record, and (2) a schedule series record.

Schedule Summary Record

A summary record describes the schedule itself. This relates to the scheduled item record in much the same manner as the agency history record relates to the bibliographic record. It provides an overall explanation of a records schedule, its purpose, and how dispositions were determined, and it links all the scheduled items to it.

Scheduled Series Record

This record may represent either actual records that have been scheduled or types of records that have been scheduled. Users will be able to distinguish actual records from types of series by the presence of a corporate author, volume, and dates. Each schedule series record will be linked to a schedule summary record, if applicable.

Required Fields in Online AMC Schedule Summary Record

A. Fixed Fields

   RTYP-record type: There is no special RTYP value for schedule summary records. Users will input schedule summary records in the CATalog function, and the system will automatically assign an RTYP value of "d." The ARChival control segment, which is required for every AMC record, must contain values in AAN or MATI, in ACT and in TAC, TFAC, or AIR.

   DCF-descriptive cataloging form: Schedule summary records do not correspond to the principles outlines in <u>Archives, Personal Papers, and Manuscripts</u> and should, therefore, use a DCF value of blank.

Figure 15-3. (Continued)

PP - : Place of publication or production code/repository code: use a PP value of XX.

L - : Language code: use three blanks in this field.

PC - : Type of data code: use value "n."

PD - : Dates: use blanks, as is appropriate when PC is "n."

CC- : Cataloging category: use value "9554" (or "9556" for non-RLG members). Records containing less data in the variable fields than specified below should value "9994" (or "9996 for non-RLG members).

B. Variable Fields

040 - Cataloging source: subfields a and c should contain the NUC symbol of the institution performing the cataloging (subfield a) and the institution creating the machine- readable record (subfield c).

245 - Title: only subfield a (title proper) is required for schedule summary records. Construct a title entry according to the following form: (name of agency) (level of agency (type of records) (type of schedule); the second and third descriptors are optional.

And so forth.

Required Fields in Online AMC Schedule Series Record

A. Fixed Fields

RTYP-record type: There is no special RTYP for schedule series records. Users will input schedule series records in the CATalog function, and the system will automatically assign an RTYP value of "d." The ARChival control segment, which is required for every AMC record, must contain values in ACCN or MATL, in ACT, and in TAC, TFAC, or AIR.

DCF-descriptive cataloging form: Schedule series records do not correspond to the principles outlines in Archives, Personal Papers, and Manuscripts and should, therefore, use a DCF value of blank; for actual records the value should be 'a" when following Hensen.

PP - : Place of publication or production code/repository code: For actual records use this field to code the repository's location. For types of records use the value "XX."

L - : Language code: use three blanks in this field; actual records should be coded for the language of the material.

PC - : Type of data code: for actual records use values "i" or "s." For types of records use value "n."

Figure 15-3. (Continued)

> PD - : Dates: for actual records enter the appropriation dates. For types of records use blanks, as is appropriate when PC is "n."
>
> CC- : Cataloging category: use value "9554" (or "9556" for non-RLG members). Records containing less data in the variable fields than specified below should value "9994" (or "9996 for non-RLG members).
> [Note: the above reflects practice after the standard has been approved; until such time, these records should be coded as nonstandard]
>
> B. Variable Fields
>
> 040 - Cataloging source: subfields a and c should contain the NUC symbol of the institution performing the cataloging (subfield a) and the institution creating the machine- readable record (subfield c).
>
> And so forth.
>
> **LDA/LDB**
>
> Use these local data elements as needed for retention and disposition information.
>
> 851- Location: for actual record give relevant location. For types of record give an explanation of possible locations.

The demands of the MARC AMC format and RLIN make standardized descriptive and appraisal practices desirable. The Appraisal Worksheet makes possible a uniform approach to both. Each analyst collects uniformly comprehensive data, from series to series, and is then able to follow written procedures for appraisal. The worksheet promotes efficiency and has reduced the number of return visits needed to complete documentation of a series. Within the archives, analysts now have a common language to discuss and share appraisal findings.

Information on the worksheet relates directly to MARC fields, and is easily translatable to disposal schedules, series descriptions in MARC AMC format, and LDA and LDB entries. The completed worksheet becomes a resource for analysts or others who may be describing the series weeks or even months after the analyst's initial survey. Analysts now share a common language with processing and reference archivists to identify records series and their context, and to discuss processing needs and reference uses of series. This promotes collaboration and has increased particularly the volume and quality of contextual information in series descriptions and authority records created by staff as a whole.

Figure 15-4. Guidelines for LDA/LDB.*

A. LDA: Used to record a brief but clear summary of the appraisal decision. The field consists of a narrative statement identifying the reasons for the retention or disposition.

   1. Introductory wording: "Appraisal Statement:"

   2. Controlled value terms:

      a. Primary: value to the creating or succeeding agency.

      b. Secondary: value outside the creating or succeeding agency.

      c. Administrative: usefulness to creating/succeeding agency in the continuing conduct of its duties.

      d. Fiscal: usefulness to creating/succeeding agency in conducting fianancual affairs; prudent or required documentation thereof.

      e. Legal: usefulness to creating/succeeding agency in conduct of current or future legal business; required to prudent evidence of legal rights fo the agency, its employees, or those people and insitutions it dealt with.

      f. Evidential: degree to which records provide authentic and adequate documentation of the creating agency's organization and functioning.

      g. Informational: historical or research value; information about persons, places, topics, and the like which would be potentially useful to historians or other researchers.

      h. Limited: limited appraisal information available (this control word can be used to screen out such records from a search result).

      Clarification on the Use of These Terms:

      The appraisal statement should provide the rationale for assigning any of the above values to a series in a brief, clear explanation. It is not sufficient to simply state that a record "has evidential value." Why? Evidence about what? Similarly, rather than saying, "this series has administrative value," explain why: "this series has administrative value because it is the central information file for this bureau." The reason need not be lengthy. The informational content and the function of the record series should be clearly described in the 520 field. Further, why the information is considered valuable, and to what extent, should be explained here in the LDA.

   3. Legal citations for laws that require retention or influence the decision should be included, as should the year that the appraisal is completed.

---

* Based on "LDA/LDB Guidelines and Functional Testing Areas: Final Recommendations," submitted to the GRP steering committee by the appraisal working group, August 30, 1989 (see Nelson, 1989).

Figure 15-4. (Continued)

4. Other information which should be included where relevant to the decision is:

    If the series related to other series within the agency, or to series created by any other body, and the relationship affects the decision, this should be noted and a citation of the related series should be included.

    Duplication of information, either in another series, or if the records themselves have been duplicated.

    Any other variables such as condition, volume, and accessibility.

    Agency background history that has had a special impact on the appraisal decision.

    Name of reviewer and the citation/location of the full documentation (appraisal report) may be cited if desired for purposes of local use.

5. Note if recommendations made by appraisal archivists differ from the retention/disposition specified in the LDB field, and provide a brief explanation.

6. Minimum LDA Information Required

    The appraisal statement must make clear why the series has been assigned its final disposition: why it is being kept, or why it is considered disposable. If this information is not available, the controlled value term "limited" must be used (e.g., "limited appraisal information available"). They year the appraisal was completed should be included in all records.

B. LDB: Used to record the retention period for a single record series as specified through an appraisal report or a records schedule, and also to record the final disposition of the series.

1. Introductory wording: "Retention and Disposition:"

2. The retention note may be begun with such phrases as "retain," "hold," or "store," and should include the retention period (expressed in years or months), the trigger event (if any), and final disposition.

3. Also noted should be any special circumstances that may modify the retention or disposition, or special disposition conditions that may result from sensitive record content.

4. The schedule number, title or name of the person or body which issued final approval of the retention/diposition, and the year in which approval was issued may also be included if desired for local use purposes.

5. Definition of terms used:

    a. Retention period: minimum period of time (unless otherwise noted) that the records are to be retained before they are transferred to a new location, and/or before they reach their final disposition. (Initial retention period begins at date of creation, unless otherwise specified.) Retention period may be expressed in years or months.

Figure 15-4. (Continued)

    b. Trigger event: that event which makes the records inactive. Records are considered inactive when they are no longer actively used in the course of business.

6. Minimum LDB Information Required. At the very least, the LDB statement must give the retention period and the final disposition.

Figure 15-5. Appraisal Worksheet.*

Date: _____ Person Completing: _____

Location: _____

1. CREATING ENTITY (include origin, function, citations, predecessors):

2. PREFERRED SERIES TITLE (title should include form and function):

    Alternative title (when citing spine title, form #, etc., use quotation marks): _____

3. FUNCTION OF SERIES (include citations as appropriate):

4. INFORMATION CONTAINED IN SERIES (include "daa elements" if form or type of information):

5. ORGANIZATION (enumerate subseries, if any):

    Arranged: __ alpha. __ numer. __ chrono. __ other, by _____

6. PHYSICAL DESCRIPTION (number and size of boxes, volumes, bundles, etc.):

    Volume in cubic feet:

7. SPAN DATES: _____ BULK DATES: _____

    Annual accumulation: _____

8. LOSSES OR GAPS IN SERIES: _____

---

* In Figure 15-5, item 1 relates to the creator of the series; items 2 through 8 collect information about the function, content, format, and extent of the series. For government records, item 9, statutory or regulatory provisions restricting access, is a major concern. Items 10, 11, and 14 refer to the appraisal paradigm established by Schellenberg (1956), still the most influential and widely used appraisal methodology among public archives. Items 12 and 13 gauge the series' level of uniqueness. In item 15, the appraiser analyzes the information gathered about the context, function, content, condition, uniqueness, and values of the record series, and formulates appraisal and disposition recommendations.

Figure 15-5. (Continued)

9. RESTRICTIONS (cite statute or regulations governing access to records): _____

10. PERIOD OF PRIMARY VALUE (note the administrative, legal, and fiscal uses to which the series is, and the expiration of these values):

11. AGENCY OPINION ON SECONDARY VALUE OF RECORDS (note agency opinion on historical or evidential values of records, and potential research uses; include names and phone numbers of contacts):

12. DUPLICATE OR SUMMARY INFORMATION IN UNPUBLISHED SOURCES (where appropriate, include media, condition, function, retention, etc. of related/duplicate information)

13. DUPLICATE OR SUMMARY INFORMATION IN PUBLISHED SOURCES:

14. ARCHIVISTS/EXPERTS OPINION ON SECONDARY VALUE OR RECORDS (note opinion on historical or evidential values of records, and potential research uses; include names and phone numbers of contacts):

15. APPRAISER'S RECOMMENDATIONS ON DISPOSITION OF SERIES:

Entries Written by Analysts

Of the 2,600 RLIN records it entered during the two-year grant, the archives input 2,224 series descriptions. Some 789 of the descriptions, or about 35 percent, were contributed by the records management unit. They included descriptions of three classes of series: some entries describe archival series, increments of which will eventually be transferred to the archives; some describe permanently valuable local government records which by law cannot be transferred to the archives, but must be retained permanently by their creators; and some descriptions contain information about nonarchival series, created and held at either the local or state level.

Most of these descriptions were generated from new surveys in government offices. In these cases, records series were identified, appraised, and described as an integral part of the creation of new disposal schedules. When any major survey was planned, analysts were asked to complete MARC format descriptions for entry into RLIN, and to provide contextual and agency history information to processing archivists for the development of authority records.

Like the other GRP participants, we also converted data contained in existing disposal schedules to MARC format descriptions. Schedules were selected for conversion based on the importance of the records for research, or for documenting the functions of the creator. Specific agency schedules were converted, as were a selected number of general schedules (for definitions of schedule types, see Figure 15-2).

Comparative Appraisal

Comparative appraisal, sometimes called "shared appraisal," is based on the premise that parallel series exist in similar institutions, and that it is useful to compare appraisers' analyses of parallel series. Parallel series are created in different locations, but result from the same or similar function. Such series occur frequently in government since classes of governmental entities perform the same basic functions; similar activities are carried out, which generate similar records series. This is also true of hospitals, schools, and universities, and classes of commercial enterprises, such as insurance companies and law firms.

During the process of appraising records series, analysts were asked to search the database for descriptions of parallel series entered by other states, and to look particularly for those containing appraisal and disposition information in the LDA and LDB fields. In testing the database in this way, we discovered several ways in which parallel series information is useful, such as identifying relevant citations, potential research uses, and federal offices of record. Despite the fact that analysts locate information needed for comparative appraisal in about 15 percent of the searches conducted in RLIN, exposure to other appraisers' analyses sharpens their thinking about appraisal and improves the quality of their work.

BENEFITS AND OBSTACLES IN USING MARC AMC FOR RECORDS MANAGEMENT

Using the MARC AMC format in an archival setting for records management activities has several benefits, including the enhancement of intellectual control over records and the exchange of data. Obstacles to the successful use of the format include the unintelligibility of nonstandard MARC formats for life-cycle control, the higher standard of description needed for comparative appraisal, and the lack of standards for documentation and exchange of appraisal information. Some steps can be taken to alleviate these problems, although despite these barriers, the MARC AMC format continues to be useful for records management activities.

Benefits

Perhaps even more than pre-MARC archivists, records managers have operated in a vacuum, apart from other managers and from archivists and librarians in their own institutions. The most significant benefit of the MARC AMC format for records management is the integration of management activities into the full records life cycle, and enhancement of the exchange of information among institutions. Using MARC to exchange information both within and outside their own organizations, records managers can improve the efficiency of records management tasks and the the quality of their appraisal decisions.

Benefit: Enhanced Control and Communication

Records management addresses records early in their life cycle. Records are created, maintained in the office, moved to off-site storage when they become inactive, and, when their value ceases to the creator, either destroyed or, if they have secondary value, transferred to the archives. Records management is involved in all of those steps but the last, and, in the case of the Massachusetts Archives, even the last as the responsibility for acquisitions, preprocessing, and transfer rests with the records management unit. Why should standardized description and intellectual control begin so late in the life cycle, when records are moved to archival vaults?

The application of standards can begin when records are identified in the office of the creator. Standard series titles and control numbers can be assigned as records are surveyed, and MARC AMC format descriptions and authority records prepared. When series are appraised and scheduled, appraisal and disposition notes in the form of LDAs and LDBs can be appended to descriptions. When this information is entered into the database, records series, regardless of their physical location, are available for research or for administrative activities.

An example of one such activity is the tracking of archival records still in agency hands; through the use of standard terms in subject access fields or through the Archival Control segment (ARC) on the RLIN system, the archives can identify series which have been appraised but not accessioned.[3] Accessioning records series is another activity enhanced by the use of MARC AMC format early in the records life cycle. When records are physically transferred to the archives, they have already been identified and described. The description can be quickly updated, and made available in online and printed finding aids. Since little descriptive work needs to be done, the records can be processed more rapidly.

There is no doubt that the use of common standards and vocabularies enhances communications among records managers, archivists, and reference staff. An additional benefit is the ease with which information about records can be returned to the creating entity. Each time a description is updated, from the first survey to the accession of new increments of a series, a copy can be sent to the creator. This informs the creating entity of actions taken by the records management and archival staff on its records, and reminds the entity that nonarchival records are scheduled and that disposition may be carried out, and that the records documenting its corporate memory are retained and available in the archives.

Benefit: Comparative Appraisal

Analysts at the archives conduct RLIN searches as a regular part of the scheduling and appraisal process. This pool of experiences has taught us that there are a variety of ways in which exchange of information about records series and their analysis can increase the accuracy and efficiency of records management tasks.

Federal statutes and regulations govern many state and local government records; because they are consistent from state to state, it is useful to identify relevant citations contained in parallel series descriptions. In one instance, an analyst found descriptions of a parallel series entered by three different states, each attributing a different retention period to the

---

[3] Nelson (1989) describes the use of standard index terms for appraised records, including the use of the terms "Appraised," "Scheduled," and "Permanent" in the 690 field.

same federal statute; in checking the citation, he discovered that the law had been revised, and only one state was retaining the records for the correct period of time. In most cases, citations in parallel series provide a shortcut, making analysts' work easier; in this case, it made the work of several states more accurate (see Cyphers, 1990a,b).

The articulation of the appraisal process found in some LDAs helps to broaden analysts' thinking about how they appraise records. What variables are considered, how are they weighed, and how can that process be communicated and documented? Questions like these sharpen appraisers' analytical skills and improve appraisal practice.

Since state law varies, assessment of primary values - administrative, fiscal, and legal usefulness - is generally less uniform from state to state; and the existence of state guidelines usually makes primary values easier to determine. As a result, analysts frequently find that it is the assessment of secondary values - particularly informational value - in which they could benefit from dialogue. Informational value, the usefulness of a series for subject studies in such areas as medicine, the social sciences, public policy, natural science, and history, must be based on a wide-ranging knowledge of the archives' holdings, holdings of other institutions, research methods, and trends. The knowledge brought by one analyst to the appraisal of a parallel series can be useful to an analyst in another state.

Comparative appraisal is the first step towards cooperative appraisal, where an institution's retention of a parallel or related series is influenced by the retention of the series by other institutions. Cooperative appraisal is more practical between, rather than within, jurisdictions. Local governments may request to destroy reports submitted to state entities if reports are retained permanently by the state. Likewise, state information retained by the federal government might be destroyed at the state level. The area of intergovernmental cooperative appraisal explored by the IRP may be one of the most significant contributions of the several experiments in sharing appraisal information. Cooperative appraisal is not restricted solely to government entities. An insurance company library, in considering retention of its records, could use a utility like RLIN to discover that the state department of insurance retains for only 10 years the sample policies and reports submitted by the company, but that a copy of the company's charter is retained permanently by the Secretary of State.

Obstacles

The barriers preventing the effective use of the MARC AMC format for records management spring from the relative novelty of the application. Usages and standards have not yet been perfected through years of practice, and institutions employing the format may not have recognized the need for programmatic change to accommodate it successfully.

Obstacle: General Schedule Records and "Real Records"

Midway through the GRP, it became apparent that the use of these nonstandard MARC AMC records was causing problems for some RLIN users. Some subscribers from research libraries, manuscript collections, and other private institutions, accustomed to traditional MARC records, were confused by the appearance of these unfamiliar authority and bibliographic records in the database. Other RLIN users, both persons in and outside the project, were disturbed by the limited descriptive information these records often contain. Descriptions of general schedule series rarely include volume amounts, or inclusive dates, and cannot note the specific locations of all offices where the series might exist. Additionally, since many of the general and schedule series records were created by conversion, contextual and descriptive data were often sketchy. Some RLIN users argued that such entries did not describe "real records," and had no place in a bibliographic database.

GRP participants supported the inclusion of schedule records in RLIN, despite their nonstandard appearance, arguing that the information they contain is important and useful to researchers, appraisal archivists, and archival administrators (Appraisal Working Group, 1990, p. 3). Such records describe series which are a part of the information universe, and which are available for access by researchers in archives or in the offices of creators. In some states, local government records of permanent value are not acquired by the state archives, but are maintained by their creators. As there may be tens of counties or hundreds of municipalities, it is not practical to survey them all, and many states manage local records exclusively through general schedules; if there is to be any documentation of these series in RLIN, it must be through a general schedule series record.

The appraisal and disposition information contained in schedule series records and general schedule series records, for both archival and nonarchival series, can be useful for comparative appraisal. Surveys of parallel series in RLIN have been used to test or support appraisal decisions, and to gain a better understanding of records values that may have been overlooked.

The controversy engendered by the appearance of these nonstandard MARC AMC records in the database is far from being resolved. The proposed usages have not yet been approved by RLG, and no timeline has been set for their approval or further development. The requirements of cataloging standards make the construction of corporate name and series title entries for these records difficult and awkward, adding to database users' confusion. It is likely that further testing and refinement of the nonstandard records will be necessary.

Obstacle: Description

Poor descriptive practices affect the usefulness of the records to identify series for research purposes, and have a direct bearing on the usefulness of the records for records management. For example, in conducting a test of records in the RLIN database, the IRP found that description was deficient exactly where detailed information was most necessary: in identifying intergovernmental records series for comparative appraisal.

The IRP reported that while not uncommon in RLIN, limited descriptive information is particularly problematic in descriptions of scheduled records, which are usually culled from existing disposal schedules;

> When records were scheduled sometime in the past, it is not easy to produce supplementary information to flesh out otherwise sketchy descriptive information because the records are most often not in the institution's custody. (National Archives and Records Administration, 1990, pp. 101-102)

Additional flaws are: the lack of information about the intergovernmental nature of the records, thereby making more difficult the establishment of clear relationships across jurisdictions; and the lack of details, such as form numbers and titles, applicable state and federal citations, and the names of submitting (or requiring) offices, which could be helpful in identifying and comparing records and their dispositions (Ibid., pp. 102-103).

Effective descriptions of intergovernmental records are possible; the IRP pointed to records entered by the Massachusetts Archives as "models of descriptions" (Ibid., p. 101). We created these records by investing the time required to newly survey the subject series, using the Appraisal Worksheet and related guidelines, to develop complete series descriptions and appraisal notes. Not every GRP participant was able to devote the necessary resources to produce this kind of detailed description; and certainly we could not do so for every record we entered. However, the development of comprehensive research databases that are useful to researchers and records administrators alike requires that more institutions expend the resources needed to produce thoughtful, complete, and detailed descriptions.

Obstacle: Comparative Appraisal

All three projects which experimented with comparative appraisal, the SSP, GRP, and IRP, identified some obstacles to successful sharing of appraisal data. Difficulties in locating and identifying parallel series relate in part to variation in access terms and descriptive practices, and are the same problems that would be faced by any researcher using the database.

A problem unique to the use of the MARC AMC format for records management is the inadequacy of the appraisal note information for sharing. Appraisal notes entered during the SSP "lacked the needed elements of information to make them comprehensible to others" (Ruller, 1990, p. 17). The GRP did not improve upon the first project's efforts: a survey of appraisal practices of GRP participants revealed that despite nearly universal agreement in appraisal methodology, little consistency existed in the "methods in which appraisal decisions are corroborated and documented" (Ibid., p. 1). In fact, "only a minimum number of data elements about the appraisal decision" were recorded; "without standards similar to those used to make archival description common to most institutions, archival appraisal documentation cannot be useful outside the institution" (Ibid., p. 18). In the absence of standards, institutions will have no impetus to improve documentation of appraisal decisions, and no way to insure an accurate exchange of data.

The first step in the development of standards for appraisal documentation and data sharing is the acceptance of the LDA and LDB as full-fledged MARC AMC fields. This is crucial for two reasons. First, while they are experimental and subject to varying interpretations from institution to institution, they will never reach their full potential for data exchange. And, second, the usefulness of the database for comparative appraisal depends in part on the quantity as well as the quality of appraisal note entries; this means that the adoption of the LDA and LDB by many institutions is key to successful sharing. But, what institution will willingly alter its current practices and document appraisal in the LDA if the investment, in the absence of standards, may prove to be worthless? Constructive, profession-wide discussion about appraisal documentation standards can only begin when steps are made for the formal acceptance of these records management fields.

CONCLUSION

Historically, librarians, archivists, and records managers have worked independently to ensure the best service to their clientele. Conditions in today's workplace have begun to blur the distinctions between these professions. The demand for more inclusive information combined with diminishing budgets and the rise of automation have prepared the ground for integration of processes. Currently records managers have had available to them software designed to control the location of records, but not to describe records' content or value. Archivists have been able to chose from a selection of software packages designed to manage bibliographic descriptions, but none that track records throughout their life cycle.

The experiences of the Massachusetts Archives in participating in the Government Records Project led us to conclude that the MARC AMC format has the potential to link the two by setting compatible standards. The format, however, cannot operate independently of a system, and systems are created by the demand of the market. Records managers must articulate their needs so that systems are designed to provide for life-cycle tracking and integration of information. Only an integrated life-cycle system can insure the preservation of corporate memory, the continued usefulness of information for institutional administrative purposes, and the provision of access to a more comprehensive universe of information for research. Librarians have been in the forefront of standards and automated systems development; those who also have the dual responsibilities of archivist and records manager are in an excellent position to effect this transition.

REFERENCES

Appraisal Working Group, RLG Government Records Project. "Position Paper Supporting the Inclusion of Schedule Records in the RLIN AMSC Database." Unpublished paper, April 1990.

Cyphers, James E. "Adventures in Shared Appraisal: A Case Study," *The GRP Standard* 1 (June 1990a): 3.

Cyphers, James E. "Further Adventures in Shared Appraisal," *The GRP Standard* 1 (October 1990b): 3.

National Archives and Records Administration, Intergovernmental Records Project. *Phase I Report.* Washington, DC: National Archives, July 1990.

Nelson, Sharon R. "The Changing Faces of Appraisal in the RLG Government Records Projects." Unpublished paper presented at the Annual Meeting of the National Association of Government Archives and Records Administrators, Boston, Massachusetts, July 1990.

Nelson, Sharon. "LDA/LDB Guidelines and Functional Testing Areas: Final Recommendations." Memorandum to Government Records Project Participants, August 30, 1989.

"Report of the Working Group on Standards for Archival Description," *The American Archivist* 52 (Fall 1989): 440-461.

Roe, Kathleen D. "The Automation Odyssey: Library and Archives System Design Considerations," *Cataloging and Classification Quarterly* 11 (1990): 145-162.

Ruller, Thomas J. "Appraisal Documentation as an Impediment to Sharing Appraisal Data: A Survey of Appraisal Documentation in State Government Archival Repositories." Unpublished paper presented at the Annual Meeting of the Society of American Archivists, Seattle, Washington, September 1990.

Schellenberg, Theodore R. *The Appraisal of Modern Public Records*. Chicago, IL: University of Chicago Press, 1956.
Weber, Lisa B. "Record Formatting: MARC AMC," *Cataloging and Classification Quarterly* 11 (1990): 117-143.

Chapter Sixteen

Records Management at the Massachusetts Bay Transportation Authority: Creating an Integrated Information Management System

by Toby Pearlstein

The Massachusetts Bay Transportation Authority (MBTA) is a regional transit authority that serves more than 150 cities and towns in Eastern Massachusetts and employs more than 7,000 people. The MBTA came into official existence in 1964, but is actually the successor, through various business mergers and legislative enactments, to a variety of public and private companies that have provided public transportation services in the Boston Metropolitan Area since the early 19th century.

The modern formal records management program at the MBTA began in 1983 with the hiring of a Chief Librariar & Archivist. The duties included, as the title might suggest, the establishment of a library as well as an archives/records management program. Prior to this time several efforts had been made to bring the agency's voluminous records under some physical and intellectual control, but these were only pursued as time and resources allowed and with no long-term goals or plan in mind.

THE GENERAL CONTEXT

While the basic principles of records management are no different from one organization to the next, their implementation is very parochial because records management is unique to a firm's needs, business environment, and history. A librarian in a situation like that at the MBTA, where records management had not been a traditional institutional priority, needs to begin by establishing a framework for information management activity beyond the library's traditional scope. This information management framework will be predicated on the kind of organization, its regulatory or business environment, and the resources it is willing to dedicate to the information management task.

The framework we set out to create at the MBTA had two major components: a desire to control three information trails in the organization, and a realization that in a truly integrated information management system an organization's vital information is under control from its creation through all its useful phases, and is disposed of appropriately.

There are two reasons why librarians should be involved in the creation of such a system. First, if they are to do their jobs well they must be able to provide information, in whatever form, from whatever source, that will satisfy their client's needs. Second, they must be able to obtain this information in the most cost-effective and efficient way. An integrated system enables them to do this. Involvement in records management activities greatly expands the pool of information available for them to use. Because this information is a resource internal to the company, it can be utilized in a very cost-effective way.

New technologies have forced us to rethink both the physical and intellectual parameters of information. How librarians respond to these new parameters may well mean the difference between professional failure or success. Within the context of the daily working environment librarians need to think of information as existing on a continuum. This continuum or life cycle begins at the point of records creation and runs through records maintenance and use, ending with appropriate disposition of the information. Whether you call it records management, archives, or library science, it is all part of the same thing. As information managers we need to be aware of and involved in judgments about the administrative, legal, and historical uses of information in our organization so that we can make sure its value is maximized not only for our own purposes but for the company's overall benefit as well.

THE INFORMATION TRAILS

There are at least three information trails in any organization, including government agencies. Librarians seem to be most familiar with the first of these, the external trail that ends in the library through the acquisition of published or otherwise packaged information from outside the organization. The second of these trails is internal to the organization and also often ends in the library when it becomes the repository for an organization's own published or other products. The third trail, also internal, consists of the unpublished day-to-day records, files, drawings, and electronic information that keep the organization operating.

More often than not, the librarian's role is one of information maintenance and disposition as it relates to the first two trails, those involving published information. Creating an integrated information system at the MBTA meant that librarians would have to become involved with the third day-to-day records trail as well. Keeping to the view that information exists along a continuum, this third trail can be incorporated into the concept of an integrated system. This would help expand the pool of information available for use and would help the organization by bringing a valuable asset under control.

AN INTEGRATED INFORMATION MANAGEMENT SYSTEM

How were we to reconcile records management responsibility with our typical library duties? A point worth stressing here is that the value of day-to-day business records is often grossly underestimated as the final component in a complete system of information management. However, how could we work towards the creation of an integrated information system? The only way was to understand the broad scope of the information trail that involves day-to-day business records. Through involvement in records management librarians can increase their value to the organization by bringing an important asset under control. To gain control of these daily business records at the MBTA we realized we had to:

o   Determine the flow of information through the agency;

o   Identify how that information was being captured, that is, in what type of instrument (paper document, tape, magnetic disk, etc.);

o   Determine how long the information had to be kept, by whom, and where;

o   Provide for access to the information; and

o   Provide for appropriate disposition of the information.

And while these were not typical library tasks, it was easy to see how our skills as information professionals could be brought to bear to accomplish them.

Of primary importance had to be the fact that the MBTA is a public agency and, therefore, subject to both state and federal requirements for recordkeeping. On the state level these requirement are promulgated and administered by the Records Conservation Board, a division of the Office of the Secretary of State. The Board provides guidance for the establishment of retention and disposition schedules and must approve any actions related to the destruction of agency records. Its interest is primarily that the records of public agencies be accessible to the citizens of the Commonwealth of Massachusetts. So one of the criteria on which our information framework would be based was dictated by state-level regulatory requirements.

A second criteria was dictated by our primary grantor agency, the U.S. Urban Mass Transportation Administration (UMTA). During the past 25 years the MBTA has received more than $2 billion in federal funds. UMTA requires that all documents related to the receipt of its grant funds be kept for a period of three years following the close of the grant. This requirement overrides any shorter term retention schedule that might be recommended by the state. Explicit in this requirement is the caveat that an inability to document the expenditure of such funds may result in having to pay money back to the federal government.

A good example of how a conflict in these differing regulatory requirements can result in prolonged retention periods arose when we attempted to schedule a records series called "time cards." Five thousand of the MBTA's employees complete daily time cards from which their weekly pay is calculated. On these cards they utilize cost codes that indicate to which accounts their time is being charged. Thus, these cards can contain grant-related as well as non-grant-related charges.

Since they contain some grant-related charges they become grant-related records for purposes of retention scheduling. State guidelines require that time cards be kept for seven years. Federal guidelines call for three years beyond the close of a grant -- and some grants may remain open 10-15 years! In the absence of a microfilm program or other changes in time-charging practices, the retention schedule for these records was set at 20 years. This resulted in literally millions of time cards being stored in computer punch-card boxes.

We have sought reduced retention requirements based on regular short-term audits, but have been unsuccessful. Microfilming has been proposed as a means of gaining physical control but other budget priorities will not allow for it. And, we have sought accounting changes so that grant-related charges may be isolated thereby reducing the quantity of cards that are being retained for long periods of time. This latter is just becoming a reality with the introduction of a new accounting system, but it is unclear how new time-card-type documentation will be retained and for how long. Meanwhile, the quantity of these records in storage inexorably increases as does the inability to retrieve information from them when needed. This complication was repeated many times as we set out to schedule other financial records.

The threat of actual monetary loss due to poor records management had been part of what contributed to the hiring of a Chief Librarian & Archivist. The State Transportation Library was just being created and was to be under the administrative auspices of the Transit Authority, although its primary charge was that it be a centralized information resource for all the state's transportation agencies. Since my professional background was in archives and records management as well as library science, the agency felt I could serve a dual purpose and help with control of its records as well as with the library. In theory, this made perfect sense, but in practice it has created some problems. The problems center around the resource demands made by an integrated information system. If the system is to function successfully, adequate resources must be supplied for all components, otherwise some flourish and others languish.

Specifically, the MBTA was faced with having to gain control over its grant-related records. These records were being stored all over Metropolitan Boston in a variety of unacceptable environments, and were virtually inaccessible to federal auditors. Not knowing where something was, or what information was contained in particular files, made documentation of activity almost impossible. This was compounded by the growing feeling that an organization the size of the MBTA, with thousands of employees and an annual budget of over $500 million, should have ready access to its day-to-day business records. Based on these considerations, the goal of the records management component of the integrated system was to gain control of the Authority's documentation with special emphasis on federal grant-related documents.

The activities and thought processes at work were really not that different from how we were simultaneously approaching establishing accessibility to the library's collections. The library was being created from a mixture of smaller collections, some of which had never really been organized in a professional way. Methods of inventory, means of access, circulation, preservation, and outreach were equally pertinent to records management and required the same skills and techniques which are applied to establish library collections and services.

With the library, however, we had already established physical control in that all of the various materials going into the collection had been moved to the same place. With the records management component the problem was essentially that most departments had no idea either where the records they had sent to storage had gone, or what information those records contained. More often than not, when asked to supply a particular file or piece of information, people simply said it was not available.

Program Focus

Having defined the general problem, a three-part plan of attack was developed focusing on the Construction Division, the office with primary responsibility for administering grant-related funds. The first part was a retrospective inventory designed to identify those documents already in "dead storage" but not necessarily inactive. This meant locating all the off-site storage areas and sending people to them to complete inventory worksheets (see Figure 16-1).

Figure 16-1. MBTA – Records Inventory Worksheet.

Department :	Inventory conducted by	Date
Manager :		
Section :	Dept. Liaison	Location
Director :		Phone ext.
Record Series Title		Form #
(sample attached)		Retention Schedule #
Inclusive dates	Description (including function)	Space (cu. ft.)

Sequence	Identification	Equipment
[ ] alphabetical [ ] numerical [ ] other (identify)	[ ] original [ ] copy [ ] information	[ ] letter size [ ] legal size [ ] other (identify)

Reference Activity	Classification	Capacity
[ ] daily [ ] weekly [ ] monthly [ ] quarterly [ ] annually [ ] other	[ ] active [ ] semi-active [ ] inactive [ ] vital [ ] historical [ ] microfilmed	[ ] 3-drawer [ ] 4-drawer [ ] 5-drawer [ ] other (identify)

Who uses records?

When do records become inactive?

How often are records transferred to records center?

Is record subject to any audits?   [ ] No   [ ] Yes (identify)

Length of retention

_____ Office   _____ Charlestown

_____ UG-16 Storage   _____ State Records Center

Additional comments :

Part two was to be an inventory of current records, those now being held in offices and still being created. Part three was to be the heart of the program, the prospective plan for managing the Authority's information, the plan that would build in controls to guide the creation of documents and the capturing of information in the future. Simply stated, we wanted to identify all the records that were in storage, all the records currently utilized in offices, and then recommend procedures and guidelines for the continuation, modification, or addition of certain recordkeeping practices.

The first major product was to be a series of flow diagrams, one for each record series identified. Each diagram would begin with the originating office, and would then follow the record through its life cycle until it had fulfilled its purpose and was ready for appropriate disposition. Once it was clear how various information flowed from department to department, we could make judgments about the uses of that information.

Finally, an analysis would be undertaken to examine whether or not information was being captured in the originating office in the most efficient way as well as whether or not there were multiple needs for that information that could be satisfied with a single instrument. Recommendations about combining forms or files, altering offices of record, and setting appropriate disposition schedules would follow.

Program Refocus

We quickly discovered during this inventory process that we could not simply isolate one department and concentrate only on its records. No department in the MBTA exists in isolation; operating and capital responsibilities overlap as do the uses of the information in various record series. A decision about the office of record for particular series could not be made without examining all these corollary uses. Rather, we had to look at the whole organization and examine how people used the information in these records before we could determine anything about their disposition.

In some ways this meant a complete refocusing of the program. Where the scope of the project had originally seemed manageable, this revised view of the way information was needed and used on an organizational rather than a departmental scale almost overwhelmed us. We had to revise our plan of a three-part chronologically sequenced attack in which we could treat each group of records - the retrospective, the current, and the future - as distinct. The realization came that all three groups of records and their uses would have to be examined simultaneously.

Staffing

Staffing became a critical concern and was to set the constraints within which the records management component could operate. Of the 7,000 employees in the organization, only one-half of one position, the Chief Librarian's, was initially assigned to records management activity. The other half of the time was spent managing the library, which serves six other agencies besides the Transit Authority. It was not until more than two years into the program that a full-time professional and a full-time clerical position were added and dedicated to records management work.

The early stages of any records management program are highly labor intensive. Surveys must be done, inventories compiled, schedules filled out, educational programs and politicking undertaken. Alternative staffing arrangements became a must if we were to gain desired controls in a reasonable time period. Our program operated during these initial two years with a staff of student interns. They accomplished most of the initial inventory work, including reboxing and moving thousands of cubic feet of documents. This was by no means the ideal situation because adequate supervision was difficult while these interns were working in remote storage areas (including an abandoned subway tunnel). Since they had no previous records management experience, they could not be expected to make educated judgments about records series and their disposition. However, these were small drawbacks compared to the alternative of having no staff at all.

The issue of managing the records management program then became increasingly important. In our new and revised view of how to proceed, the issue of where the information manager was situated in the organizational hierarchy became critical. We realized that if we could not affect the decisions being made concerning the company's information assets from the earliest point in the life cycle, it would be difficult if not impossible to integrate all of the information functions.

It also became clear that good records management practices could not be dictated. Rather, we would have to educate, cajole, and even outright beg an office to implement our recommendations. This is a long and involved process of creating relationships, trust, and goodwill. These relationships are the greatest asset for what the program is trying to accomplish. It takes people, however, to develop them.

CAN THE INTEGRATED INFORMATION MANAGEMENT SYSTEM BECOME A REALITY?

This is the very real question we face. In retrospect, in our particular situation, it appears not to have been the best decision to combine library and records management activity because the early success of the library has masked the true resource needs of the records management program. Although this would not necessarily be the case in another environment, here are some issues that seem to be impeding success in our agency.

As was mentioned earlier, an integrated information management system exists on a continuum. While the same skills can be used to manage information at any point along that continuum, an organization cannot expect that the same amount of resources traditionally allotted to one aspect of the system, for example, the library, can be spread out to cover all aspects. Some components will inevitably thrive while others wither.

For example, a typical records management program in a mid- to large-size organization, like the MBTA, should employ several records analysts, at least two clerks, and a micrographics staff. A library of our size, approximately 30,000 volumes, employs four professional librarians, a clerk, and two interns. Theoretically, these would be companion staffs under the umbrella of an integrated information service. On rare occasions they might work interchangeably, but the magnitude of each task requires that adequate resources be given to both.

In the MBTA, however, there is only one full-time records analyst, one part-time program manager/records analyst, and one clerk. While the library flourishes with a staff in proportion to the size of its collection and the various services offered, the records program only plods along. What results is a large backlog of tasks needing to be accomplished. While the library's success as a central information resource is well recognized by management, it seems to have blinded them to the resource demands of a records management program.

PROGRESS IN SPITE OF OURSELVES

This has not deterred us from making progress towards the integrated system we have envisioned. One of our information trails, the external, is under excellent control and we are making progress on controlling the internal products of the second trail. We are at least able now to focus on the third trail, the daily business records.

In the early stages of the records program, as was mentioned above, great strides were made in disposing of obsolete material, in consolidating off-site storage areas, and in inventorying materials held there. Offices of Record for particular series were identified, enabling us to dispose of large quantities of superfluous documentation.

We were even able to make progress by mandating appropriate storage containers. One of the thorniest problems at the MBTA had always been storage boxes. People were in the habit of raiding the photocopy room when they needed a box to store records in, or worse, because we had moved within the past couple of years, we had an abundance of oversized moving boxes on hand. Records were stored in whatever kind of box could be acquired. Sometimes this worked out well and the box was neatly packed and labeled. For the most part, however, offices created back-breakers. Anyone who has ever tried to lift a typical moving company box which has been loaded to the brim with 4 or 5 cubic feet of records can appreciate the difficulty. They do not fit on standard shelving and when stacked in twos or threes inevitably collapse. As simple as it may sound, one of the records program's greatest accomplishments was the standardization of storage containers. A standard 1 cubic-foot box can now be ordered by each office through the central purchasing process. No records are accepted for storage if they are not in these standard containers.

The rate of progress more than doubled when a full-time professional archivist and a clerk with data entry experience were hired. This Senior Archivist worked full time with departmental records liaisons and other individuals to make considerable progress in understanding the use and scheduling of many previously uncontrolled records series. The clerk started to computerize the inventory as well as to assist office personnel in preparing their records for storage or disposal.

One of the most deleterious obstacles we faced, though, was that many abortive attempts at records management had been made throughout the Authority over the years and most employees had become immune to the hope that progress could be made. Their hopes had been raised so many times, only to fall prey to agency apathy and crisis management. We knew a great deal of time would have to be spent on trying to get people to understand that even though the records manager could not be included in every discussion that involved the capture of the agency's vital information, everyone who was involved must at least be aware of the parameters of the issue.

The best way to ensure that a records management staff member rather than the trash man was the first one called when there was a storage problem, for example, was to make sure every employee understood what records must be kept and why. Even if they could not be made to understand completely why something was being kept, convincing them to stop and call a records professional first would make a big difference.

If there was a storage problem, we knew it was our job to address it as quickly as possible so that people did not get discouraged and take the easy way out. By the same token, it was equally useful to demonstrate to employees that three existing forms could fulfill the same function and might better be combined into one form, thus reducing the paperwork that they must struggle over.

A major accomplishment toward the above ends was the issuance of a "Records Management Manual." For the first time, employees had a handy and easy-to-use guide to assist them in preparing their records for scheduling and disposition. This Manual will be the basis for a renewed outreach program to all employees to reinforce the records management program goals. Even with these dramatic increases in what we have been able to attain, so much more remains to be done. The program is not yet positioned sufficiently high in the organization's management scheme for staff to be a part of the daily decisions being made about how vital business information is being managed. As professional information managers we have completely accepted the idea of the integrated information management system but we have not been totally successful in selling it to upper management. Records management is still a long-term goal rather than an immediate solution to a very real business problem, and the amount of resources devoted to it are correspondingly affected.

The resultant inactivity has led to one of the worst fears an information manager can imagine -- that of being unable to fulfill a client's expectations. For example, if we convince employees to turn their inactive files over to the records center they do so with the understanding that when they need a file it will be forthcoming within a reasonable amount of time. If it is not, the service reputation we are trying to build will suffer.

The very nature of a records management outreach program is the same as that of the library's outreach activity; the purpose is to convince people of what you can do for them. Part of this convincing is accomplished by successfully demonstrating that the activity you are advocating does work. Nothing is more frustrating or detrimental to your goals than having to turn these clients away when the system fails.

CONCLUSION

Has the MBTA created an integrated information system? The answer would have to be yes and no. The lack of personnel and financial support for records management activity has not affected the resources for library activities. The library is flourishing. There seems to be little question as to the value that information management in a library setting offers. We have not yet been successful enough in redefining for upper management how valuable the information contained in daily business records is and how its lack of control can be a drain on the organization's resources. Even though the original impetus for the program - control of grant-related records - is still valid, time and the intervention of one or another crisis seems to have dimmed the urgency.

What must not be forgotten, however, is that as a public agency we are governed by criteria that go beyond a company needing simply to protect the vital documentation of its daily business activity. We have responsibilities to two levels of government and to the citizenry at large; responsibilities which have both financial and political consequences.

We are convinced that integrated information management is the way to go. The three information trails discussed earlier have to be integrated into one unified management system. Given even our limited success, we have seen how valuable the knowledge of the Authority's inner workings, gained through records management activities, has been in daily library activities.

Finally, records management is not like riding a bicycle. Once you stop doing it for a while you cannot just jump right back and begin where you left off. The briefest inattention to the life-cycle phases can send a company's records into chaos. The integrated information system we have sought to establish as information managers at the MBTA cannot be accomplished in a vacuum. We must insert ourselves into the process of records creation so that the information needed by our organization to function, and needed by posterity to understand that functioning, is appropriately managed. Resources and tangible institutional support, however, are essential. All the goodwill you can muster and all the converts you gain will not matter if organizational resources are not forthcoming to back you up.

Like a record, a records management program has its own life cycle. It goes through a creation, maintenance and use, and disposition phase. Ideally speaking, it would be classified as vital and, therefore, tagged for permanent retention. So often, however, like libraries, records management programs are considered luxuries.

There is no doubt that librarians, especially those in government agencies, can and must expand their role to include records management activities, thereby increasing their value in the workplace. At the MBTA through involvement in records management activities we have increased not only our value to the organization by beginning to bring under control an important asset, but also the body of information we have to draw on when responding to our client's information needs.

Whether an organization is a public agency or a private corporation, the stakes are high. As information managers we cannot ignore the third information trail, that of day-to-day business records, if we are to provide an integrated information management system for our employers. The establishment of such a system is one way to ensure that information professionals become an integral part of our organization's life rather than a luxury to be foregone when times get tough.

Chapter Seventeen

Records Management, Librarians, and the Future

This text has attempted to introduce the principles and practices of records management to an audience familiar with library settings. Unfamiliar concepts and routines (such as inventory, appraisal, and retention) have been explored in some depth. In the case of activities common to both fields (for instance, database management, preservation, and micrographics management), the emphasis has been on aspects which differ from normal library procedures. Managerial endeavors common to all institutions (staffing, manual writing, budgeting, systems analysis, and evaluating services) have been delineated for their contribution to the smooth functioning of records management operations. Information resources management and information policy are both fields of study with which forward looking librarians and records managers must be familiar, and each has been briefly introduced.

Given this much commonality between records management and librarianship, it is hardly surprising that these two groups will share similar problems and challenges in the future. The professional literatures of both fields exhibit the same overall concerns with proving value to management, coping with technological change, interpreting tasks and responsibilities in competition with other information processing departments in an organization, and finding appropriate educational models.

EDUCATION FOR RECORDS MANAGEMENT

Over the past decade, schools of library and information science (LIS), especially those with an emphasis either on information resources management or archival studies, have added courses in records management to their curricula. Pemberton (1991c) points out that a course or two hardly constitutes a complete program of study, but he also admits that he could not find a single instance of a records management major at the graduate or undergraduate level in any American institution of higher learning. He is of the opinion that library and information science is a logical home for records management, but feels that the lack of a market for graduates, and the lack of a body of theory and research to give records management academic credibility, will discourage LIS programs developing fuller curricula for records management.

On the other hand, many such schools are now in the process of self-examination and reassessment, especially in light of budgetary cutbacks, shrinking student pools, and an unusually high number of school closings (see Stieg, 1991). There is a trend towards interdisciplinarity, as programs attempt to reflect in course content a change which was reflected mostly in name only in the 1970s (typically from "library science" to "library and information science" or "information studies"). Similarly, records managers are beginning to concern themselves with the role that they play in the entire information life cycle in an organization, and this too is reflected in new titles such as "records and information manager" or "information resources manager."

It would certainly appear that the two fields are moving closer together, and indeed at least one LIS school (the School of Information Studies at Syracuse University) has developed a degree program in information resources management. Such alliances can provide a context for the study of records management within existing bodies of theory and research in fields such as information science, computer science, and management science. An advanced degree would also give records managers the academic credentials needed to compete for position and power, something that the CRM (Certified Records Manager) certificate alone cannot do (Pemberton, 1991b).

IMAGE AND "TURF"

Records management is a relatively young field, and is not well understood. Morddel (1991) surveyed British job descriptions appearing in the *Bulletin* of the Records Management Society, and found that while the job titles were easily understood, the accompanying descriptions indicated that either the company had little understanding of what records managers were supposed to do, or that they were looking for advanced filing clerks. The situation in North America is somewhat better, thanks in large part to the efforts of ARMA. However, Carroll's (1991) experience in exploring records management as a result of taking a course during her M.L.S. degree at Catholic University suggests that there is no clear-cut career path into records management, and that the position which records managers occupy in the corporate structure is ambiguous and ill defined. Discussions with records managers in local ARMA chapters bear this out -- they come from a wide variety of academic backgrounds, often fall into records management almost by accident, and frequently assume positions of responsibility by rising through the ranks rather than by virtue of external training and education.

Credibility, or "image," is a concern for records managers, as it is for librarians. Librarians have the advantage of being in the public eye, and while they may be misunderstood, at least the term "librarian" is part of the basic lexicon of everyday life. The same could hardly be said of the description "records manager," even within the information professions. Librarians also have the advantage of a well-established professional community, with a number of general and specialized associations, a nationally accredited professional degree, several possible doctoral degree paths, and quite well-defined positional breakdowns (pre- or paraprofessional, entry-level professional, and managerial). The interest shown by records managers in forging relationships with library education is one indicator of the quest for a professional identity. Another is the call for a code of ethics for records managers (Pemberton and Pendergraft, 1990), and yet a third is the concern with what constitutes the domain of records management, as distinct from other related groups.

One corporation will frequently have a number of different units which are concerned with information handling, such as libraries, archives, data processing, and records management. In many cases these units do not communicate with each other in any meaningful way, although the ties between libraries and archives tend to be close. Each contributes to the effective management of information assets, but each also competes with the other for fiscal and other forms of corporate support. From the organization's point of view, cooperation among these units would reduce redundancy and promote efficiency, but individual unit managers see the most likely form of enforced cooperation as merger and takeover (especially in times when layoffs are common). Wright (1991) goes so far as to suggest that records managers take over libraries, and strive to streamline operations (largely by reducing internal collections and relying on external services for on-demand source provision).

Records managers seem to view data processing departments as the biggest threat to their existence. Records managers, like librarians, have certainly taken to new information technologies for information handling, and have done so quite ably. However, they do also have to maintain large paper files, and so the *perceptions* of management are that data processing departments are better prepared to manage the computer-based information resources of an organization (although *in fact*, records managers probably have a better overall understanding of corporate information life cycles). Phillips (1991) reasonably suggests that the appropriate model is one of teamwork. Records managers who are well versed in the latest technologies (especially with respect to networking, image handling, and technological standards) can contribute to decision making when computer-based systems are being considered, and can increase their visibility and credibility.

Within an organization, both libraries and records management departments are cost centers, and face the challenge of proving their value (especially when economies are being considered). This has been well covered in the library literature (see, for instance, Matarazzo, Prusack and Gauthier, 1990) and appears in records management as well. Summerville (1992) calls for records managers to position themselves as planners and shapers, leaders who understand the value of information as a corporate and social asset. Pemberton (1991a) emphasizes the importance to records managers of meeting the information needs of senior management by expanding the domain of records management to include comprehensive integrated information services. He feels that the identity of records management needs to be more clearly delineated. Both authors feel that these goals can be accomplished through the development of educational programs, and the concomitant development of a body of theory and research pertinent to records management.

LOOKING TOWARD THE FUTURE

For the librarian who is interested in records management, either as a separate career option or as a function within library operations, the prevalent issues and trends in both fields are closely related. A thorough knowledge of current and emerging information technologies (including electronic data interchange, voice and image handling, local and wide-area networks, desktop publishing, and computer-aided design and manufacture) is essential. Abilities in systems analysis, strategic planning, and evaluation are also critical. Librarians and records managers must have broad visions and missions which encompass information resources in all formats. This is especially problematic as information tasks are decentralized through widespread local microprocessing. Perhaps most important to both is the ability to adapt to a changing environment, and to be prepared to "live in interesting times."

As the decade of the 1990s unfolds, libraries and information centers, as well as other organizations, will continue to experience financial stringencies while trying to cope with the information and electronic ages. These organizations, as well as government agencies, are showing increased interest in meeting the information needs of their clientele and in better managing information resources. With the availability of digital library collections and remote access to information on the rise, "it will be necessary both to support the old information sources and reinvest in the new ones as well as in the infrastructure to support them" (Lynch, 1991, p. 20). Clearly, there is growing interest in the dissemination of information and "widespread effective access to information," especially the *gray* literature (Ibid., p. 7). While attention focuses on access issues, other aspects of the life-cycle process and information resources management remain important.

The decade will see mounting interest in IRM and information policy issues, as records managers cope with the challenges and opportunities of change. Change "is any planned or unplanned alternation in the status quo that affects an organization's structure, services, programs, or allocation of resources" (Hernon and McClure, 1990, p. 224). Already in this decade, organizations, including businesses and industries, are experiencing fundamental change, and the repercussions are being felt by the work force. Within such an environment, it is important that records managers engage in planning and ensure that the organization's memory, be it in print or electronic form, is retained and at the disposal of those needing access to it. This book has shown that records managers have other responsibilities as well, in that they support the organization in meeting its responsibilities and in making decisions.

The challenges are many but so too are the opportunities. Now is an ideal time for individuals to plan careers as records and information resource managers. Those already in such positions may need additional training and education. The readings suggested in this book offer a helpful first step, since they are far-reaching and serve to unite records management with library and information science, as well as other disciplines.

Records management will remain a cross-disciplinary field. Herein are both its strengths and weaknesses. It can benefit from the theory, research, and practices of different disciplines and professions. On the other hand, it will experience difficulties in developing its own identity within academe and in attracting a work force having broad cross-disciplinary backgrounds. Perhaps, though, this last point may not pose a significant barrier.

Change and planning necessitate that organizations and records managers support and engage in research as well as ensure that the professional literature of records management improves in quality and not merely quantity. Records managers will need to strengthen their skills as consumers and doers of research, especially evaluation and policy research. For records management to reach its potential in this decade and beyond, it must realize the importance of research to better management of change, and the importance of a high quality and useful professional literature. That literature must challenge, educate, and provide assistance. Clearly, records management faces some significant but not insurmountable hurdles, but there are definite advantages (as well as risks) for records managers to be associated with change agents. By understanding the present and looking toward the future, records managers can play a key role within organizations, and assist those at center stage.

REFERENCES

Carroll, Eireann. "In Search of . . . Records Management," *ARMA Records Management Quarterly* 25 (October 1991): 32-36.

Hernon, Peter and Charles R. McClure. *Evaluation and Library Decision*

Making. Norwood, NJ: Ablex Pub. Corp.. 1990.
Lynch, Clifford A. "The Development of Electronic Publishing and Digital Library Collections on the NREN," *Electronic Networking* 1 (Winter 1991): 6-22.
Matarazzo, James M., Laurence Prusak, and Michael R. Gauthier. *Valuing Corporate Libraries : A Survey of Senior Managers*. Washington, DC: Special Libraries Association (in cooperation with Temple, Barker & Sloan, Inc.), 1990.
Morddel, Anne. "Records Management Jobs in Britain . . . After a Fashion," *ARMA Records Management Quarterly* 25 (July 1991): 40-42.
Pemberton, J. Michael. "Does Records Management Have a Future?," *ARMA Records Management Quarterly* 25 (January 1991a): 38-41.
Pemberton, J. Michael. "Education for Records Management: Rigor Mortis or New Directions?," *ARMA Records Management Quarterly*, 25 (July 1991b): 50-54.
Pemberton, J. Michael. "If Being a CRM Is the Answer, What Is the Question?," *ARMA Records Management Quarterly* 25 (April 1991c): 50-53, 57.
Pemberton, J. Michael and Lee O. Pendergraft. "Toward a Code of Ethics: Social Relevance and the Professionalization of Records Management," *ARMA Records Management Quarterly* 24 (April 1990): 3,8.
Phillips, John T., Jr. "Records Management and Data Processing - A Good Strategic Alliance," *ARMA Records Management Quarterly* 25 (April 1991): 44-48, 57.
Stieg, Margaret. *Change and Challenge in Library and Information Science Education*. Chicago, IL: American Library Association, 1991.
Summerville, John R. "Records Management: A 'Now' Kinda Thing?," *Records Management Quarterly* 26 (January 1992): 10-13.
Wright, Craig W. "The Corporate Information Challenge: Streamlining External Information," *ARMA Records Management Quarterly* 25 (July 1991): 14-16.

List of Contributors

Kathryn Hammond Baker is Assistant Archivist for Records Management and Acquisitions at the Massachusetts Archives (Boston, MA 02125), and prior to that was Diocesan Archivist for the Episcopal Diocese of Massachusetts. She has provided consultative services to groups such as the Department of Social Services (MA), Needham Public Library, the Supreme Council of the Northern Masonic Jurisdiction, and the Somerville Historical Society. Recent among her numerous presentations was an Intermediate Workshop on Appraisal for the New England Archivists (NEA). Ms. Hammond Baker holds a B.A. in American Studies and an M.A. in History and Archival Methods. She is Editor of the NEA *Newsletter*, and is on the Board of the National Association of Government Archives and Records Administrators.

Peter Hernon is Professor, Graduate School of Library and Information Science, Simmons College (300 The Fenway, Boston, MA 02115). This is his 28th book, and he is the author of more than 75 articles. He writes, researches, and teaches primarily in the areas of government information policy, research methods, evaluation of library services, and access to U.S. national government information. Dr. Hernon is Editor of the journal *Government Information Quarterly*.

Kate Jones-Randall holds the position of Business Reference Librarian at the University of Massachusetts Dartmouth (North Dartmouth, MA 02747), and is in charge of Project ASC, the University's fee-based information service. She is also the Director of Randall Research Associates, specializing in indexing and records management in libraries. Ms. Jones-Randall has a B.F.A. in Theatre Arts and an M.S. in Library and Information Science. She is currently editor of the *Simmons Librarian*, an alumni newsletter, and has been published in *Computers in Libraries*.

Toby Pearlstein has held the position of Chief Librarian and Archivist for the State Transportation Library of Massachusetts (10 Park Plaza, Boston MA 02116) since 1983, and in that capacity she also served as Records Manager for the Massachusetts Bay Transportation Authority. Dr. Pearlstein has a B.A. and an M.A. in History, an M.S. in Library Science, and a D.A. in Library Administration. She is currently Editor of the Special Libraries Association Transportation Division *Bulletin*, and recently co-authored "General Transportation" section of *Sources of Information in Transportation*, produced by the Division and published by Vance Bibliographies.

Nancy Richard holds the position of Curator at the Massachusetts Archives (Boston, MA 02125), where she was Inventory Archivist from 1984 to 1986. Ms. Richard has served as a consultant to the Smithsonian Institution, the Harvard Graduate School of Education, the Supreme Council of the Northern Masonic Jurisdiction, the Wayside Inn, and the Aids Action Committee. She holds a B.A. in Women's Studies and an M.L.S. in Archives Administration. Ms. Richard is active in New England Archivists (NEA), and has published for the Harvard Graduate School of Education, NEA *Newsletter*, *OMIS Newsletter*, and *Government Records Project Newsletter*. She has made presentations on topics such as management of large collections, and photographic research.

Candy Schwartz is Associate Professor, Graduate School of Library and Information Science, Simmons College (300 The Fenway, Boston, MA 02115). She teaches courses related to online searching, database design, indexing, and records management. Dr. Schwartz holds a B.A. and M.L.S. from McGill University, and Ph. D. in Information Science from Syracuse University. She serves on the ASIS Board of Directors and is President of the Board of Directors of Documentation Abstracts, Inc. Her recent publications include articles in *CD-ROM Professional* and chapters in monographs on online searching, CD-ROM collections, and library and information science research.

Author Index

The author and subject indexes were prepared by Marie Rodgers. The author index includes references in the text and in the *References* sections at the end of each chapter. It does not include references in the *Readings* section which accompany many chapters, or which appear in figures. Page numbers referring to the *References* sections are underlined.

A
Akoka, J., 188, 193
Argyris, C., 159, 175
Avrin, L., 20, 35

B
Balough, A., 180, 187, 188, 193
Barber, D.T., 127, 130
Barton, J.P., 135, 140
Bass, G., 208, 209, 210, 211, 212, 219, 229, 236
Bassett, E.D., 113, 130
Bearman, T.C., 234, 235
Bergeron, P., 208, 210, 212, 220
Betton, V.L., 76, 90
Bishop, A.P., 208, 210, 212, 220, 226, 236
Blake, F., 234, 236
Bommer, M.R.W., 188, 194
Boss, R.W., 165, 176
Boyce, B.R., 52, 53
Brathal, D.A., 147, 154
Brinberg, H.R., 234, 235
Brown, G.F., 1, 16, 44, 52, 54
Bulgawicz, S.L., 135, 140
Burk, C.F., 170, 171, 176, 180, 194, 201, 202, 217, 219

C
Cabell, C., 208, 210, 219
Cameron, C.A., 66, 71
Carlson, D.H., 52, 53
Carroll, E., 293, 296
Carroll, J.S., 40, 53
Caudle, S.L, 213, 215, 219
Chartrand, R.L., 226, 235
Chelton, M.K., 234, 236
Chorba, R.W., 188, 194
Clark, P.M., 190, 194
Connolly, M.J., 64, 71, 83, 90
Crix, F.C., 146, 154
Cyphers, J.E., 274, 278

D
d'Alleyrand, M.R., 111, 111
Diamond, S.Z., 25, 35
Diebold, J., 213, 219
Dmytrenko, A., 95, 112
Doty, P., 208, 210, 212, 220, 226, 236
Dunlap, L.W., 22, 35

E
Eddison, E.B., 107, 111
Emmerson, P., 2, 16, 60, 71
England, C., 135, 140
England, P., 189, 194
Eulenberg, J.N., 136, 140
Evans, K., 135, 140

F
Fingerman, J., 188, 194
Fosegan, J.S., 113, 130
Freeman, H.E, 45, 54, 180, 195

G

Garbarino, J., 164, 165, 176
Gauthier, M.R., 295, 297
Gill, S.L., 113, 130
Gilmore, V.K., 113, 130
Goodman, D.G., 113, 130
Gow, K.F., 163, 171, 176

H

Hagerty-Roach, L., 189, 194
Harris, M.H., 22, 35
Hernon, P., 41, 44, 47, 52, 53, 174, 176, 184, 187, 191, 194, 197, 219, 224, 236, 296, 296
Hitt, M.A., 158, 176
Horton, F.W., Jr., 170, 171, 176, 180, 194, 201, 202, 217, 219

J

Jackson, J.H., 165, 176
Janis, I.L., 161, 176
Jenkins, T., 147, 154
Johnson, E.D., 21, 22, 35
Johnson, E.J., 40, 53
Johnson, E.R., 183, 194
Josey, E.J., 234, 236
Joyce, J.M., 145, 154

K

Kaser, D., 234, 236
Kast, F.E., 158, 159, 176
Koontz, H., 159, 176
Kraft, D.H., 52, 53
Kroll, R.H., 165, 176

L

Langemo, M., 127, 130, 147, 154
Leahy, E., 66, 71
Leary, W.H., 113, 130, 153, 154
Lee, J.A., 66, 72
Lundeen, G., 95, 111
Luthans, F., 159, 176
Lynch, C.A., 295, 297

Lynch, M.J., 181, 183, 184, 186, 194

M

Maedke, W.O., 1, 16, 44, 52, 54
Malinconcio, S.M., 234, 236
Mann, L., 161, 176
Marchand, D.A., 201, 213, 215, 219, 220
Mason, M.G., 222, 236
Matarazzo, J.M., 295, 297
Mathis, R.L., 158, 165, 176
McClure, C.R., 41, 44, 47, 48, 53, 54, 157, 159, 174, 176, 177, 181, 183, 184, 185, 186, 188, 189, 191, 194, 195, 208, 210, 212, 217, 220, 224, 226, 236, 296, 296
McFarland, D.E., 163, 164, 176
Middlemist, R.D., 158, 176
Miller, N.G., 113, 131
Moran, B.B., 158, 176
Morddel, A., 26, 35, 52, 54, 60, 70, 72, 80, 90, 293, 297
Morris, J., 135, 140
Myers, G., 145, 154

N

Nadler, D.A., 41, 54
Nelson, S.R., 260, 267, 273, 278
Nolan, C.E., 135, 140
Nygren, W., 145, 154

O

O'Brien, J.A., 101, 111
O'Donnell, C., 159, 176
Oglesby, T.R., 113, 130, 153, 154
Orr, R.H., 185, 194
Osteen, C.E., 145, 155
Owen, A., 181, 183, 194

P

Pemberton, J.M., 292, 293, 294, 295, 297
Pendergraft, L.O., 294, 297

Penn, I.A., 26, 35, 52, 54, 60, 70, 71, 80, 90
Pennix, G., 26, 35, 52, 54, 60, 70, 71, 80, 90
Phillips, J.T., Jr., 95, 111, 294, 297
Pings, V.M., 183, 195
Plocher, D., 208, 209, 210, 211, 212, 219
Porat, M., 224, 236
Posner, E., 25, 35
Prusack, L., 295, 297

R
Radack, S.M., 29, 36, 230, 236
Raikes, D., 165, 176
Relyea, H.C., 197, 220
Ricks, B.R., 163, 171, 176
Rider, A.D., 21, 36
Robek, M.E., 1, 16, 44, 52, 54
Rodger, E.J., 186, 195
Roe, K.D., 256, 278
Rosenbaum, H., 226, 236
Rosenberg, V., 234, 236
Rosenzweig, J.E., 158, 159, 176
Rossi, P.H., 45, 54, 180, 195
Rubinstein, G., 210, 220
Ruller, T.J., 277, 278
Ruth, L., 189, 194

S
Saffady, W., 111, 111, 147, 155
Samuels, A.R., 159, 176
Schellenberg, T.R., 269, 279
Schubert, D.R., 66, 72
Schwartz, K.D., 25, 36
Semprevivo, P.C., 43, 52, 55
Skillman, J., 95, 112
Smith, K., 26, 35, 52, 54, 60, 70, 71, 80, 90
Smith, M.D., 66, 71
Socolar, M.J., 207, 220
Sprehe, J.T., 200, 204, 220
Stieg, M., 293, 297
Stone, N., 212, 220
Strain, P.M., 172, 176
Stueart, R.D., 158, 176
Suchman, E.A., 191, 195
Sullivan, P., 234, 236
Summerville, J.R., 295, 297
Swartz, R., 234, 236
Swisher, R., 174, 177, 183, 195
Synnott, W.R., 202, 220

T
Tenopir, C., 95, 111
Thompson, L.H., 199, 200, 220
Triano, C., 229, 236
Tushman, M.L., 41, 54

V
Van House, N.A., 181, 183, 184, 185, 186, 194, 195, 217, 220
Vrooman, J.W., 23, 36

W
Waegemann, C.P., 113, 131, 154, 155
Wagner, A., 95, 111
Wallace, P.E., 66, 72
Weber, L.B., 255, 279
Wellheiser, J.G., 135, 140
Weil, B., 184, 185, 186, 195, 217, 220
Williams, R.V., 4, 16
Wolchak, W.H., 47, 54
Wren, D.A., 159, 177
Wright, C.W., 294, 297

Y
Yates, J., 23, 24, 36
Young, J., 113, 131

Z
Zweizig, D.L., 181, 183, 184, 186, 194, 195

Subject Index

Titles are given in italics.

A
ABI/Inform, 197
Action research, 174, 183-184
Active records, 62
Administrative environment, of an organization, 157-160
Administrative value, of records, 75, 81, 274
The Affirmation, 9
AIIM Monthly Monitor, 8
AIM Network, 8
Alphabetical name filing, 119-120
American Bar Association, 77
American Institute of Certified Public Accountants, 77
American Library Association, 119, 135, 255
American Medical Records Association, 10
American National Standards Institution, 148
American Records Management Association, 7; see also Association of Records Managers and Administrators
Aperture cards, 114-115, 148
Appraisal, records, 74-80, 82
  at Massachusetts Archives, 261, 266, 270
Approval cycle, in retention scheduling, 84
Archival records, 62, 256
Archives, government, 25
Archives management
  educational requirements for, 4
  compared with records management, 2-5
ARMA *see* Association of Records Managers and Administrators
ARMA News, Notes and Quotes, 7
Art and Architecture Thesaurus, 258
Aslib Information, 10, 12
Associated Information Managers, 8; *see also* Association for Information Management (AIM)
Association for Federal Information Resources Management, 9
Association for Information and Image Management, 8, 10, 148, 154
Association for Information Management (AIM), 8
Association for Information Management (Aslib), 9, 11, 12
Association of Commercial Records Centers, 9
Association of Records Executives and Administrators, 7; *see also* Association of Records Managers and Administrators
Association of Records Managers and Administrators, 7-8, 56, 60, 116, 119, 128, 133, 163, 173, 293
  publications, 10, 77, 95, 113, 135

304   Records Management and the Library

Associations, professional, 5-10, 77
Attorney General, of the United States, 229
Audiotapes, 61, 115
Automation; *see also* Computer assisted retrieval; Computers; Database management; Data processing; Decision support systems
   benefits of, 110-111
   costs of, 110
   at Massachusetts Archives, 255-278
   at Weston Public Library, 246-254

B
Boxtrax, 93
British Library, 235
Brown-Ferguson Act (1953), 26
Buckley Amendments, 27
Budget and Accounting Act (1921), 213
Budgeting, 168-171
Bulletin (Records Management Society), 293
Bureau of Efficiency, 26
Bureau of National Affairs, 226
Bureau of the Budget, 213; *see also* Office of Management and Budget
Burglary, protection against, 118
Bush, George, 203, 226
Business Forms Management Association, 10
Business Periodicals Index, 197
Business records, history of, 19-25

C
Cameras
   planetary, 150
   rotary, 150
   step and repeat, 150

Canadian Institute for Research on Policy, 235
Canadian Library Association, 135
Catholic University, 293
CD-ROM, 115
CD-ROM Professional, 104
Certification, for records managers, 4, 7-8
Charge-out forms, 87-88
Classification of records, by function, 74-75
Clay tablets, used for business records, 22
Clean Water Act (1977), 260
Code of Federal Regulations, 32, 76-77, 153, 229, 232
Coding systems, in records retention, 83
Color coding, 127
Commercial records centers, 77, 128-129
Commission on Federal Paperwork, 202, 208-209
Commission on Organization of the Executive Branch of the Government, 26
Compactable files, 117-118
Comparative appraisal, 271-276
Computer Assisted Retrieval (CAR), 150
Computer diskettes, 115, 134
Computers; *see also* Automation; Database management; Data processing; Decision support systems
   storage media, 61, 115, 134, 136, 152-153
   technologies, 152-154
Computer Output Microfilm (COM), 114, 152
Computers in Libraries, 104
Computer tapes, 115, 134
Conference Proceedings (AIM), 8

Subject Index 305

Congress, 26, 32, 205, 209, 213, 226-227, 233
Copy machines, 146; *see also* Reprographics
Copy of record, 61, 84
Corporate culture, 158
Correspondence management, 142, 144
Costs, of database management, 110
Council on Competitiveness, 229
Courts of Appeal, 228
Critical path analysis, 50
Critical path methods, 50-52

D
Data collection and entry, 47, 63, 107, 217
Data dictionaries, 96-98, 101, 104, 107
Data processing, 24, 145
Data structure, 104
Database management, 93-111
  at Weston Public Library, 246-254
Database management software, 104, 108
Data Processing Management Association, 10
dBase, 95, 190
Decision-making, 160-161, 174-175
Decision support systems, 188-191
Department of Agriculture, 28
Department of Justice, 229
Descriptive statistics, 187
Dewey, Melville, 24
Directives, 142-143; *see also* Reports
Directory of Collegiate Schools Offering Courses and Majors in Records and Information Management, 7

Directory of Microcomputer Software, 50
Directory of State Archives and Records Management Programs, 9
Disaster
  causes of, 135-136
  kit, 137-138
  management, 133, 135-139
  prevention, 137-138
Disaster Plan Workbook, 135
Disintegrators, 89
Diskettes, 115, 134
Disposal methods, for records, 87, 89
Documentation of procedures, for database management, 108-109; *see also* Manuals
Domestic Council, 234

E
Education
  for archivists, 4
  for librarians, 4, 293
  for records managers, 4, 173, 292-293
Eisenhower, Dwight D., 26-27
Electronic Library, 104
Electronic media, 61, 115, 134
ELF (Eliminate Legal Files), 116
Environmental Protection Agency, 260
Evaluation
  of database management software, 98-104
  of databases, 108-109
  as part of the planning process, 178-181
  accountability in, 192-193
  obstacles to, 191-192
  of vital records program, 134
Evidential value, of records, 75, 80

F

F3 Pro Designer, 145
Fair Credit Reporting Act (1970), 27
Feasibility studies
  for micrographics project, 152
  as part of systems analysis, 48
Federal District Courts, 228
Federal Emergency Management Agency, 28
Federal government
  and information life-cycle, 197, 199-200, 213
  and information policy, 226-235
  and information resources management, 197, 199, 202-207
  and inventory/locator system, 208-213
  records management activities in, 25-33, 213
Federal Information Centers, 29
Federal Information Locator System, 209-211
Federal Information Resources Management Act (1989), 205-207
The Federal Information Sources and Systems, 212
Federal Property and Administrative Services Act (1949), 26, 230
Federal Records Act (Hoover Commission), 26
Federal Records Act (1950), 26-27
Federal Records Act (1968), 230
Federal Records Centers, 33-34
Federal Records Management Amendments (1976), 27
Federal Register, 32, 76-77, 229, 232
Federal Reports Act (1942), 213
Federal Water Pollution Control Act (1972), 260
File management software, 101-102, 104, 108
Filing equipment, 116
  resistance to burglary, 118
  cabinets, 117
  coding schemes, 63
  resistance to fire, 117-118
  history of, 24
  types of
    compactable, 117-118
    flat, 24
    lateral, 117
    open, 117
    pigeonhole, 24
    Shannon, 24
    spindle, 24
    vertical, 24, 117, 122
Filing errors, 122, 127
Filing methods
  alphabetic, 119-120
  color coding, 127
  geographic, 119, 121
  numeric, 119, 121-123
    chronological, 121
    consecutive, 121-122
    terminal, 122-123
  phonetic, 118-119, 121
  subject, 119, 122, 124-126
  tickler, 87
Filing procedures, 127-128
Films, 61, 115
Filmstrips, 115
Fire, protection against, 117-118
Fiscal value, of records, 75, 77, 81, 274
Flat file software, 101-102
Flat files, 24
Ford, Gerald, 234
Formative evaluation, 180
Formats, physical, 61, 113-116; *see also* Records, types of
Forms; *see also* Worksheets

Subject Index 307

charge-out, 87-88
records appraisal, 81-82
records inventory, 66-70, 247-248
records transfer, 85-86
reference request, 86
retention authorization, 81
Forms management, 144-145
Formtool, 50, 145
For the Record, 9
Freedom of Information Act (1966), 27, 208, 233
Friday Memo, 8
fyi/im, 8

G
Gantt charts, 50-52
General Accounting Office, 207
General Records Disposal Act (1889), 26, 213
General Services Administration, 26-30, 212, 229-230
Geographic filing, 119, 121
Glenerin Declaration, 235
Government Printing Office, 209, 233
Government Records Issues, 9
Government Records Project, 255, 258, 260-261, 262-265, 271, 275-278
Great Society, 233
Guide to Record Retention Requirements in the Code of Federal Regulations, 26, 32, 77-78
Gutenberg, Johannes, 23

H
High-Performance Computing Act (1991), 226
Historical value, of records, 4, 23, 80
Hoover, Herbert, 26

Housekeeping records, 74

I
ICRM Newsletter, 7
IMC Journal, 9-10
IMC Newsletter, 9
Important records, 133
Inactive records, 62, 128-129, 254
Indexing services, 12-15
Inferential statistics, 187
InfoFind, 212
InfoMapper, 190, 212
Inform, 8, 10
Informational value, of records, 75, 80, 274
Information and Image Management, 8
Information Industry Association, 8
Information life cycle, 60, 197, 199-200, 208, 213, 222
Information Management Sourcebook, 8
Information policy, 217, 222-235
Information Policy Act (1989), 205
Information Resources Directory, 212
Information resources management, 197-218
Information Resources Management, 163
Information Resources Management Handbook, 29
Information Resources Management Service, 29, 153, 230
Information Science Abstracts, 13, 197
Information Sources, 8
Information Times, 8
INMAGIC, 95, 104, 190, 246, 249, 252, 254
Institute of Certified Records

Managers, 4, 7
Instructional Guide, 32, 113
Intergovernmental Records Project, 260, 274, 276
Internal records, 2
Internal Revenue Service, 77
International Information Management Congress, 9-10
International Journal of Information Management, 10-11
International Micrographic Congress, 9; *see also* International Information Management Congress
Inventory forms, *see* Records inventory forms
Inventory/locator system, 208-212
 and records management, 213-214, 216-217

J
Job analysis, 163
Job description, 163
Johnson, Lyndon, 233
Joint Committee on Printing, 233
Journals, professional, 5, 12

L
Lateral files, 117
Leahy, Emmett J., 26
Legal value, of records, 75-77, 81, 274
Librarianship
 educational requirements for, 4, 293
 compared with records management, 2-5, 142, 292-296
Libraries, types of, 22-23
Library and Information Science Abstracts, 13
Library Bureau, 24

Library Hi-Tech, 104
Library Literature, 13, 197
Library of Congress, 244, 255
Library Software Reviews, 104
Life-cycle of information, 60, 197, 199-200, 208, 213, 222
Lodge-Brown Act, 26
Lotus 1-2-3, 190, 246

M
Machine-Readable Form of Bibliographic Information, 255
Machine-readable records, 61, 115, 134, 136, 152-153; *see also* MARC
Mainframes, 189
Management styles, 159-160
Manager (software package), 50
Manuals; *see also* Documentation
 for machine/readable records, 153
 at MBTA, 289
 for records management, 166-168
MARC, 93-94, 255-256, 266, 271-272, 275
MARC AMC, 255-258, 261, 266, 272-275, 277-278
Massachusetts Archives, 255, 258, 261, 272, 276, 278
Massachusetts Bay Transportation Authority (MBTA), 280-296
Media, types of, *see* Formats, physical
Membership Directory (AFFIRM), 9
Membership Directory (ICRM), 7
Microcomputers, 98, 152, 188-190
Microfiches, 114-115, 148-150
Microfilm, 114-115, 134, 147-152
Microforms, 114-115; *see also* Microfilm; Microfiches

Subject Index 309

Micrographics, 4, 142, 147-152
Minaret, 94
Minuteman Library Network, 240
MIS Quarterly, 9

N
NAGARA Clearinghouse, 9
National and International Information Policies, 226
National Archives, 26
National Archives and Records Administration, 28-29, 31, 80, 212, 229-230, 258, 260
  publications, 12, 32, 113, 153
National Archives and Records Service, 26-28
National Association of Government Archives and Records Administrators, 9
National Bureau of Standards, 29; see also National Institute of Science and Technology
National Commission on Libraries and Information Science, 235
National Fire Protection Association, 118, 139
National Historical Publications and Records Commission, 257-258
National information policy, 234-235
National Information Policy, 234
National Information Systems Task Force, 255
National Institute of Science and Technology, 28-29, 229-230
National Microfilm Association, 8; see also Association for Information and Image Management
National Micrographics Association, 8; see also Association for Information and Image Management
National Records Management Council, 9, 26
National Research and Education Network, 226
Needs assessment, in database management, 96
Network, 9
New Deal, 233
Newsletters, professional, 10-12
New York University Library, Preservation Committee, 135
Non-records, definition of, 61
NREN, 226
Numeric filing, 119, 121-123

O
Office of Administrative Support, 28
Office of Federal Records Centers, 29, 32, 113, 122
Office of General Services, 26
Office of Information and Regulatory Affairs, 27-28, 32, 203, 205, 209
Office of Information Resources Management, 28
Office of Legal Counsel/Office of Legal Policy, 229
Office of Management and Budget, 27-28, 32, 200, 203, 205, 209-213, 229, 233
Office of Records Administration, 29, 32
Office of Records Management, 27
Office of Technical Assistance, 29
Office of Technological Assessment, 223
Office of the Federal Register, 32, 77
Office of the President, 32, 227-

229, 234-235
Online search services, 12-15
Open files, 117
Open system, 38-41
Optex, 93
Optical media, 61, 115, 134, 152-153
Organizational charts, 161-163

P
Paper, as a format, 61, 107, 114-115, 128, 134, 147
Paperwork Reduction Act (1980), 27, 32, 203-205, 209-210, 217, 234
Paperwork Reduction and Federal Information Resources Management Act (1989), 205
Paradox, 95, 190
PC-FILE, 95
PC Magazine, 104
PC Sources, 104
PC Week, 104
Perform (software package), 145
Performance measures, 184-187
Permanent records, 62
Personnel, 163-166
PFS Professional File, 95, 104-106
Phonetic filing, 119, 121
Photographs, 115
Physical records inventory, 66-70
Pigeonhole files, 24
Planetary cameras, 150
Planning, 178, 181-183
Planning/scheduling charts, 49-52
Preliminary records survey, 62-66
Preparing for the CRM Examination, 7-8
Primary value, of records, 75, 274
Printing, 23-24
Printing press, 23
Privacy Act (1974), 27, 208
Problem solving, in systems analysis, 42-45
Proceedings (SIM), 9
Procurement of ADP Resources by the Federal Government (Brooks) Act (1965), 230
Professional associations, 5-10, 77
Professional journals, 5, 10-12
Professional newsletters, 12
Program Evaluation and Review Technique (PERT), 50-52
Project management software, 50
Protection, of records, 134-135
Public Administration Review, 197
Public Records Office Act (U.K., 1938), 25
Pulpers, 89
Pulverizers, 89

Q
Quayle, Dan, 229

R
Reader/printers, microfilm, 149-150
Readers, microfilm, 149-150
Reagan, Ronald, 32, 203, 229
Recordfacts Update, 12
Records & Retrieval Report, 12, 77
Records Administration Information Center, 12, 32
Records appraisal, 74-80, 82
Records centers, 128-129, 134
Records, classification, by function, 74-75
Records Conservation Board, 282
Records, definition of, 60-61
Records disposal, 87-89
Records Disposal Act (1943), 26
Records inventory, 56-71
  at MBTA, 284, 286
  at Weston Public Library, 245-249
Records inventory forms, 66-70, 82

Subject Index

at MBTA, 285
at Weston Public Library, 245-250
Records management; *see also* Records managers
  compared with archives management, 2-5
  as a career, 4, 142, 172-173, 292-296
  in corporate environment, 294-295
  defense of, 56-60
  definition of, 1-2
  educational requirements for, 4, 173, 292-293
  history of, 19-28
  image of, 293-295
  and information resources management, 213-214
  legal consequences of, 58-59
  compared with librarianship, 2-5, 142, 292-296
  manuals, 166-168
  at MBTA, 289
  at Weston Public Library, 240-254
  as recorded history, 59-60
  personnel, 163-166
  software, 93-104, 189-190
  and U.S. government, 25-34
Records Management Bureau, 26
Records Management Division (National Archives and Records Service), 26; *see also* General Services Administration
Records Management Handbook, 113
Records Management Journal, 10-12
Records Management Quarterly, 7, 10
Records Management Society, 293

Records managers; *see also* Records management
  as administrators, 157
  certification for, 4, 7-8
  duties of, 13, 16, 142
  and information policy, 222
  and information resources management, 216-217
Records, protection of, 134
Records recovery, 136
Records requests, 86-88
Records series, 60, 74-75, 79-87, 119, 121, 271, 286
Records transfer, 84-86
Records, types of
  active, 62
  archival, 62, 256
  housekeeping, 74
  important, 133
  inactive, 62, 128-129, 254
  internal, 2
  permanent, 62
  reference, 74
  transactional, 74
  vital, 38, 62, 74, 118, 133-135
    at Weston Public Library, 246
Reference records, 74
Reflex (software package), 190
Relational database software, 102-103, 246
Reports, 107-108, 142-143; *see also* Directives
Reports inventory, 143
Reprographics, 142, 146-147
Research, action, 174, 183-184
Research Libraries Group, 256-258, 261, 275
Research Libraries Information Network, 256-260, 266, 271, 273-276
Research, for efficient records management, 174-175, 183-184

Research value, of records, 75, 79
Resource allocation, *see* Budgeting
Resource Center Index, 8
Retention, 74-90
 at MBTA, 283-284
Retention scheduling, 80-87
 at MBTA, 283
Retention value, of records, 80-81
Roll microfilm, 114-115, 148-150
Roosevelt, Franklin D., 233
Rotary cameras, 150

S
Safes, 118
Safety nets, in government information, 233-234
Scheduling charts, 49-52
Scientific value, of records, 75, 79
SearchMAGIC, 249, 252
Secondary services, 12-15
Secondary value, of records, 75, 80, 274
Second Commission on Organization of the Executive Branch of the Government, 26-27
Securities and Exchange Commission, 77
Senate, 205, 207, 227
Serialized microfilm, 114-115, 148-150
Seven States Project, 256-258, 260-261, 276-277
Shannon files, 24
Sholes, Christopher Latham, 23
Shredders, 89
Skills inventory, 165
Skupsky, Donald, 81
Slides, 115
Social Sciences Citation Index, 197
Societies, professional, 5-10, 77

Society for Information Management, 8-9
Society of American Archivists, 255
Software
 database management, 101-104, 108, 246
 decision support system, 190
 forms management, 145
 project management, 50
Space management, 171-172
Spindle files, 24
Staffing, 163-166
 at MBTA library, 286-289
 at Weston Public Library, 241
Statistics, 187
Step and repeat cameras, 150
Storage, *see* Filing equipment
Subject filing, 119, 122, 124-126
 at Weston Public Library, 244-245
Summative evaluation, 180
Supreme Court, 228
Systems analysis, 38-53
 at Weston Public Library, 244
Systems development, 43-45

T
Tapes, computer, 115, 134
Task Force on Paperwork, 26
Task Force on Regulatory Relief, 229
Theft, protection against, 118
Tickler files, 87
Trade & Industry Index, 197
Transactional records, 74
Truman, Harry, 26
Typewriters, history of, 23

U
Ultramicrofiches, 114

Uniform Photographic Copies of Business and Public Records in Evidence Act, 147
Uniform Rules of Evidence Act, 147

(Note: Agencies whose names are commonly preceded by "United States" or "U.S" are listed alphabetically by name.)

United States Code, 209, 227, 230-232
United States Statutes at Large, 32
Unitized microfilm, 114-115, 148-150
Upper management, records managers and, 56, 58, 161
Urban Mass Transportation Administration, 282-283

V

Values, of records
  administrative, 75, 81, 274
  evidential, 75, 80
  fiscal, 75, 77, 81, 274
  historical, 4, 23, 80
  informational, 75, 80, 274
  legal, 75-77, 81, 274
  primary, 75, 274
  research, 75, 79, 81
  retention, 80-81
  scientific, 75, 79
  secondary, 75, 80, 274
Vaults, 118
Vertical files, 24, 117, 122
Videodiscs, 115, 153
Videotapes, 115
Vital records, 38, 62, 74, 118, 133-135
  at Weston Public Library, 246

W

Weston Public Library, 239-254
Who's Who in Information Management, 8
Word processing, 24
Worksheets
  appraisal, 269-270
  records inventory, 285
Writing systems, history of, 20-22